COLLATERAL DAMAGES

LANDLORDS AND THE URBAN HOUSING CRISIS

MEREDITH J. GREIF

D1565869

A Volume in the American Sociological Association's
Rose Series in Sociology

Russell Sage Foundation • New York

Library of Congress Cataloging-in-Publication Data

Names: Greif, Meredith J., author.
Title: Collateral damages : landlords and the urban housing crisis /
   Meredith J. Greif.
Description: New York, NY : Russell Sage Foundation, [2022] | Series:
   The American sociological association rose series in sociology | Includes
   bibliographical references and index. | Summary: "Collateral Damages
   looks to answer the question: why do federal, state, and local laws which are
   meant to protect renters from disadvantageous landlord practices fall short?
   Indeed, it is the job of city authorities, including the PHA, court system, and
   building departments, to protect vulnerable renters and neighborhoods from
   landlord practices which can pose harm, including discriminatory screening,
   tenant harassment, and subpar property maintenance. The central premise
   of this book is that federal, state, and local laws create circumstances which
   are suitable for landlords to develop motivation and justification to treat
   tenants and their properties as disposable, and the opportunity to do so
   with low risk of sanctions. As part of its key contribution, Collateral Damages
   demonstrates that policies and procedures which are meant to protect
   tenants, and even appear 'race neutral,' can in fact produce negative
   consequences for lower-income tenants, and particularly tenants of color" —
   Provided by publisher.
Identifiers: LCCN 2021060005 (print) | LCCN 2021060006 (ebook) |
   ISBN 9780871544711 (paperback) | ISBN 9781610449007 (ebook)
Subjects: LCSH: Housing policy. | Housing. | Landlord and tenant. |
   Rental housing.
Classification: LCC HD7287.3 .G75 2022 (print) | LCC HD7287.3 (ebook) |
   DDC 363.5/561 — dc23/eng/20220215
LC record available at https://lccn.loc.gov/2021060005
LC ebook record available at https://lccn.loc.gov/2021060006

The paper used in this publication meets the minimum requirements of
American National Standard for Information Sciences—Permanence of Paper
for Printed Library Materials. ANSI Z39.48-1992.

Text design by Suzanne Nichols.

RUSSELL SAGE FOUNDATION
112 East 64th Street, New York, New York 10065
10 9 8 7 6 5 4 3 2 1

The Russell Sage Foundation

The Russell Sage Foundation, one of the oldest of America's general purpose foundations, was established in 1907 by Mrs. Margaret Olivia Sage for "the improvement of social and living conditions in the United States." The foundation seeks to fulfill this mandate by fostering the development and dissemination of knowledge about the country's political, social, and economic problems. While the foundation endeavors to assure the accuracy and objectivity of each book it publishes, the conclusions and interpretations in Russell Sage Foundation publications are those of the authors and not of the foundation, its trustees, or its staff. Publication by Russell Sage, therefore, does not imply foundation endorsement.

Previous Volumes
in the Series

American Memories: Atrocities and the Law
Joachim J. Savelsberg and Ryan D. King

America's Newcomers and the Dynamics of Diversity
Frank D. Bean and Gillian Stevens

Beyond the Boycott: Labor Rights, Human Rights, and Transnational Activism
Gay W. Seidman

Beyond College For All: Career Paths for the Forgotten Half
James E. Rosenbaum

Changing Rhythms of the American Family
Suzanne M. Bianchi, John Robinson, and Melissa Milkie

The Company We Keep: Interracial Friendships and Romantic Relationships from Adolescence to Adulthood
Grace Kao, Kara Joyner, and Kelly Stamper Balistreri

Counted Out: Same-Sex Relations and Americans' Definitions of Family
Brian Powell, Lala Carr Steelman, Catherine Bolzendahl, and Claudi Giest

Divergent Social Worlds: Neighborhood Crime and the Racial-Spatial Divide
Ruth D. Peterson and Lauren J. Krivo

Egalitarian Capitalism: Jobs, Incomes, and Growth in Affluent Countries
Lane Kenworthy

Ethnic Origins: History, Politics, Culture, and the Adaptation of Cambodian and Hmong Refugees in Four American Cities
Jeremy Hein

Family Consequences of Children's Disabilities
Denis Hogan

Golden Years? Social Inequality in Later Life
Deborah Carr

Good Jobs, Bad Jobs: The Rise of Polarized and Precarious Employment Systems in the United States, 1970s to 2000s
Arne L. Kalleberg

The Long Shadow: Family Background, Disadvantaged Urban Youth, and the Transition to Adulthood
Karl Alexander, Doris Entwisle, and Linda Olson

Making Hate a Crime: From Social Movement to Law Enforcement
Valerie Jenness and Ryken Grattet

Market Friendly or Family Friendly? The State and Gender Inequality in Old Age
Madonna Harrington Meyer and Pamela Herd

Nurturing Dads: Social Initiatives for Contemporary Fatherhood
William Marsiglio and Kevin Roy

Passing the Torch: Does Higher Education for the Disadvantaged Pay Off Across the Generations?
Paul Attewell and David Lavin

Pension Puzzles: Social Security and the Great Debate
Melissa Hardy and Lawrence Hazelrigg

A Pound of Flesh: Monetary Sanctions as Punishment for the Poor
Alexes Harris

Sites Unseen: Uncovering Hidden Hazards in American Cities
Scott Frickel and James R. Elliott

Social Movements in the World-System: The Politics of Crisis and Transformation
Dawn Wiest and Jackie Smith

They Say Cut Back, We Say Fight Back! Welfare Activism in an Era of Retrenchment
Ellen Reese

Trust in Schools: A Core Resource for Improvement
Anthony S. Bryk and Barbara Schneider

Forthcoming Titles

Chains of Discrimination
Reginald A. Byron and Vincent J. Roscigno

Counting on College: The Far-Reaching Benefits for Low-Likelihood College Graduates
Jennie E. Brand

Horatio Alger Livers in Brooklyn, but Check His Papers
Robert C. Smith

Immigrant Growth Machines: Urban Growth Politics in Koreatown and Monterey Park
Angie Y. Chung, Jan Lin, and Sookhee Oh

The Journey to Adulthood in Uncertain Times
Robert Crosnoe and Shannon E. Cavanagh

Learning to Lead: The Intersectional Politics of the Second Generation
Veronica Terriquez

The Rose Series in Sociology

The American Sociological Association's Rose Series in Sociology publishes books that integrate knowledge and address controversies from a sociological perspective. Books in the Rose Series are at the forefront of sociological knowledge. They are lively and often involve timely and fundamental issues on significant social concerns. The series is intended for broad dissemination throughout sociology, across social science and other professional communities, and to policy audiences. The series was established in 1967 by a bequest to ASA from Arnold and Caroline Rose to support innovations in scholarly publishing.

AMY ADAMCZYK
RICHARD D. ALBA
LYNN SHARON CHANCER
NANCY FONER
PHILIP KASINITZ
GREGORY SMITHSIMON

EDITORS

This book is dedicated to James.

Contents

List of Illustrations   xv

About the Author   xvii

Acknowledgments   xix

CHAPTER 1   Introduction   1

CHAPTER 2   The Uneven Fortunes of Cleveland's
              Neighborhoods   21

CHAPTER 3   "I May Just Have to Walk Away"   41

CHAPTER 4   "If I Got Him Paranoid Enough, I Knew
              He Would Go"   63

CHAPTER 5   "What Kills Me Now Is the Water"   81

CHAPTER 6   "You Said You're Section 8 . . . That's *Why*
              I Don't Want to Get in Touch with You"   104

CHAPTER 7   Conclusion   131

              Study Methodology   147

              Notes   149

              References   159

              Index   169

List of Illustrations

Figure 1.1   Map of Cleveland Metropolitan Region,
              Percent White   7
Figure 1.2   Map of Cleveland Metropolitan Region,
              Percent Black   7
Figure 1.3   Map of Cleveland Metropolitan Region,
              Percent Asian   8
Figure 1.4   Map of Cleveland Metropolitan Region,
              Percent Hispanic   8
Figure 2.1   Maps of Cleveland, Properties Graded D or F
              and Housing Complaints, 2015   32

═ About the Author ═

Meredith J. Greif is assistant research professor of sociology at Johns Hopkins University.

Acknowledgments

THIS BOOK WAS made possible by the generous support and contributions of numerous people and organizations.

I have a great deal of gratitude to the over one hundred participants in this study for their willingness to share their perspectives and their enthusiasm. I am especially grateful to Judge Pianka and the Cleveland Municipal Housing Court staff for providing numerous formal and informal opportunities for me to learn from them. Other local officials were extraordinarily generous in sharing their time and insights to further this research.

I am extremely grateful to the Russell Sage Foundation for its deep investment in this work. The Rose Series editors—Amy Adamczyk, Richard Alba, Lynn Chancer, Nancy Foner, Philip Kasinitz, Leslie Paik, and Gregory Smithsimon—worked closely with me to sharpen my ideas and provided extremely useful feedback and encouragement throughout the writing process. The Rose Series workshop was instrumental to the book's development, thanks to the wealth of sharp insights provided by its participants, including Thomas Angotti, Nicholas Bloom, Susan Brown, Sheldon Danziger, Kathy Edin, Ingrid Ellen, Lance Freeman, Jessica Halliday Hardie, Sophie House, Yana Kucheva, Robert Lake, John Mollenkopf, Tim Nelson, Gretchen Purser, Wendy Roth, and Kristen Seefeldt. Anonymous reviewers read the manuscript extremely closely and provided incisive, extensive commentary that led me to clarify my arguments. Suzanne Nichols, director of publications at the Russell Sage Foundation Press, provided important guidance and direction during this entire process.

Kathy Edin's boundless, unwavering support as colleague, mentor, and friend was crucial to this work. Draft after draft, conversation after conversation, she encouraged me to see the big picture and to savor all of its nuances. Stefanie DeLuca supported me from the very beginning and provided inspiration and mentorship for which I am deeply grateful. Tim Nelson closely read the manuscript numerous times and provided invaluable insights throughout this journey. Andy Cherlin provided valuable feedback on early versions of the work, and as a mentor more generally.

Eva Rosen and Phillip Garboden were both key contributors to this research: they collected data, shared ideas, and provided indispensable feedback. The work was further facilitated through the contributions of additional members of the research team who conducted interviews and ethnographic observations, including Barbara Kiviat, Stephen Wong, and Anna Rhodes.

My family deserves my utmost gratitude. My parents, Susan and Barry, showed endless patience and enthusiasm for reading and discussing the work, providing sharp commentary and becoming honorary sociologists in the process. James Taylor believed in this work and did everything in his power to bring it to fruition, through countless hours spent discussing, reading, editing, and drawing on whiteboards, as well as making home-cooked meals and taking long walks through Cleveland and Baltimore.

Finally, this research was made possible through support from the U.S. Department of Housing and Urban Development, the Annie E. Casey Foundation, and the Furman Center for Real Estate and Urban Policy.

$=$ Chapter 1 $=$

Introduction

"I GUESS I think I should be making more money. For everything I'm doing," said a chagrined Trevor, a Black landlord in his fifties who participated in our research study on landlords and who provided low-cost rental housing in the Cleveland metropolitan area. Like other landlords who housed low-income tenants, he insisted that his profit margins were slim. Citing low rent amounts and his tenants' obstacles to paying rent consistently, Trevor moaned to me and my colleague over coffee at the McDonald's where we first met, "The only way that you can really make any extra money is to spend less." To ensure some certainty in his rent revenue, he decided to rent primarily to subsidized tenants ("Section 8") so that he could receive partial rent payment from the government. To receive government rent payments, however, landlords' housing units must pass the quality standard inspections performed by the local public housing authority (PHA). In fact, the PHA scheduled an inspection at one of Trevor's units later that week. "Yep, you can come by," he agreed before driving away in a pickup truck piled with a toolbox, hedge clippers, a lawn mower, and other tools he used to maintain the properties.

The address he provided was on a street in one of the most poverty-stricken communities in the city of Cleveland. The block was exceedingly quiet, without a sound or flutter of movement from a nearby neighbor or car. Trevor's two-story, mustard yellow house had spots of peeling paint and shingles that curled upwards. Two tall, dense green bushes stretched across the front of the long porch, ensuring that its patch of rotting wood was only visible from several feet away. Other houses lining the quiet street showed similar signs of disrepair.

Trevor rushed us researchers through the kitchen, leading roaches to scatter under the cabinets, and we stopped in the center of a spare living room space with tattered wood floors. He disappeared into a side room to finish repair work before the inspector arrived, leaving us to speak with his tenant, Marla, a wiry, forty-something Black woman. She greeted us with a warm smile that revealed she was

1

missing her front teeth. Trevor's hammering grew more frenetic, and she suddenly asked, "Do you want to see the place?" Without waiting for a response, she opened door after door to reveal crumbled ceramic tiles in the bathroom, sagging shelves in the closet, and a caving ceiling in her bedroom at the front of the house. "This was *supposed* to have been fixed right after we moved in!" she declared furiously. Pointing to an even larger patch of graying, water-damaged ceiling tiles, and seeing my phone in hand, she whispered urgently, "Take pictures!"

Talking rapidly, Marla explained that the apartment was in terrible shape before she signed the lease. She and her daughter had been pressed to find housing, however, and Trevor had promised to fix the ceiling and floors after they moved in. Clearly, Trevor had not. Marla grew fed up with the conditions and called the PHA, leading them to schedule a "special" inspection, well ahead of the yearly one. Prior to the inspector's arrival, we watched her yelp out "Damnit!" as a splinter lodged into her bare foot as she thumped across the aging floors.

When the inspector did arrive, he immediately examined the condition of the floors and ceiling. Then he announced that the property failed the inspection as a result of these problems. If Trevor didn't fix them in a timely manner, his tenant would have to move, once again.

"Let's go outside," Trevor said to us afterwards, appearing stung. "Why did the inspector have a list? They don't usually come with a list." Kicking at pebbles in the driveway with his boots, he pouted, "If I knew they were going to care about those things, I wouldn't have spent so much time mowing the lawn." Clearly, he could not fathom that his tenant had filed a complaint. It wasn't common in his experience, or that of other landlords who provided low-cost rental housing, for tenants to file complaints. The stakes were high for low-income tenants, as a staff member at a local tenants' rights organization insisted to us. Having few housing options, low-income tenants feared their landlord's retaliation if they filed a complaint.

We had one last question for Trevor that day. How did the property pass its first inspection despite several code violations that seemed impossible to ignore? As it turned out, he had a personal relationship with the inspector. "He sometimes lets me off easy, you know?" he said plainly.

It is the job of city authorities, including the PHA, the court system, and building departments, to protect vulnerable renters and neighborhoods from landlord practices that can pose harm, including discriminatory screening, tenant harassment, and subpar property maintenance. So why do federal, state, and local laws that are meant to protect renters from disadvantageous landlord practices fall short?

The central premise of *Collateral Damages* is that federal, state, and local laws create conditions that motivate landlords to treat tenants and their properties as disposable, give them opportunities to do so with low risk of sanctions, and enable them to justify these actions. One key contribution of this book is to demonstrate that policies and procedures that are meant to protect tenants, and that even appear "race-neutral," can in fact produce negative consequences for lower-income tenants, and particularly for tenants of color.

More than ever, it is important to understand the business practices of private landlords—particularly small, "mom-and-pop" landlords as well as those with midsized property holdings. These landlords provide the majority of the low-cost units available to marginalized tenants nationwide, and especially in low-growth cities, including Cleveland, Baltimore, and Milwaukee.[1] Typically, these landlords provide single-family dwellings or small apartment buildings that are generally older and therefore more costly to maintain adequately.[2]

Several recent shifts in federal housing policy have positioned these small urban landlords as the primary providers of affordable rental units to low-income households nationwide. First, the federal government chose to demolish some of the nation's large, dense public housing developments, beginning in the 1990s, through the HOPE VI program. The developments had become sites of concentrated poverty whose ill effects were increasingly revealed by researchers.[3] Accordingly, the government rebuilt public housing units in mixed-income areas so as to deconcentrate poverty among public housing residents. That process led to a net loss of affordable public housing units, however, and forced some low-income renters to secure housing with private landlords.[4]

The Housing Choice Voucher Program (HCVP), originally "Section 8" of the Housing and Community Development Act of 1974, then further expanded small landlords' role in providing affordable rental housing. The HCVP provides low-income renters with a rent subsidy that can be used to secure housing in the private market. The program ensures that renters do not become "housing cost burdened" by ensuring that they pay no more than 30 percent of their household income on rent; the government pays the landlord the remainder of the total rent amount.

Even though they provide most of the affordable housing units for the nation's poor renters, there is limited sociological knowledge of these small and midsized landlords' business practices. Some attention has been paid to the business practices of large corporate landlords, for instance, in Milwaukee.[5] Further, the body of literature that seeks to understand these small urban landlords has focused on their personal financial goals, their interactions with their tenants, and, when applicable, their experiences with the local public housing authority that administers housing vouchers.[6] In this book, I argue that the existing literature on landlords who house marginalized tenants lacks a crucial component to understanding their business practices: landlords' interactions with the system of federal, state, and local laws that regulate them.

Some attention has been given to landlords' experiences with the local public housing authority that administers housing vouchers, when applicable, to explain their consequential business practices. For instance, researchers have demonstrated that landlords' interest in housing a subsidized tenant depends to an extent on the rent amount they can command from the PHA, as well as the extent to which they experience the voucher program's quality inspection process as burdensome.[7] Together these works show that landlords' business decisions, specifically those pertaining to voucher holders, reflect incentives and disincentives fueled by a particular government agency's policies and practices. Notably, only one in four families who are eligible to receive a housing subsidy on the basis of low income ever receive one.[8]

Accordingly, I argue that the existing literature on the business practices of landlords who house marginalized tenants, including unsubsidized tenants, does not account for their interactions with the larger system of federal, state, and local laws that regulate them.[9] This book shows how a system of laws meant to benefit marginalized tenants and communities instead amplifies their disadvantage by raising landlords' financial precarity and increasing their mistrust toward both authorities and tenants. Landlords are thus motivated to evade laws meant to protect the interests of renters and their communities in the belief that they are justified in doing so.

This work began with a three-year study of sixty small and midsized landlords who provided affordable rental housing to lower- and moderate-income renters in the Cleveland, Ohio, metropolitan region. The Cleveland metro area, which includes the central city of Cleveland and its fifty-seven inner- and outer-ring suburbs in Cuyahoga County, has much in common with other postindustrial cities (for example, Milwaukee, Baltimore, Detroit, Pittsburgh, and St. Louis), including high levels of poverty, unemployment, and racial segregation.[10] And like these cities, the Cleveland region's sizable stock of vacant and deteriorated homes has greatly reduced home values.[11]

Between 2013 and 2015, I, along with a team of experienced qualitative researchers, including faculty, graduate students, and undergraduate students, conducted semistructured, in-depth interviews with landlords who operated in the Cleveland metropolitan region; some of these landlords were also followed longitudinally. The semistructured interviews with landlords lasted approximately two to three hours.

In these interviews, we asked respondents to "tell us the whole story" of how they became landlords. We wanted to know about their current and past rental properties; their business practices and goals; their experiences and decision-making regarding rent collection, evictions, unit inspections, and repairs; and their participation in housing subsidy programs. Some landlords were eager to talk about the business and excited, even incredulous, that we were keen to learn about them. Others were wary and reticent at first, but often surprised us and even themselves when conversations continued for many hours, ending with invitations to join them for a "day in the life" of a landlord. We made ethnographic observations as we accompanied eight of these landlords on their daily rounds and directly observed their interactions with tenants, housing inspectors, lawyers, magistrates, and bailiffs.

The racial composition of the landlord sample reflected the Cleveland metropolitan area's racial demographics, which will be discussed in more detail later. Close to half of the landlords were Black (45 percent), and close to half were White (45 percent). Asian respondents constituted the remaining 10 percent of the sample. The majority of these landlords (70 percent) were male.

The majority of the landlords in this sample had small or midsized property holdings. Approximately one-quarter (27 percent) had "small" property holdings: they rented out six or fewer units, which were located in single-family homes or small multifamily buildings. Fewer than half (43 percent) had "medium-sized" holdings: they owned between seven and thirty units, which were spread across single-family homes and small, multi-unit buildings. Meanwhile, nearly one-quarter (23 percent) had "large" real estate portfolios: these landlords owned (or in select cases acted as primary managers for) over thirty but fewer than one hundred units. Only a small portion (7 percent) owned or oversaw over one hundred units, typically across a handful of midsized multifamily buildings.

These landlords had several key motivations to enter the rental business, but the primary ones were profit maximization and wealth accumulation. Indeed, financial incentives strongly drove these landlords' business practices, in contrast with landlords who entered the business "circumstantially" as a result of life transitions, such as an inheritance.[12] The vast majority entered the business primarily driven by a specific interest in short-term cash flow. Most commonly, they purchased their first rental property either to supplement their wages at a full-time job or with a plan to build a sustainable rental business so that they could exit their current job. The latter were dissatisfied with the wages, hours, and lack of autonomy in their current position. Still others first entered the business because they struggled to find a job, or had recently lost one. Slightly fewer than one-fifth of the landlords entered the business with a goal of building a nest egg to sustain them during their retirement years. Finally, a select few were driven by an interest in providing decent housing for vulnerable renters, including those who struggled to secure housing given obstacles pertaining to mental health and addiction.

The landlords in the sample rented properties in the central city as well as suburban communities across the region, and thus I was able to examine how market dynamics drove their business practices. As in Baltimore, Dallas, Milwaukee, Chicago, New York, and numerous other cities nationwide, the Cleveland metropolitan area is highly segregated on the basis of race and class.[13] The region's Black residents, who constitute just under one-third of its population, are concentrated in communities on the city's East Side and in its inner-ring suburbs to the east. Its White residents constitute nearly two-thirds of the population and are largely concentrated on the city's West Side and in its inner- and outer-ring suburban communities to the west. Asian and Latino residents represent smaller percentages of the metropolitan region's population (3 percent and 6 percent, respectively). The region's Latino population is concentrated on the city's West Side and in its inner-ring suburbs to the west, while the region's Asian population is primarily located in communities that are just east of central downtown (see figures 1.1, 1.2, 1.3, and 1.4).[14]

By and large, the city of Cleveland's East Side communities show the starkest disadvantage, with elevated levels of poverty and unemployment and lower median household income.[15] These communities also experienced the sharpest fallout from the housing market crash, which had hit the northeastern Ohio region hard by the mid-2000s.[16] The property values in the East Side's predominantly Black communities declined precipitously, following a wave of foreclosures and subsequent vacancies, deteriorating property conditions, and spiking crime rates.[17]

The region's predominantly White communities generally show the greatest economic advantage, with lower levels of poverty and unemployment and higher median household income. While these predominantly White communities also faced decline resulting from decreased property values brought on by the housing market crash, their recovery far outpaced that of other communities in the region. Yet there continue to be persistent pockets of White poverty in Cleveland, notably on the city's West Side.[18]

Some of the city's inner-ring suburbs to the east also struggled in the wake of the housing market crash. The wave of foreclosures and ensuing drop in property values led to the wide-scale conversion of

Figure 1.1   Map of Cleveland Metropolitan Region, Percent White

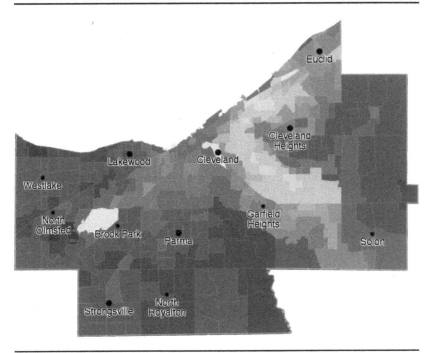

Source: ACS 2016–2020d.

Figure 1.2   Map of Cleveland Metropolitan Region, Percent Black

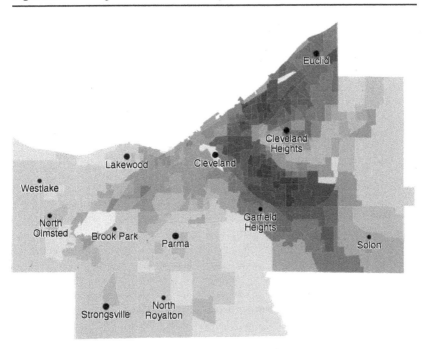

Source: ACS 2016–2020b.

Figure 1.3   Map of Cleveland Metropolitan Region, Percent Asian

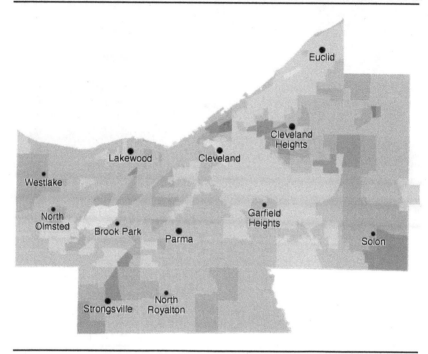

Source: ACS 2016–2020a.

Figure 1.4   Map of Cleveland Metropolitan Region, Percent Hispanic

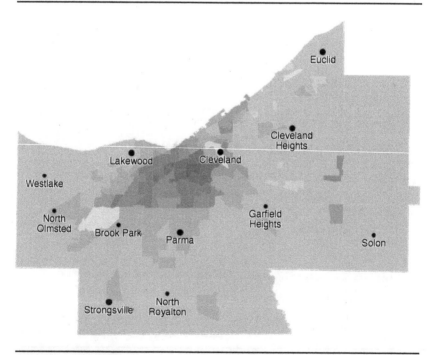

Source: ACS 2016–2020c.

owner-occupied homes into rentals. Owners who hoped to sell their home but failed to command their desired sale price decided to rent them out instead. The increased availability of rental housing and falling rent prices in these communities enabled the entrance of lower-income renters, who had previously been priced out. As these communities' lower-income renter population grew, so too did its population of Black residents and voucher holders.[19]

Two-fifths of these landlords primarily rented properties in struggling communities on the city's East Side, which had sizable Black populations (approximately 40 percent or more of residents) and relatively high levels of poverty (more than 20 percent of residents below the poverty line). The landlords who operated in these marginalized communities had followed a diverse range of professional trajectories. Some had entered the business a decade or more earlier, taking out mortgages to purchase single-family and small multifamily properties at modest prices (approximately $40,000 to $85,000 in the 1980s, 1990s, and early 2000s). Still others had entered the business after the housing crash, when they purchased properties for prices as low as $2,000 and up to $25,000, typically paying cash for them. Some landlords who had invested in these communities decades earlier continued to purchase properties at low prices after the housing market crash.

Close to one-third (30 percent) of the landlords in this sample primarily rented their properties in communities with a sizable Black population and relatively low poverty levels (fewer than 20 percent of residents with household incomes below the poverty line). Most of these communities were inner-ring suburban communities to the east. Some of the landlords in these communities had entered the business with substantial investment prior to the housing market crash and were still paying off mortgages. Falling sale prices spurred yet other landlords to purchase properties in the communities after the crash; typically they paid in cash or used hard money lenders to acquire single-family properties for as little as $18,000 or multifamily properties going for as much as $59,000.

Slightly more than one-fifth (22 percent) of the landlords in the sample primarily operated in communities on the city's West Side where White residents constituted close to a majority of the residential population and where poverty levels were low. Some of these landlords had entered the business prior to the housing market crash and invested substantially in mortgages and now, as of 2014, bemoaned being "underwater"—owing more to the bank than the property was worth. They struggled to remit mortgage payments with the rent payments from their increasingly struggling tenant population.

The remaining 8 percent of the sample primarily rented in communities where the majority of residents were White and poverty levels were elevated (above 20 percent). Indeed, pockets of White poverty persist on the city's West Side, despite recovery in most of its other White communities. Several of these landlords purchased the properties at modest prices well before the housing crash, in the 1980s and 1990s, while others purchased their properties for lower prices in the years surrounding the housing crash.

These landlords followed a diverse range of trajectories in the business. They varied in the time period when they entered the business, in the markets where they primarily invested, and, relatedly, in the amount of their investment. They had different motivations to enter the business: some bought properties in order to generate short-term cash flow, while others were attempting to build a long-term safety net that would sustain them on into their retirement years. As stated earlier, there was noteworthy diversity in these landlords' racial composition. That this investor population showed diversity along many lines, yet engaged in a wide range of behaviors that harmed tenants and the surrounding community—including property divestment, discriminatory screening practices, tenant intimidation, and informal evictions—underscores that there were systematic factors at play.

Collateral Damages focuses on two interrelated themes. First, it demonstrates how recent macro-level shifts—including changes in federal housing and cash assistance programs, the rise of mass incarceration, and the War on Drugs—have rendered tenants vulnerable to harmful landlord practices by intensifying their financial struggles and social stigma and deepening their mistrust toward government authorities. Second, this book makes the key contribution of showing that local laws can perpetuate disadvantage for marginalized tenants. They do so by creating financial precarity for landlords, thereby motivating them to engage in disadvantageous business practices to stay afloat, and by fostering landlords' mistrust toward both authorities and their marginalized tenants and thus leading them to believe that they are justified in pursuing harmful business practices.

The Impact of Macro-Level Shifts on Tenant Vulnerability

Several macro-level societal shifts in the latter part of the twentieth century have contributed to tenants' vulnerability to landlord practices that contribute to housing insecurity. These include factors that fueled tenants' financial precarity and, relatedly, landlords' financial precarity, which was widespread among the landlords in this sample. Here I define "financial precarity" for landlords as real or perceived uncertainty about whether the revenue earned in their business is sufficient to cover the multitude of "costs of doing business" while also producing a satisfactory take-home profit. Notably, financial precarity is an especially valuable concept for understanding landlords' business practices, as it can provide motivation to engage in illegitimate practices for economic gain, including discriminatory screening, poor property upkeep, and illegal soft evictions.[20]

"Good jobs"—those that provide a living wage, stable work hours, and benefits, including health insurance and retirement plans—have disappeared from the U.S. economy.[21] As a result, renters have increasingly become "housing-cost-burdened," that is, compelled to pay more than 30 percent of their household income toward housing costs. This burden leaves them vulnerable to losing their housing through eviction.[22] Nationwide, 47 percent of renters are housing-cost-burdened.[23]

In the Cleveland metropolitan area, slightly more than half of renters are housing-cost-burdened. Even more striking, nearly one-third of renters in the Cleveland metro area are considered "severely" housing-cost-burdened because they pay more than half of their income toward housing costs.[24]

Creating even more financial and housing insecurity for renters—and relatedly, their landlords—has been the wholesale collapse of the cash-based safety net. In 1996, the nation's cash welfare program for low-income households, Aid to Families with Dependent Children (AFDC), was terminated. It was replaced by the provisions of the Personal Responsibility and Work Opportunity Reconciliation Act of 1996 (PRWORA), which imposed time limits on government assistance and made receipt of benefits contingent on participation in work-related activities.[25] Dwindling government cash assistance places renters at risk of falling behind on rent payment as a result of an economic shock—a cutback in work hours, for example, or an unexpected medical bill—and subsequently losing access to their housing. Tenants need liquid cash, not in-kind subsidies such as food or health care, to pay the landlord rent money so as to avoid eviction.

The growth of the carceral state, seen by the rise of mass incarceration, is another shift that has undermined tenants' access to decent, affordable rental housing. Black renters, and in particular Black men, face some of the greatest barriers to housing as a result of the expansion of the carceral state. Black men are incarcerated at disproportionately high rates, leading to significant reductions in their income and obstacles to their employment that undermine their capacity to afford rent.[26]

The Impact of Local Laws

The findings presented in this book illustrate how local laws and practices perpetuate disadvantage among marginalized populations and communities in ways that are hidden and sometimes unintended. They do so by amplifying the sense of financial precarity and suspicion toward tenants felt by landlords that have already been set in motion by the macro-level shifts discussed earlier. Notably, these laws not only fall short of their goals by failing to account for landlords' financial precarity but also spark additional mechanisms by which landlords come to perceive the business as financially unsustainable, and their tenants as untrustworthy.

The process to evict a tenant in court, which varies across municipalities nationwide, provides one example of unintended consequences of local laws. At one end of the spectrum are cities, including Baltimore, where tenants may have to move out of their rental housing less than three weeks after the landlord files to evict.[27] In other municipalities, including the city of Cleveland and its surrounding suburbs, the process typically unfolds over the course of four to five weeks.[28] In other municipalities, including Washington, D.C., the court eviction process may take several months to complete.

A longer court eviction process, which extends the time frame for finding new housing after a landlord has filed to evict, should be more beneficial for tenants. Long eviction processes can also be counterproductive, however, with unintended consequences for tenants, as I show here. The small landlords in this study said that the greater amount of time necessary to remove a tenant through a court eviction hearing increased their sense of financial precarity. The length of the court eviction process and its associated costs, including court filing fees, motivated landlords to pursue illegitimate means to remove tenants hastily and without cost so as to protect their bottom line. "Why should I pay for my own demise?" Curtis, a Black man in his forties, wondered aloud as he related his account of chasing out a tenant by taking off the front door rather than incurring the costs to evict her in court. Informal evictions can have disastrous consequences for tenants by leading them to secure worse-quality housing and triggering emotional trauma.[29]

Other local laws increase landlords' sense of financial anxiety and make them more likely to evade laws that are meant to protect tenants. Communities in the Cleveland metropolitan area and across the country are increasingly enacting laws that make the landlord responsible for deterring their tenants' illegal or undesirable activity on their property. The pace at which these laws were passed began to speed up in the mid-2000s, when more and more properties in the region were deteriorating in the midst of the flailing economy and housing market crash. Under these laws, a landlord can incur financial penalties, and even criminal sanctions, for failing to abate tenants' illegal drug use on the property or other "undesirable" behaviors, including loud noise and repeated calls for police assistance with emergencies, including domestic violence. In response to these criminal activity nuisance ordinances being passed in cities nationwide, landlords can avoid incurring city sanctions by evicting their tenants.[30]

Landlords accordingly looked to screen out tenants who, they believed, would put them at risk of incurring nuisance sanctions through behavior on the property that could attract police attention. They turned away applicants who had experienced domestic violence or were marked by a criminal conviction. As shown here, landlords did indeed adhere to prescribed court procedures to remove tenants who police claimed engaged in "nuisance" behavior, but they also evicted tenants through off-the-record informal evictions triggered by unfounded suspicions of illegal activity.

Another set of laws even more routinely trigger financial precarity for landlords. Water bills are skyrocketing in cities nationwide as the costs of upgrading aging water infrastructure are passed on to consumers. In the Cleveland metropolitan region and others across the nation—including Baltimore, New York City, and Seattle—water billing regulations hold that the landlord is responsible for paying the municipal water bill, even if the lease requires the tenant to pay the water bill or if the account is in the tenant's name.

In light of the rapidly rising cost of water, landlords became unduly agitated about tenants' water usage. They closely scrutinized prospective tenants in search of clues that they would use water excessively, rejecting applicants who lacked employment and those with large households, thereby deepening their ongoing struggle to access decent, affordable housing. Furthermore, current tenants' water usage faced close surveillance from landlords. Mundane activities such as doing laundry or watering the lawn could confirm or even spark a landlord's belief that tenants were irresponsible or untrustworthy. Subject to landlords' extreme scrutiny, tenants' routine behaviors on the property became sources of contention. Ramped-up surveillance can lead tenants to experience their homes as a "carceral environment" and a source of distress, not a place of safety and stability.[31]

Besides laws and regulations that stoke landlords' financial precarity and mistrust toward tenants, another factor justifies landlords' business practices but disadvantages tenants: mistrust toward the authorities who hold them accountable for tenant behavior over which they perceive themselves as having little control. "Not a constituent" is how some landlords in the sample believed that they were treated by the authorities who implemented laws meant to protect renters or the community. Seeing lawmakers as biased in favor of the interests of the tenant or the community weakened landlords' sense of obligation to play by the rules, whether moral or legal. These observations fall in line with research on the societal factors that lead people to engage in morally dubious or illegal behaviors.[32] Their belief that city authorities had not considered the interests of small landlords when implementing these and other laws fueled landlords' justification to evade laws, to the detriment of tenants.

The Significance of Race

Race is an essential component of this story. First, Black Americans in particular face stark racial discrimination in the housing market, whether they are searching to purchase a home or to rent one.[33] As noted earlier, the systemic obstacles that Black Americans face in securing steady jobs that pay livable wages may also undermine the success of their housing search.[34]

Race-based stereotypes provided landlords with justification for business practices that disadvantaged their marginalized tenants. Indeed, landlords routinely invoked beliefs about tenants' "culture of poverty": their view of certain tenants as irresponsible, lazy, and even deviant reflected the racialized stereotypes that have become deeply entrenched in the nation's discourse.[35] These perceptions fueled landlords' belief that marginalized tenants did not deserve good-quality housing or respectable treatment and neutralized any misgivings they might have had in pursuing business practices that harmed tenants.[36] Importantly, landlords of all racial backgrounds, whether Black, White, or Asian, invoked tropes about their marginalized tenants' irresponsibility. These findings reflect patterns seen in studies of other "street-level bureaucrats" who serve lower-income Americans—notably welfare caseworkers—who dole out rewards and sanctions on the basis of clients' race rather than their own racial background.[37]

Local laws even served to amplify landlords' race- and class-based biases about tenants. Laws pertaining to water billing and nuisance behavior led landlords to become unduly aggrieved about certain tenant characteristics—unemployment, large family size, and criminal convictions—that had been cast as evidence of irresponsibility and deviance in the societal dialogue on welfare recipients.[38] Racial stereotypes about Black Americans' irresponsibility or deviance were amplified by landlords' observations of behaviors that seemed to align with them.[39] As a consequence, legal circumstances that led landlords to hyperscrutinize tenants' behavior on the property, deem their mundane behavior as negligent, and explain it through readily available "culture of poverty" arguments served to deepen landlords' stereotypes about marginalized tenants and even reinforce their justifications for business practices that could disadvantage these tenants.

Shifts in government assistance programs and the criminal justice system have created additional obstacles to lower-income and African American renters' access to decent, affordable rental housing. Negative interactions with any one government institution can provoke mistrust toward that institution and toward "the system" more generally.[40] Indeed, lower-income people, and Black people in particular, disproportionately interact with government authorities, including police officers and welfare caseworkers, and in ways that provoke feelings of alienation, degradation, fear, and powerlessness.[41] This is relevant to the current story because systemic mistrust can motivate "system avoidance" whereby individuals avoid interactions with government institutions.[42] Thus, marginalized tenants experience disincentives to interact with authorities who enforce laws that are meant to protect them.

To ensure that this study of landlords' business practices did not rely exclusively on the perspective of landlords, members of the research team and I also interviewed thirty officials who implemented and enforced laws meant to protect renters and the housing stock. These interviewees included actors within the court system: a judge, magistrates, mediators, and bailiffs at the Cleveland Municipal Housing Court and the Cleveland Heights Municipal Court. We also conducted in-depth interviews with administrators who worked in the Building and Housing Department, the Health Department, and the Police Department in the city of Cleveland and one of its suburbs, Shaker Heights. Additional interviews were conducted with elected city council members in the city of Cleveland, as well as administrators and inspectors who worked for the region's largest public housing authority, the Cuyahoga Metropolitan Housing Authority (CMHA).

Also informing this analysis are interviews with and observations of nonprofit housing agencies in the region, including the Cleveland Tenants Organization (CTO) and the Legal Aid Society, which both looked to protect renters' rights. We also met with senior officials who worked for organizations fighting against community decline, including the Vacant and Abandoned Property Action Council (VAPAC) and the Cuyahoga County Land Reutilization Corporation ("Cuyahoga Land Bank").

The research team and I made ethnographic observations of a subset of these officials by joining bailiffs and movers as they performed the grim work of setting out tenants who had been evicted from their home, watching as court staff mediated landlord-tenant disputes, and observing magistrates and the judge in courtroom hearings.

Using landlords as a lens into the city and conversations with city officials who oversaw housing and landlord matters, this book contributes to the literature on urban politics and government. Douglas Massey and Nancy Denton, Patrick Sharkey, and Richard Rothstein have provided sweeping accounts of how federal and local policies and practices create and perpetuate spatial and social disadvantage.[43] This volume builds on these works by revealing policies and practices that foster disadvantage but have gone under the radar, including housing code enforcement, nuisance ordinances, and decisions about who is ultimately responsible for paying the price of water.

The findings in this book illuminate the processes by which local laws and practices can appear "neutral" on the basis of race and class but still create disadvantage for marginalized tenants and communities. Ultimately, it is the marginalized tenant who suffers the "collateral damages" of laws that fail to consider the economic and social positions of landlords and tenants.

The Outline of the Book

Chapter 2 examines the laws and institutions that regulate landlords' behavior as they interact with the local agencies that implement and provide counsel on codes meant to protect renters, including the staff who work for the local court system, building code inspectors, and organizations that protect tenants' rights. The chapter shows the central challenges that these agencies face in ensuring that renters benefit from their protections, such as the disappearance of "good jobs," which has increased tenants' financial struggles. Left without resources to pay rent, tenants see their housing options shrink and feel little incentive to report to authorities their landlords' violation of housing laws, out of fear of a retaliatory eviction and loss of housing.

The expansion of the carceral state provides further disincentives to take advantage of the laws that protect tenants: by fueling their mistrust toward authorities, the carceral state not only removes tenants' incentives to report their landlords' code violations but motivates them to avoid interactions with authorities. These outcomes of the expanding carceral state make renters particularly vulnerable to experiencing the fallout of landlords' illegitimate business practices in cities—including Cleveland—where housing codes are enforced reactively, largely in response to renters' and residents' complaints, rather than through systematic inspections. The findings reported in this book show that laws meant to protect renters are unlikely to be effective if they fail to consider their social and economic circumstances.

The following four chapters revisit this book's central theme—how a system of laws meant to benefit marginalized tenants and communities instead amplifies their disadvantage through the behavior that the system encourages in landlords. These chapters illustrate how these laws produce harmful and often unintended consequences for marginalized tenants, especially by raising landlords' financial precarity and mistrust toward authorities and tenants and thus providing them with motivation and justification to evade laws meant to protect the interests of renters and their communities.

Chapter 3 takes a close look at the circumstances that perpetuate disadvantage in the region's most marginalized communities. It focuses on how city and state codes meant to protect renters and the housing stock in these communities fall especially short, and even have counterproductive effects, through the ways in which landlords react to them. The chapter details the structural and social forces that motivate landlords to evade housing laws in the belief that they are justified in doing so.

Landlords in the sample who rented properties in poor and predominantly Black communities made rational economic arguments to justify evading housing codes: they insisted that the rent amounts they could command were too low, and their tenants' rent payments too inconsistent, to generate sufficient revenue to invest back in their properties. The landlords in these communities seemed most starkly cynical toward local authorities, who, in their view, enforced health and safety codes capriciously and enacted laws that, they believed, unfairly disadvantaged landlords. Tenants' marginalized status was another important part of this story, in that it led landlords to justify subpar property conditions and even their callous treatment of tenants. The findings reported in this chapter show the "perfect storm" of circumstances in marginalized communities that perpetuates their disadvantage.

Chapter 4 shows how another set of city housing laws, criminal activity nuisance ordinances (CANOs), undermine access to affordable housing in municipalities across the region, though most often in predominantly White, middle-income communities with high rates of homeownership.[44] This chapter shows that CANOs ultimately punish marginalized tenants. Landlords screened out prospective tenants based on unfounded assumptions about how likely they were to engage in "nuisance" activity. Moreover, landlords moved to evict tenants—whether through legal court channels or illegal informal eviction—in order to hastily eliminate a "nuisance" out of fear of fines. Additionally, landlords' concerns about nuisance sanctions drove them to turn away prospective tenants on the basis of characteristics that, for other reasons, also contribute to housing insecurity, and especially among Black renters, including a criminal record and the experience of surviving domestic violence.

Chapter 5 examines water billing regulations and measures taken by municipalities to collect on delinquent water bills. These regulations provide additional examples of laws that appear race-neutral on paper but, by disproportionately affecting communities of color, are far from it in practice. In Cleveland and most other cities, landlords are ultimately responsible for water bill payment and face financial penalties, financial liens, and property seizure for delinquent water bills, even when the account is registered under the tenant's name. Above all other threats to landlords' bottom line (short of nonpayment of rent), and because of the severe penalties involved and their inability to observe or control tenants' water use, no other interaction with the city evoked a greater sense of financial insecurity for landlords.

Financial precarity triggered by water billing regulations motivated landlords to screen tenants based on expectations about their water usage, to the detriment of those who lacked employment, held housing vouchers, or had larger families. These were some of the same characteristics that blocked marginalized tenants' access to decent, affordable housing; as a result, water billing regulations exact a "double penalty" on tenants who struggle to secure stable housing. The prospect of exceedingly large and unpredictable water bills that could cancel out their net revenue led small-time landlords in particular to scrutinize tenants' water usage, harass them, and look upon even routine water usage as "irresponsible," a view reinforced by their beliefs about their marginalized tenants' irresponsibility.

The chapter further demonstrates that, aside from raising water costs, municipalities attempt to recoup vital resources to fund water infrastructure upgrades by contracting with private corporations to pressure owners to pay delinquent water bills and astronomical fees—or else lose their homes to foreclosure. Black owners and communities face the sharpest fallout from this practice.

Chapter 6 discusses the reasons why government-subsidized housing programs fall short of their goal to secure access for lower-income renters to decent, affordable rental housing. The Housing Choice Voucher Program (HCVP, or "Section 8") provides landlords with the opportunity to receive rent payments directly from the government for housing low-income tenants, thereby minimizing landlords' financial strain and, relatedly, their motivation to fall behind on property maintenance or harass tenants to pay rent. This chapter shows that financial incentives are insufficient to attract or retain landlords who offer housing of decent quality and who also "play by the rules."

In struggling regions such as the Cleveland metropolitan area, a low fair market rent (FMR), which determines the maximum rent, deters landlords from participating in the voucher program when they can secure higher-paying, unsubsidized tenants, largely owing to their units' location in safe, resource-rich communities. Other aspects of the program, including housing quality inspections, lead landlords to determine that the financial costs and losses associated with housing a voucher tenant outweigh the benefits of participating in the program. Yet deeply entrenched biases regarding voucher holders' irresponsibility also enable landlords to justify turning down their applications.

The scope of this chapter extends beyond the issue of subsidized tenants' access to housing to examine the quality and safety conditions of the housing that landlords provide subsidized tenants. Landlords in the sample who agreed to rent to subsidized tenants, particularly those with units in distressed communities, typically sought ways to do so while investing few resources to make their properties decent or safe.

This chapter builds on current knowledge about the impact of landlords' decisions regarding the voucher program's perpetuation of segregation.[45] It shows that several factors underlie landlords' decisions about whether, where, and how well to house voucher holders, including their motivation for entering the business, the profit they generate in it, the size of their real estate portfolio, and the markets where they operate.

Chapter 7 summarizes the claims made in previous chapters about landlords' financial precarity, legal cynicism, and biases toward tenants, as triggered by federal and local laws, being a central dynamic in prompting and justifying their disadvantageous behavior. In short, the small-time landlords who provide the majority of housing in low-growth American cities can easily dip into the red in such markets. Beyond these market forces, landlords' perceived financial uncertainty is driven not only by their bottom line but also by a broad array of forces that they feel unable to either predict or control, owing to the dynamics outlined here.

Chapter 7 then offers policy recommendations, including incremental measures to benefit landlords and tenants, such as mediation and property management assistance. I argue that deep investment by the federal government will be necessary to assist poor cities, at least in the short term, to proactively enforce housing codes that motivate owners to maintain their properties and reduce the cynicism that arises from a sense that the city has turned a "blind eye" to the problems of its marginalized neighborhoods. Federal funds to help cities rebuild their water and sewer infrastructure are also necessary, not only in order to leave more money in the pockets of poor renters but also to decrease landlords' discriminatory screening practices, undue monitoring of tenants and threats, and mistrust toward tenants due to fear of overwhelming water bills.

Measures to reverse, at least in part, the neoliberal turn in housing policy are in order. Taking us closer to this goal would be more hard-unit public housing—not development similar to the high-rise towers of the past, but an explicit deconcentration strategy to ensure that subsidized families have access to high-opportunity neighborhoods. Measures to increase affordable homeownership for low-income households would further limit marginalized renters' dependence on the private market to provide housing. Chapter 7 further recommends putting more money in all renters' pockets in the form of a renter's tax credit, which would open doors by making housing more affordable and do so without the stigma or administrative burden faced by subsidized tenants.

We cannot forget that even with the support of the federal government, city institutions alone cannot fix the nation's housing crises. The findings in *Collateral Damages* demonstrate the consequences of the disappearance of stable work. Researchers continue to uncover the many implications of unemployment, including the insufficient resources available to the unemployed to pay for basic needs.[46] This book illustrates yet another of these implications: landlords' beliefs about whether poor tenants deserve access to stable, decent, affordable housing. Accordingly, the ills of poor tenants, the landlords who house them, and the cities struggling to deal with a housing crisis can only be addressed with new, bold solutions to ensure that all of the nation's people, whatever their employment or income status, can be decently housed.

= Chapter 2 =

The Uneven Fortunes of Cleveland's Neighborhoods

R ENTERS IN the Cleveland metropolitan region—and nationwide—
face mounting obstacles to accessing decent, stable, affordable
housing. The region's renters have become increasingly "housing-
cost-burdened": many pay more than 30 percent of their gross household
income for housing.[1] The housing affordability crisis among the region's
renters stems from their low and stagnant incomes, not from rapidly
rising rents.[2] Despite pockets of economic development, the region's rents
have remained relatively low as the problem of excess housing and population loss continues. The region's median gross rent, $809 per month for
a two-bedroom unit, is still out of reach for renters who struggle to secure
"good jobs" that pay stable, livable wages in a regional economy whose
stable manufacturing jobs were shed and replaced by low-paying jobs
in the growing service sector.[3] As has happened in other postindustrial
cities, including Baltimore, Detroit, Pittsburgh, and Milwaukee, Cleveland's
housing affordability crisis largely reflects national and regional economic
trends, not exorbitant rents.[4]

Renters' financial struggles make them vulnerable to losing their housing through eviction. In Cleveland, 4.53 percent of renter-occupied households experienced an eviction in 2016. Other cities with similar eviction
rates—the number of evictions per 100 renter-occupied households—
include Detroit, Michigan (5.20 percent), Memphis, Tennessee (4.89 percent),
Cincinnati, Ohio (4.70 percent), Kansas City, Missouri (4.59 percent), and
Milwaukee, Wisconsin (4.25 percent). At the national level, 2.3 percent of
renter households experienced an eviction in 2016.[5]

Renters face mounting housing insecurity and risk an eviction filing for
reasons besides having insufficient funds to pay rent to their landlords,
as we will learn in this chapter from the staff who perform important
work at the region's housing agencies, including the Cleveland Municipal
Housing Court, the Cleveland Building and Housing Department, and
the nonprofit Cleveland Tenants Organization (CTO). Our interactions
with and observations of these authorities reveal additional mechanisms

that make low-income renters vulnerable to unstable, unsafe housing and its fallout, despite state and local laws designed to protect them. Indeed, states nationwide have enacted landlord-tenant legislation to protect tenants' housing security and ensure the quality of the housing stock.[6] Ohio's Tenant-Landlord Law of 1974 requires landlords to maintain their rental properties in "fit and habitable condition," free of health hazards, such as bug infestations and collapsing structures, and with access to basic amenities, including running water and electricity. The law prohibits landlords from pursuing "informal evictions"—terminating utilities or services, removing tenants' belongings, changing locks, or engaging in other tactics to remove tenants from the property without the due process of a court hearing.[7]

This chapter shows that laws fail to account for the obstacles and disincentives faced by the renters and residents intended to benefit from them. For instance, renters may be unaware of the full range of protections available to them under the law. Furthermore, some benefits can be accessed only by interacting directly with authorities—a disincentive for those who live in marginalized communities, which show high levels of mistrust toward authorities.[8]

Tenants are doubly penalized by their lack of resources, knowledge, and trust in government if they live in cities where housing codes are not enforced systematically, with regular inspections by authorities, but rather reactively, driven by residents' complaints. Cleveland is one of many cities—including Cincinnati, Ohio, Houston, Texas, San Antonio, Texas, and Santa Barbara, California—that enforce housing codes reactively.[9] Without systematic surveillance over housing conditions, marginalized renters and communities face an undue burden in seeking to benefit from the laws meant to protect them.

This chapter features a central theme found throughout the book: the system that best protects the rights and interests of all residents is one that accounts for their financial and social circumstances.

Cleveland's lower-income and Black renters and communities were marginalized through processes common to cities nationwide. As will be seen, the region continues to be a site of vigorous housing advocacy meant to defend vulnerable renters and residents. Yet an individual agency is limited in the protections it can provide for marginalized populations whose deep disadvantage reflects large-scale systemic forces.

Cleveland was once a place of great prosperity. By the late 1800s, it had become a booming industrial center, and some of the country's wealthiest entrepreneurs, including John D. Rockefeller, had earned their fortunes there through manufacturing and oil industries. Millionaire's Row, lined with mansions and their lush gardens, advertised that Cleveland was a place where dreams were made. Its population grew substantially in the 1920s, as did its arts, medical, and education sectors. By 1930, Cleveland had become the sixth-largest city in the nation.[10]

Then Cleveland's trajectory toward high segregation on the basis of race and class began, a result of local policies but also of federal policies that were contributing to stark segregation in other cities as well, including Baltimore, Philadelphia, and Chicago.[11] Black Americans who migrated to Cleveland and other northern cities in the early and mid-1900s in search of work and to flee racial violence settled in overcrowded, central-city communities. Simultaneously, wealthy White residents began to move to the suburbs and were replaced by Black residents who paid higher rents to reside in what eventually became poorly maintained units.[12]

White flight to the suburbs began to deplete the central city's tax dollars, which funded essential services, including police, fire departments, schools, and housing inspectors. The resulting declines in safety and services led to even more population loss.[13] Still further flight from the central city was brought on by Federal Housing Authority (FHA) practices that enabled the government to underwrite and insure mortgages. The creation of the Home Owners' Loan Corporation (HOLC) in 1933 helped families purchase homes, as guided by risk assessments provided by local real estate experts. The grades that were assigned to neighborhoods—A, B, C, or D—determined the property's eligibility for a government-issued mortgage and reflected the neighborhood's racial composition. Families trying to buy a home in a D-graded neighborhood—colored in red because of a large presence of Black residents—were denied access to a mortgage insured by the federal government. The "redlining" maps that displayed these grades would lay the groundwork for decades of divestment, especially in Black communities.[14]

Redlining, combined with realtor steering practices and racial threats, made it nearly impossible for Black residents to obtain housing in the region's mixed-race or predominantly White communities. By the late 1950s, some of the city's formerly White communities had transitioned to predominantly Black. Population loss in the central city of Cleveland further strained its capacity to fund important systems; the resulting spikes in crime and failing schools fueled even more White flight.[15]

Racial tensions mounted over the course of the 1960s. The U.S. Commission on Civil Rights visited Cleveland in 1966 to assess the conditions faced by its Black population. Testimony from interviews with several dozen Black residents revealed their ongoing concerns about obstacles to securing stable jobs and good-quality housing and about their negative encounters with police.[16] Carl Stokes was subsequently elected, in 1967, as the first Black mayor of a large American city, and he vowed to improve conditions for Cleveland's Black residents. Nonetheless, racial tensions exploded in the 1968 "Glenville Shootout"— a nearly weeklong period of violence between Black residents and Cleveland police officers that resulted in fatalities on both sides.[17] In triggering more White flight, these incidents all but ensured that the racially segregated spaces created by federal and local policies would remain that way.

Eventually Black residents of Cleveland, who constitute the largest racial minority in the region, became concentrated in the central city's East Side communities and in its inner-ring suburbs to the east. These communities have some of the highest rates of poverty in the region. Meanwhile, the White population is concentrated in working-class and middle-income communities on the city's West Side and in its suburbs to the west.[18]

The gradual decline of the city of Cleveland's predominantly Black communities to the east did not go unnoticed by local housing advocates. In the 1950s, a local housing advocacy community began to coalesce. It made sizable gains in the 1970s, including the establishment of the nonprofit Cleveland Tenants Organization (CTO), which protects renters' rights, and the creation, through a grassroots campaign, of the Cleveland Municipal Housing Court, which has jurisdiction over the city's housing-related matters and is led by a single judge.[19]

The Cleveland Municipal Housing Court has two branches—civil and criminal. The civil side hears cases pertaining to the eviction process, which has two parts. "First-cause" eviction hearings pertain to possession of the property. In first-cause hearings, the landlord presents evidence that the tenant has lost the right to stay in the property because of a breach of the lease. "Second-cause" cases pertain to money matters. In second-cause hearings, landlords attempt to collect on the tenant's debt that has accumulated through missed rent, unpaid utility bills, or costs associated with excessive wear-and-tear on the property. On the court's criminal side (discussed later in this chapter), the court hears cases pertaining to housing code violations.

Landlords are wary of renting to applicants with the mark of an eviction on their record.[20] But for those who have experienced it, eviction can be devastating and often exacts an emotional toll, such as through higher rates of depression and anxiety.[21] Children suffer the consequences of eviction as well, and poor performance in school can be one result.[22] The majority of tenants who attend eviction hearings in the Housing Court are Black, female heads of households with children, very low income, and a high housing cost burden.[23]

"We Are Witnessing Somebody's Worst Day of Their Life in Court"

First-cause eviction hearings take place in a wood-paneled courtroom where tenants, landlords, and lawyers sit on long wooden benches, sometimes packed shoulder to shoulder, waiting for their cases to be called. Some sit motionless and silent, and others fidget and sigh. A black-robed magistrate hears the cases from behind a tall, wooden desk in the front of the room. Court bailiffs, wearing white button-down shirts and dark pants, stand staunchly, keeping watch over the crowd. The court mediator, a White, forty-something man wearing a brown houndstooth blazer, charges authoritatively through the aisles, snapping his fingers at visitors who talk loudly or pull out a cell phone.

Magistrates press landlords who have filed for eviction, asking, "Did this person live in your property?" and "Why are you evicting them?" and "Did you serve a three-day notice?" They ask tenants questions too, including: "Did you live there?" and "When did you last pay rent?" Over 90 percent of eviction cases that come before the court are for nonpayment of rent.[24] Notably, tenants' nonpayment of rent does not necessarily reflect insufficient funds. Some tenants are motivated to withhold rent so as to compel landlords to remediate subpar or hazardous property conditions, even though doing so renders them vulnerable to losing their housing through an eviction.[25] Indeed, nonpayment of rent is the most "cut-and-dry" breach of lease that will lead the court to decide in the landlord's favor.

When a landlord presents legitimate evidence that a tenant has violated lease terms by failing to remit rent payment on time and in full, the landlord will most likely receive a writ of restitution, permitting them to take back possession of the property. Upon announcing a verdict in favor of the landlord, magistrates typically press tenants who are present at the hearing for more information. "Are you a veteran? Are you over the age of sixty? Are you receiving any type of social services for disability, mental health?" If the tenant responds "yes" to any of these questions, their move-out period may be extended past the typical seven to ten business days. Social workers sit in on courtroom hearings to determine whether a tenant who just received a verdict of eviction qualifies for financial assistance; to help them move out; or to help them find new housing, including through the U.S. Department of Veterans Affairs, the Cleveland Department of Aging, and other city service agencies.

The court then schedules a move-out date, typically seven to ten business days after the hearing. If the tenant does not vacate the property by the move-out date, the landlord must request assistance from court bailiffs to remove the tenant. Under these circumstances, landlords must hire licensed, court-approved movers to remove tenants' belongings from the property and bring them to the curb. The span of time between the date the landlord serves the tenant a notice of their intent to evict and the date of the court-ordered move-out is approximately five weeks.

A court staff member who oversaw eviction cases marveled at the gravity of the work the staff performed each day. "We are witnessing somebody's worst day of their life in court every single day," he observed solemnly. Wearing a pinched expression, he remarked, "This is a really serious crisis moment when [tenants] are leaving this court," referring to tenants who received a judgment against them in an eviction hearing. "They're walking out with their children, and people are devastated."

Often tenants do not appear at an eviction hearing, which then proceeds with just the plaintiff—the landlord—who is sometimes joined by an attorney.[26] Tenants have a variety of reasons for not appearing at a court eviction hearing. The scheduled hearing date may conflict with their work or child care obligations. If the landlord holds legitimate evidence that a tenant has breached the lease—for example, through nonpayment of rent—the tenant may see little benefit to attending the hearing, especially if it necessitates being absent from work or forgoing other obligations. The tenant's appearance at an eviction hearing increases not only the amount of time spent on each case but also the likelihood of the tenant receiving a verdict in their favor. In an in-depth study of Cleveland Municipal Housing Court eviction case outcomes, 61 percent of cases were decided in favor of the landlord when a tenant was not present, and only 47 percent were decided in the landlord's favor when the tenant attended the hearing.[27]

The Housing Court sees the worrisome consequences of an increasingly cashless economy, for both tenants and landlords, as staff adjudicate disputes over tenants' alleged nonpayment of rent in an alternative "currency," notably labor. Tenants' struggles to garner sufficient cash to pay rent prompts some landlords to accept their labor, such as painting or carpentry, as full or partial payment, but such payments are difficult to quantify and document as "rent." In these circumstances, Housing Court staff find it difficult to render verdicts that protect renters' access to housing. A magistrate remarked that these arrangements, though not illegal, are "ill advised." "It puts everybody at risk," she explained slowly. "The landlord has a harder time proving no rent was paid, because the tenant is like, 'Yes, but I painted a quarter of that wall.'" Squinting in concentration, she wondered, "So, is that partial payment of rent for that month?" Of course, she noted, "it is just easier to keep that stuff separate," but "that is not reality." Shaking her head, the magistrate admitted, "People don't have the money to keep it separate."

"Like Collecting Blood from a Stone"

In second-cause hearings, landlords and tenants dispute money matters. Landlords may pursue tenants to collect on debt, whether accrued through unpaid rent or the costs to reimburse them for excessive property damages. Second-cause hearings are also where tenants can pursue landlords for uncollected debt—for example, an unreturned security deposit.

The crowd is much sparser at second-cause hearings. Most landlords who house low-income tenants do not attempt to collect on debt in second-cause court. They explained to me that it wasn't worth the cost to file and, when applicable, pay a lawyer or debt collection agency to pursue a debt that they believed to be uncollectible. Because a tenant must be employed in order to garnish their wages, collecting unpaid rent is "like collecting blood from a stone," a landlord told me disappointedly. It is not uncommon for a tenant who has just been evicted to have fallen behind on rent because they recently lost their job. Further, there are some sources of income that the courts do not permit landlords to garnish, including government entitlements such as Social Security, SSI (Supplemental Security Income), and SSDI (Social Security Disability Insurance).

Even if the landlord receives a judgment that permits them to garnish a tenant's wages, they must perform the legwork to verify the tenant's employment. Notably, a landlord cannot collect the debt in one lump sum, but rather can only receive payments in installments. A portion of a tenant's wages is automatically deducted from their paycheck and placed in an account maintained by the court. The court then distributes the funds to the landlord or their attorney.

Less experienced landlords are sometimes surprised to learn of the obstacles to collecting on debt from tenants. A court official mused to me, "You'll hear it every once in a while, it doesn't happen too often, but [landlords] win in court on a small claims case, and then they'll go, 'Okay, so where do I get my check?'" He chuckled, "Well, unfortunately, you're missing the point, that's not how it works. Now you have to collect on this judgment."

For many landlords, it is the obstacles to suing unemployed tenants for debt accrued through missed rent or excessive wear-and-tear on the property that fostered their belief that the unemployed are "risky" to house. Lack of employment can thus block renters' access to affordable housing for reasons besides landlords' immediate concerns about whether applicants will pay rent consistently as they turn away those who can in fact afford their rent by drawing on sources of income that cannot be garnished, including SSDI (Social Security Disability Insurance), which assists lower-income renters with a disability. This practice, by disproportionately disadvantaging renters with a disability who collect government assistance, constitutes a violation of the Fair Housing Act of 1968 and its later amendments, which protect residents from discrimination in renting or buying a home on the grounds of race, color, national origin, religion, sex, family status, or disability.[28]

In addition to cases pertaining to occupancy, eviction, and rent, the Housing Court oversees cases regarding the quality of housing conditions. All homeowners, including landlords, are required by state and local laws to maintain their properties so as to protect residents and the surrounding community. For example, state and local codes mandate that housing must be structurally safe—no caving roofs or sagging porches. The paint job must be adequate, without signs of chipping or peeling. These mandates are not simply cosmetic; they are meant to ensure the safety of residents and the vitality of the surrounding community.

Lead-based paint has been implicated in a nationwide lead exposure epidemic—chipping paint is the primary method by which children, who are most cognitively and physically affected by lead poisoning, ingest lead.[29] By fostering residents' sense of unsafety, structural problems also have implications for their mental health. Feeling unsafe can motivate families to reactively change residences, but this often hasty move can culminate in worse housing conditions, especially for lower-income families who struggle to secure housing because of slim budgets and stigma.[30]

The spread of deteriorating properties also has implications for individual residents' wealth accumulation and for city budgets as it triggers local crime and falling property values. The population loss caused by deteriorating properties and crime, with the ensuing drop in property values, leaves fewer tax dollars for the city to fund vital services, including policing, school systems, and housing code enforcement.[31] Accordingly, the court and other city agencies have strong incentives to address undesirable housing conditions in communities and curtail the vicious downward spiral that could ensue if they do not.

Systematic observations of the quality of the housing stock in the city of Cleveland, however, indicate that housing codes are not applied uniformly. Observations performed in 2015 by the nonprofit organization Western Reserve Land Conservancy revealed that the vast majority of properties graded D and F as a result of hazardous and egregious code violations were concentrated in its predominantly Black, lower-income communities to the east, where its affordable rental stock is concentrated.[32] As will be seen, tenants and residents face an undue burden through a "reactive" housing and health code enforcement system, which is largely driven by their complaints instead of city inspectors' routine inspections. Tenants' and residents' incentives (and disincentives) to report problematic properties to authorities are not distributed equally across geographic areas. Accordingly, building codes that are meant to protect all residents and renters simply do not.

The Perils of a Reactive Code Enforcement System

Few authorities lamented the city's reactive code enforcement system to me more than the Housing Court's sixth and longest-serving judge, Raymond Pianka, who repeatedly commented about the "uneven fortunes of Cleveland's neighborhoods." He took the bench in 1996, as the region's housing problems began to escalate more rapidly. Judge Pianka approached the bench with unique expertise: he was a former city council representative and the director of the highly successful Detroit Shoreway Development Corporation, a nonprofit community development corporation (CDC) that managed to reverse the downward trajectory of the West Side's working-class community. After taking the bench, he looked to build a legacy on defending the interests of ordinary residents. That goal was part of the larger vision he held— to create a "problem-solving" court that would address the root of the problems coming before it.

Each day at lunchtime, the judge, a tall man in his midsixties with sandy-colored hair and a neatly trimmed mustache, left his black robe in his court chambers to walk the city streets as an ordinary resident. Together, Judge Pianka and I walked on a quiet street in Slavic Village, a lower-income East Side community with a high proportion of low-cost rental housing. In the wake of the housing market crash, the community had been labeled "ground zero" for its high foreclosure rates and rapid decline in property values.[33] Much of the community's quaint housing stock appeared aged, with faded yellow or blue exteriors. Some properties featured a crisp paint job, new windows, or a lush garden. Newly constructed housing, with a sleek design that contrasted with the older housing stock, had even sprung up in spots. There were also flat plots of grassy land, post-demolition. Several of these lots were tidy, with lawns kept neatly trimmed; others had been overtaken by tall weeds and were peppered with stray debris. A corner lot was piled with torn clothing, stacks of bricks and wood, and a stark white rectangular sign whose red letters read: MEDICAL CENTER.

The judge's expression lit up at the sight of a family enjoying the sunny day on the porch of a small bungalow house. A Black man leaned back in a colorful red-yellow-and-blue rocking chair. Several younger boys sat on the porch stairs, balancing bowls of cereal in their laps. "That's a beautiful chair!" the judge pointed and cheered.

"Thank you," the man replied graciously, nodding.

"That house across the street," the judge said, swiveling to point toward a two-story, beige-and-brown Victorian-style house across the street with several broken windows and patches of peeling paint, "have you seen anyone in there lately? A tenant?"

"No, I have not," the man responded stoically. The boys, quietly observing the conversation, shook their heads.

"Have you seen any activity? The landlord?" Judge Pianka wondered.

"No, no one's doing anything on it. Not for a while," the man responded matter-of-factly.

"Do you have a landlord?" Judge Pianka then asked, pointing at a splintered patch of wood on the porch. They all nodded. "You should talk to him about that," he told the group earnestly. "He should really do something about that." After he wished them a good afternoon, we continued our walk. The judge told me he might look into the property's records back at the courthouse.

As Judge Pianka reminded me, his court, like all other courts, can only hear cases that are brought before it. It is not within the court's jurisdiction to conduct inspections to discover code violations, nor to legitimize reports of them; that is the duty of the city's Building and Housing Department. Upon receiving a complaint, department staff typically dispatch an inspector to assess the property conditions. If the inspector's observation legitimizes the complaint, the property owner will receive a violation notice in the mail that indicates the nature of the violation and the amount of time allotted to remediate it (typically thirty days). If, upon reinspection, an inspector discovers that the owner has failed to remediate the violation in the allotted time, the case may be forwarded to the Housing Court. At a criminal hearing in court, the owner may incur fines or even criminal misdemeanor charges for non-compliance with housing or health codes.[34]

Unlike some of its wealthier suburbs, whose tax base can support routine inspection of the rental housing stock, the city of Cleveland takes a reactive, complaint-driven approach to enforcing important building codes. Accordingly, city authorities largely learn about housing code violations—peeling paint, a leaking ceiling, a broken furnace—through complaints, whether from renters, local residents, CDCs, or city council members.[35] Among the ten thousand housing complaints received by the Building and Housing Department in 2015, close to 70 percent came from "the public" — renters and residents.

Strikingly, the geographic distribution of "public" complaints across the city does not align with the surveyors' systematic observation of the exterior conditions of the housing stock. The public complaints are distributed far more evenly than the D- and F-graded properties, which are concentrated in poor and predominantly Black communities to the east (as seen in figure 2.1).

The Empowered Homeowner and Marginalized Tenant

Housing tenure and economic advantage may begin to explain why complaints are filed about properties in the city's predominantly White communities to the west more than expected, given the assessed housing conditions. Communities that are predominantly homeowner-occupied typically show higher levels of collective efficacy — that is, a community's recognition of shared goals and willingness to work together toward them.[36] An administrator with the city of Cleveland reported that sometimes her staff received a "pile-on" of complaints from multiple homeowners, typically in a middle-income West Side community, for what could be considered a small-scale violation, such as overgrown grass. The pile-on could reflect collective efficacy, as well as homeowners' unique financial stake in the conditions in their community through the value of their property — the largest asset for most Americans. A rundown property could lower the value of the neighbor's home across the street, thereby motivating complaints about nearby property disrepair.[37] The official acknowledged that it was important for the city to respond to all complaints, though doing so diverted the overworked inspector staff away from tackling the serious conditions that were more commonly reported on the city's struggling East Side, including conditions in OVV — open, vacant, and vandalized — properties.

Renters, on the other hand, face disincentives to report housing problems in the unit where they reside, this official noted, and especially for interior code violations. As she explained, a complaint about an exterior condition, like caving porch steps, could easily originate with a neighbor, CDC representative, or other city official. Yet, she noted assuredly, "when there is a complaint about interior conditions, like mold, the landlord *has* to know it's coming from the tenant." Accordingly, the tenant may fear retaliation from the landlord, perhaps an eviction, as a result of their formal complaint. This is especially worrisome for low-income tenants who have limited housing options.

Figure 2.1   Maps of Cleveland, Properties Graded D or F and Housing Complaints, 2015

A. Properties graded D/F in 2015

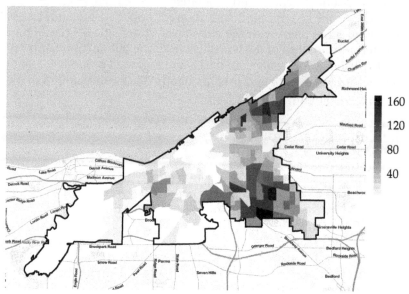

B. Complaints in 2015

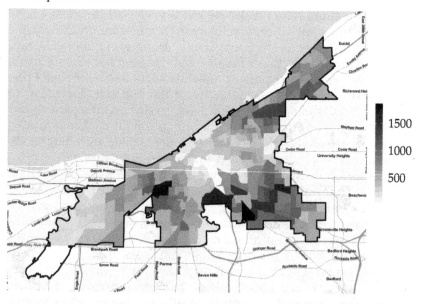

Source: Author's compilations using data from the 2015 Western Reserve Land Conservancy systematic property assessment survey and housing code complaints received by the Cleveland Building and Housing Department in 2015.

Given the high stakes of filing a formal housing complaint, marginalized tenants pursue informal, off-the-record advice about their housing concerns, as seen by staff at one of the largest nonprofit organizations in the region that defend tenants' rights, the Cleveland Tenants Organization (CTO). In 2014, the organization received over twelve thousand calls to its tenant hotline, most of them coming from renters who were lower-income, Black, and residing on the city's East Side. Interior disrepair was the most common complaint to the helpline, a CTO representative told us. "'My landlord—they supplied the stove, and I've been hounding them for five months to fix the stove, and they haven't fixed it,'" she offered as an example of a common tenant concern. Or, she continued, "'My landlord won't turn the boiler on.'"

The CTO staff then revealed an important reason why tenants are unable to benefit from housing laws meant to protect them: "administrative burden," or the "learning, psychological, and compliance costs that citizens experience in their interactions with government."[38] The representative remarked that tenants are often unaware of the legal procedures they can pursue to compel their landlords to adhere to housing laws, and without jeopardizing their access to housing. She observed the consequences of administrative burden in speaking with callers who sought advice on how to compel landlords to remediate inadequate property conditions. "We ask people when they call, 'Did you pay your rent?'" the representative noted, and then lamented to us, "In Ohio, if you haven't paid your rent, you really have little standing, even to do anything, even if you've been wronged. A lot of tenants don't know, and they withhold their rent thinking, 'Well, screw you,' and what they've really done is put themselves in peril, particularly of getting evicted."

Ohio's 1974 Tenant-Landlord Law established a "rent escrow" procedure for tenants to use in order to compel a landlord to comply with housing codes. "Basically, you put your money in with the Clerk of Courts instead of the landlord," the representative began enthusiastically. "And the idea is, of course, the minute you start withholding money from the landlord, it gives them an incentive to like, actually do something." She continued: "The landlords all know what that means, and the minute you start talking rental deposit, people know you know the law, people know you know the process. And a lot of times, it lights a fire under them." Tenants were reluctant, however, to pursue the rent escrow process, even though "you don't need a lawyer, and it's free." The representative explained that "tenants, and pretty low-income tenants, are incredibly fearful of retaliation. They're just like, 'Where else am I gonna go?'"

Mistrust toward authorities is another reason why marginalized tenants are reluctant to interact with authorities so as to benefit from codes meant to protect them. "They hear the word 'court,'" the representative said ominously. Benefiting from the rent escrow process requires that tenants interact with a legal system that can spark their mistrust toward authorities, or "legal cynicism," which can develop through firsthand negative experiences with law authorities or from learning about others' negative experiences, including through the media.[39] Importantly, legal cynicism and mistrust toward one government authority can spill over to mistrust of another authority, leading to "system avoidance"—avoiding interactions with an entire system of institutions that keep formal records, such as hospitals and schools.[40]

Practices by the Cleveland Police Department give the city's residents, and especially its Black residents, good reason to mistrust law authorities. In 2014, U.S. Attorney General Eric Holder and the Justice Department released a report on an investigation of Cleveland Police Department practices and its pattern of using excessive force that violated constitutional rights, and it recommended sweeping reforms to the police department. The Justice Department did not explicitly investigate racial profiling, but the report noted Black residents' reports of verbally and physically aggressive police behavior and described their perception of the barriers to complaining about mistreatment at the hands of Cleveland police officers.[41]

Despite landlords' profit motives for being in the business, they are occasionally willing to forgo their financial interests in exchange for a sense of procedural justice—the perception that the law is implemented in ways that are neutral, receptive to constituents' voices, and respectful.[42] Accordingly, rather than simply imposing mandates on landlords as a means to protect renters, the Housing Court attempts to bring landlords into the decision-making process, when possible, and positive outcomes for tenants can result. The next section describes the court's methods for pursuing procedural justice: a mediation program and its bailiff procedures.

Crafting an Agreement: "I Am a Neutral Party"

The court's alternative dispute resolution (ADR) services, commonly called "mediation," give both parties an opportunity to construct a resolution that could be mutually beneficial. Such resolutions stand in contrast with the first-cause or second-cause cases heard in the courtroom, which typically culminate in a "winning" party and a "losing" party as decided by magistrates, who are bound by the law in deciding cases. According to Housing Court records, close to 85 percent of the cases brought to mediation are resolved there, without the landlord and tenant having to step in front of a judge or a magistrate in the courtroom.

Before the start of eviction hearings each day, the mediator calls out to the tenants, landlords, and lawyers seated on wooden benches or standing in the back of the room, asking if they are interested in mediating their case. Throughout the day, the mediator continues to call to the crowd, which ebbs and flows as the magistrate moves through the docket. Both the landlord and the tenant must agree to the mediation, which is conducted around a table in a small, glass-walled room connected to the courtroom.

"I am a neutral party," the mediator immediately announces to those gathered around the table. After both parties have the opportunity to tell their side of the dispute, the mediator presents some alternative solutions to settle the dispute, all while maintaining order in the room. In the case of an eviction, the landlord may agree to a "voluntary vacate," which allows the tenant to avoid having a stigmatized mark of eviction on their record. Other benefits that tenants occasionally accrue in mediation include a move-out period extended beyond the seven to ten business days typically designated by magistrates. Having additional time on the property helps tenants as they try to secure new housing. Occasionally, landlords even agree to allow tenants who have fallen behind on rent payments to stay in their property, as long as they adhere to an agreed-upon payment plan to remit the rent money they owe.

Most mediation hearings unfold calmly, though occasional outbursts occur. At the start of one mediation session, I watched a Black man in his thirties, wearing neatly tied dreadlocks and a gray hooded sweatshirt, glare across the table at his landlord, an Asian Indian man wearing a plaid button-down shirt. Soon after the mediator began the session, the tenant pointed at the landlord and erupted, "This man is a slumlord! I shouldn't owe him anything." The landlord sat up stiffly and began to holler back. Within seconds, the mediator called out "Freeze!" and the room fell silent. After several minutes of discussion, the landlord agreed to a voluntary vacate—as did every landlord who brought their eviction case to mediation that day.

Landlords also benefit from having their case heard in mediation. Agreeing to a voluntary vacate spares them the cost of mover's fees to remove a tenant's belongings, if necessary, on the court-ordered move-out date. Plus, landlords whose properties are registered as limited liability corporations (LLCs) are required to have legal representation in courtroom hearings, but not in mediation.

Having a poorly maintained property also motivates some landlords to opt for settling their case in mediation. The landlord thus avoids scrutiny from a magistrate, who could order an inspection upon hearing about code violations from the tenant or their lawyer. If an inspector discovers code violations, the landlord could be required to make necessary repairs and might incur fines or even criminal sanctions. Yet another reason landlords choose to settle cases in mediation is that a tenant's airing of grievances about poor property conditions in the public courtroom amounts to negative advertising for the property.

Some combination of these motivations led to a settlement between a tenant and a landlord over a security deposit dispute. The tenant, a twenty-something Black woman wearing a short-sleeved purple silk blouse, sat slumped at the table with a dazed expression. Across the table sat her landlord, a White man in his forties wearing a blue button-down shirt; his thirty-something White property manager in a white T-shirt; and a stern-looking White man, the lawyer, dressed in a dark gray suit.

"Who wants to live in a roach-infested apartment?" the tenant choked out as tears streamed down her face. She said that when she told the property manager about her fear of bugs when she toured the vacant apartment, she had been relieved when he reassured her that wouldn't be a problem. However, roaches were scattered throughout the kitchen on the day she moved in—or attempted to. "I couldn't move in," she told the mediator, while shaking her head and dabbing tears from her cheeks. She left a voice message for the landlord to indicate that she would not be moving in, and then she found housing with a different landlord.

According to Ohio's Tenant-Landlord Law, the tenant, who had not pursued any legal procedures to formally terminate the lease, was still liable for paying the rent. Now, several months later, she sat across the table from the landlord in pursuit of her $300 security deposit. The landlord had refused to return the deposit, citing her breach of the lease in failing to either formally terminate the lease or make rent payments. To defend her decision, she took out her phone to play several messages for her that had been left by the property manager. His pale cheeks grew blotchy while listening to himself acknowledge the bug infestation and provide assurance that it would be remediated.

The mediator firmly stated, "I hope we can reach an agreement," and reminded both parties of what they stood to lose in bringing the case in front of the magistrate instead of working out an agreement in mediation. In a formal hearing, he instructed the tenant, the magistrate could decide in favor of the landlord, citing a breach of lease; in that event, she would lose the security deposit. Yet, he informed the landlord, bringing the case in front of a magistrate in the courtroom would inform the public of the building's unsanitary conditions.

The landlord, property manager, and lawyer huddled behind the table in conversation, while the tenant stared down stonily at the table.

"Okay," the lawyer finally declared, turning around and straightening his suit jacket. "She doesn't owe the deposit." Later, I asked the mediator whether the dispute would have been resolved differently in the courtroom. "Frankly, they had every right to keep the security deposit," the mediator responded matter-of-factly, reflecting on Ohio's Tenant-Landlord Law. "They didn't have to give that back." If the landlord had demanded that a magistrate hear the case in the courtroom, the mediator surmised, "they would've went in and won."

"We Can't Do This Today. Call the Landlord"

While magistrates and mediators do their work in the courthouse, "blue shirt" bailiffs go out in the field to carry out court orders, mostly for eviction move-outs. If the tenant has not vacated the property by the move-out date, the landlord may request the services of the court bailiffs, whose job is to physically remove tenants from the premises and oversee the work of the court-approved movers that landlords must hire to move tenants' belongings to the curb. Early in the morning, bailiffs set out, stony-faced, wearing bulletproof vests. Eviction set-outs can be emotionally charged, and in rare instances carrying them out has been life-threatening for bailiffs. In 2015, several bailiffs dodged gunshots from a male tenant who huddled behind his apartment door on the court-ordered move-out date. The incident ended tragically, with the tenant's self-inflicted fatal gunshot wound.[43] Not surprisingly, the bailiffs insisted that I wear a bulletproof vest when joining them on their daily rounds.

Guided by a list of property addresses for the day, the bailiffs drive up to meet the landlord, look to remove any occupants who are not lawfully entitled to be in the property, and oversee the movers' work. The bailiffs approach each situation with what several described as a "desensitized, but not callous" approach. Keenly attuned to their surroundings, they appear assertive but not aggressive.

When tenants have already vacated the property, sometimes fleeing just several hours earlier, the case is easy. There is minimal work for the bailiffs beyond maintaining safety on the scene and overseeing the work of the movers hired by the landlord—often a crew of young Black men and women. The movers descend on the property like worker ants, stoically marching in and out, dismantling the remnants of the tenants' lives. Though these crews are described as "movers," they are more accurately termed "removers": they extract belongings from a property, leave them at the curb, then begin once again at the next move-out.

The hardest work for bailiffs takes place when they discover that tenants are still on the property on the court-appointed move-out date.

These are the tenants who face the direst circumstances: they have nowhere else to go, and no family or friends to help them, and many suffer from physical or mental health problems that make it difficult or impossible to leave. In these cases, bailiffs wear many hats: as counselors calming agitated tenants, as guardians of the movers and landlords, and as caseworkers connecting tenants to services. Court officials told us that they occasionally received calls from bailiffs in the field who were concerned about the health and safety of an elderly or ill tenant whom they were about to set out.

In cases where a tenant seems to face catastrophic circumstances upon eviction, court officials will ask landlords if they would postpone the set-out by several days. With this extra time, the court attempts to connect the tenant with emergency housing or health care services. In most cases, one magistrate reported, landlords will consent to the court's request. She reflected, "Occasionally, we will extend the move-out, and I thought landlords would be having a conniption, but they are not. They are pretty good about it." Nodding slowly, she observed, "Landlords are really very patient about it if they know [staff] are legitimately working on getting something together."

I watched the court staff work with a landlord to delay the move-out of a frazzled elderly tenant. The bailiff, Sam, a stout, forty-something White man, pressed the doorbell of the tall, Victorian-style house. "Who's that?" a woman's voice called out lightly from inside. A few moments later, a petite, elderly Black woman opened the door. She first noticed Sam and the other bailiff, a tall, slim White man, standing on her front porch. Then her jaw dropped when she saw a group of mostly White men and women, the movers, standing on the street in front of a large, white moving van. A few interested bystanders clustered together on the sidewalk.

"Is everyone here, for me?" she asked incredulously, seeming tickled and in awe. Sam gently explained to her that the landlord had received a court judgment to evict her. Scanning her flat expression, he asked, "Were you aware . . . of this?" Appearing puzzled but still calm, she quipped, "You can't evict me, I'm seventy-five years old. I'm going to die tomorrow!" The movers and the growing crowd of bystanders erupted in nervous, muffled chuckles. "Not on my watch," Sam assured her.

When the bailiffs stepped inside the towering home, the tenant became even more frazzled as she tried to understand the reason for their visit. She hobbled and stumbled through the house, pulling out the contents of kitchen drawers and lifting up stacks of papers, in search of a document, a bill, anything, to demonstrate to everyone, including herself, that the rent was paid. The rent had been paid steadily for over a decade through government checks that she received for her deceased husband's military service, she explained to the bailiffs. "I don't understand," she sputtered, her frail hands twitching and shaking the papers in her hands.

Then Sam climbed the home's tall, winding staircase to assess the amount of work that the movers would need to perform. Each floor brimmed with couches, wooden cabinets, carved wooden chairs, stained-glass lamps, and ornate rugs. Poker-faced, Sam hustled back downstairs to join the other bailiff, who watched over the crowd while standing in the front door frame. Sam paced a few short, stiff steps and then broke his composure to nod and confess to his colleague, "We can't do this today. Call the landlord." Within ten minutes' time, the court staff had spoken with and received consent from the landlord to extend the move-out. A caseworker at the court would contact the tenant and refer her to an agency that could help her secure new housing, most likely the Cleveland Department of Aging or the U.S. Department of Veterans Affairs. The movers left and the crowd of onlookers slowly dissipated. The bailiffs' work there was done for the day.

As observed by Cleveland Municipal Housing Court staff, the city officials who oversee code enforcement, and representatives of local tenants rights organizations, the region's marginalized renters face extreme housing insecurity on the basis of their social and financial positions. Aside from lacking the resources to afford decent, stable housing, renters encounter obstacles to obtaining information about the laws and practices meant to protect them; they also face deterrents, including mistrust of authorities, to report disadvantageous landlord practices.

The local housing advocacy community continues its fight to protect the region's renters, despite several devastating blows. The Cleveland Tenants Organization shut down in 2018, citing difficulties in maintaining their operations in the face of the local government's funding cuts. The Legal Aid Society of Cleveland subsequently took over CTO's Tenant Information Line in 2018, ensuring renters' continued access to informal advice about their rights and responsibilities.[44] In 2019, the city of Cleveland passed an ordinance that guarantees to low-income tenants with children facing an eviction no-cost legal counsel through Right to Counsel–Cleveland (RTC-C), a partnership between the Legal Aid Society of Cleveland and United Way of Greater Cleveland.[45]

The Housing Court continues its work as a "problem-solving" institution, despite the unexpected passing of Judge Pianka in 2017. At the public memorial service for the judge, attendees received red rubber wristbands etched with "WWRD4CLE," which stood for "What Would Ray Do For Cleveland?" That question guided the court staff's ongoing work, they explained to me after his death, whether in struggling to adjudicate a difficult case or working to ensure the success of the mediation, referral, and other programs that Judge Pianka encouraged the court to devise. These programs showed continued success under the leadership of subsequent judges. Each year the referral program helped connect more residents to financial and social assistance than the year before. The mediation program's success rate remained above 80 percent, court authorities reported in 2019. New programs evolved under the leadership of subsequent judges, including a procedure enabling tenants to have their eviction records sealed so they can avoid the blocked opportunities associated with the stigma of an eviction or an eviction filing.[46]

This chapter has explained some of the macro-level and systemic forces that make it difficult for renters to benefit from their legal protections. We have seen that the goal of ensuring that all renters have access to decent, stable, affordable housing cannot be achieved without considering the landlord's perspective. Tenants' burdens and disincentives to navigate the legal system can certainly provide an opportunity for landlords to evade laws without legal or financial consequences. Yet ensuring access to decent housing for all cannot be accomplished without understanding landlords' motivations to pursue illegitimate business practices that disadvantage renters.

The following four chapters illustrate a central premise of this book: that local laws intended to protect renters and communities not only fall short but even inadvertently deepen their disadvantage. They do so by giving landlords reasons and justification for pursuing disadvantageous, unethical, and sometimes illegal business practices, including discriminatory screening, subpar property maintenance, tenant harassment, and informal evictions, in part because of characteristics they share with tenants—financial precarity and mistrust toward authorities.

Chapter 3

"I May Just Have to Walk Away"

N UMEROUS GOVERNMENT policies have created deep disadvantage in poor, predominantly Black communities. This chapter illustrates a set of present-day mechanisms by which government practices can perpetuate the struggles of those living in marginalized communities, focusing on the counterproductive effects, through landlords, of housing codes that are meant to protect renters and communities.

Contrary to the conventional wisdom that the business of renting properties to low-income tenants in struggling communities draws only investors with ill intentions, this chapter highlights the significant diversity in the origin stories of landlords who operate in these communities. Some are longtime "holders" — landlords who entered the business years earlier with significant investment, intending to rent properties over an extended period of time and maintain them in good condition, as enabled through tenants' consistent rent payment.[1] The business practices of some others model those of investors described by Alan Mallach as "milkers" — landlords who typically enter the business with little upfront payment and then collect rent, often from low-income renters, while investing little back in the property.[2] Eventually, these landlords abandon their properties.

This chapter describes the structural and social forces that motivate landlords to evade housing laws and to justify doing so whether or not they began as a "holder" or a "milker." These forces include stark financial precarity triggered by the unpredictable costs encountered in the business of providing affordable rental housing in poor communities. Landlords' sense of financial precarity was deepened by their "legal cynicism" — their belief that city authorities were not effective in enforcing codes meant to protect public safety and property values. Reinforced by the belief that city authorities did not consider the interests of small-time landlords when implementing policies, legal cynicism further weakened landlords' sense of obligation to adhere to the law.[3] For some landlords, their belief that marginalized renters did

not necessarily deserve access to good-quality housing further undermined any sense of obligation to adhere to housing codes meant to
protect renters.

Landlords' disincentives to adhere to housing codes are especially
consequential in a context where renters have disincentives to report
landlords' code violations and where authorities have disincentives
to enforce codes. As explained in chapter 2 by the representative from
the Cleveland Tenants Organization, the local tenants rights organization, low-income tenants are "incredibly fearful" about engaging
with authorities to complain about housing conditions—both because
they fear retaliatory eviction, given their limited housing options, and
because they mistrust authorities. Meanwhile, building inspectors "go
easy" in doling out citations for code violations to homeowners and
small-time investors in poor communities to spare them the expense of
costly repair work.[4] City authorities expressed concern to me, and also
reporters, that "hammering" landlords through stricter code enforcement could undermine the quality and availability of the affordable
housing stock by persuading landlords to abandon their low-valued
properties instead of investing in repairing them.

Taken together, these disincentives demonstrate that, in attempting
to address the disadvantage found in poor Black communities, as first
created through discriminatory laws, seemingly race-neutral policies
fail to account for the social and economic circumstances of landlords
and their tenants.

Reports of financial precarity were widespread among the entire sample
of landlords. I define "financial precarity" as real or perceived uncertainty about whether revenue earned in the business is sufficient to
cover the multitude of "costs of doing business," while also leaving the
landlord with a satisfactory take-home profit.

Financial precarity was most commonly reported by the landlords with
small property holdings who operated at the lowest end of the housing
market, typically in poor, often predominantly Black, communities. They
linked their financial precarity to that of the renters they had a reasonable
chance of attracting to their properties and securing as tenants, given
the rise in property deterioration and crime that follows the under-
enforcement of housing and health codes. Unlike landlords who enter
the business through "circumstantial" means, such as property inheritance,
all of these landlords in our sample entered the business in pursuit of
wealth accumulation.[5] That goal motivated these landlords to evade laws
meant to protect renters in order to conserve their scarce resources.[6]

The sociologists George Sternlieb and Robert Burchell noted that
property owners' divestment process unfolds quite predictably.[7] First,

non-essential repairs, like fixing a loose door knob or a torn window screen, are delayed. Then owners stall on making essential repairs, such as fixing a broken furnace or taking care of a ceiling leak. Their property tax payments stop—depriving cities of the resources needed to fund essential services, including police and housing inspectors. Eventually, the owner abandons the property.

"I Kinda Let It Go Downhill"

"Come by on Thursday," Quinn, a slim, middle-aged White man with buzzed blond hair, had told me over the phone. "I'll be waiting for some folks to come by."

Quinn was searching for a tenant to fill a vacancy that opened up in his duplex's three-bedroom apartment because he evicted the former tenant, a young woman, after she fell a month behind on rent. During the previous three weeks, Quinn had worked on cosmetic upgrades to attract a new tenant, including a fresh coat of yellow paint on the apartment's walls and glaze on its wood floors.

The address Quinn provided led to a tall, colonial-style house with a nicely painted dark gray exterior, white pillars, and a small patch of tidy grass in front. Quinn, wearing a white T-shirt, stood at the window of the upstairs apartment, seemingly in conversation. After noticing my arrival on the street below, he frantically pointed down toward a side door by the driveway and then disappeared from sight. A minute later he appeared at the door to hold it open, telling me breathlessly, "I've got someone here," before turning to race back up the interior stairs with the gait of a man twenty years younger. Once inside the apartment, he beelined back toward the front window to rejoin a young Black woman who wore a bright pink T-shirt and blue jeans and had hair neatly scraped into a bun. "This is Stacy," Quinn announced excitedly. She smiled shyly and said, "Hello." "She's not like the others," he beamed, extending an arm out toward her. "She's got a job!" Her expression dimmed, Stacy returned to Quinn's tour of the apartment.

"Freshly painted!" he remarked while gesturing at its yellow walls, which were a welcome change from the stark white paint jobs found in many units at the lower end of the rental market. Next, he brought her to see the kitchen, which had gray cabinets, dark gray linoleum tiles, and a bright white tiled backsplash. "It's got a pretty good amount of space, I think," Quinn informed Stacy earnestly, holding his hand up to his chest. Finally, he led her into two small bedrooms with mottled wood floors that were coated in a clear, plastic-like glaze.

"I'm going to think about it," Stacy told Quinn with an apprehensive smile, causing his eyes to glaze over. As she rummaged through her dark crossbody purse for the keys to her car out front, she explained that she wanted to see several other apartments before selecting one. "All right. You know how to reach me," Quinn said cheerily. "Let me walk you out." After holding the downstairs door open for Stacy, he called out, "Bye-bye!" and climbed the dusty staircase much more slowly than he did before. "Well, you never know," he remarked drily, raising his brow. His disappointment was clear; he didn't expect to hear from Stacy again. In his experience, tenants who held stable jobs were increasingly difficult to attract. "I try pretty hard. And I still struggle," Quinn said glumly. He lifted a yellow pad from the white kitchen counter to scratch off Stacy's name on a list of a dozen other crossed-out names of prospective tenants who told him earlier that they couldn't tour the apartment after all.

For the rest of the afternoon, Quinn paced in his bright white sneakers across the apartment's wood floors as he talked about the decline of the rental business, alternating between bursts of earnest reflection, excitement so extreme that he tripped over his words, and occasional sarcastic and off-color commentary. He had entered the rental business in the 1980s, after completing a degree in health care, with the purchase of the gray duplex. The local community drew his interest, he recalled, because it "was kind of awesome!" The neighborhood then bustled with small factories, Polish delis, and bars that drew crowds of locals each night. Working-class and middle-income renters showed interest in the area's rentals, and rents were on the rise.

As part of a successful strategy, Quinn planned to keep maintenance costs low by drawing on the carpentry and plumbing skills he learned from his father, a professional carpenter. "I looked at the way rents were going, and I knew I'd have everything paid off and I had [stock] investments," he reminisced dreamily, crossing his arms while leaning against the kitchen counter. "I said, 'You know, if I do this right, I should be able to retire and just run my rental properties by the time I hit forty-five.'"

Over the following decade, Quinn generated satisfactory profit in the business of renting to working-class tenants, but then the sharp decline of the regional economy, which began in the early 2000s, upended his business model. "Our economy. Oh my God, it went to hell in Cleveland. We were losing jobs left and right," Quinn remembered, clutching his chest. Foreclosures swept through the central city and its inner-ring suburbs. Some of his tenants fled the duplex, as well as the three other duplexes nearby that he had acquired in the 1990s. "All my good tenants went out to the suburbs, because suddenly you could [rent] a house for 500 or 600 bucks," Quinn said ruefully. Suburban rental housing had become affordable to his working-class tenants after investors bought foreclosed properties cheaply and charged low rents.

More tenants fled the duplexes after an outbreak of violent crimes in the community. "I had a nice couple that lived back here," he said, gesturing toward a small white building behind the duplex. "They were a White couple," he noted with a shrug and then, with annoyance, "They got robbed and that was it. They were gone, and they were my tenants for five years." Pointing toward the front of the house, he added, "A kid got shot down here, got in a fight in the driveway." Quinn splayed his fingers outwards, as though a bomb had exploded between them. "Boom. Gone. And I can't blame them. But whose fault is that?" he pressed, glancing back and forth. "What control do I have?"

The steadily deteriorating properties and rising violent crime rates in the community made it increasingly difficult for Quinn to secure tenants who could pay rent consistently. The costs and losses associated with renting to tenants with unstable employment—missed rent, court eviction costs, and repairs to ready the property for the next tenant—fueled his determination to secure working tenants, for reasons other than their ability to pay rent consistently. "When I hear somebody's had a job for four or five years, oh, I'm going, oh you know what, then I can garnish your wages!" he said enthusiastically and swatted his arm out. "You know, something happens, I can garnish your wages." Furthermore, the ability to garnish tenants' wages for excessive wear-and-tear made him less concerned about whether they would treat the property with care. Quinn reasoned, "It's all a matter of, what do you have to lose?"

Prospective tenants who could afford his low asking rent—$550 per month—through sources of income that could not be garnished in court, including Social Security, SSDI, and child support, were occasionally surprised when Quinn turned down their application. Yet his working tenants also occasionally fell behind on rent, not because they were irresponsible but because of the precarity of the low-wage jobs they held, mostly in the local economy's service sector. In renting to applicants with criminal records, he provided them with access to affordable housing that other landlords would not. Yet the practice simultaneously closed doors to other renters, including renters with disabilities who received government cash assistance—a form of discrimination banned by the Fair Housing Act.

Eventually the sunlight grew dim and shadows began to stretch across the apartment's yellow walls and wood floors. Quinn finally took a seat in a rickety wooden chair. "Last year, it was the worst year I ever had," he admitted grimly, in regards to profit. "Finally, rents are starting to go up a little bit, but I'm charging $550 for this now. It's the most I've ever charged for it, and it's not even a 10 percent increase in twelve years." Then he grew flummoxed as he tried to estimate his net profit from renting out the duplex and his three other duplexes nearby, as well as a single-family property, in the past year. "What did I make?" he wondered, staring up at the ceiling. As with other small-time landlords, his struggle to calculate the yearly profit in his business reflected the unpredictability in his rent collection and business costs, as well as his informal record-keeping. After tallying the past year's rent revenue and costs across his seven units, which commanded between $550 and $650 per month, he concluded disappointedly, "I made about $15,000."

Nodding at a patch of crumbling paint in the kitchen—a lead poisoning hazard for small children—he noted wistfully, "I kinda let it go downhill. I'm kinda like, I'm torn between how much time am I really gonna spend on it." Pointing toward a corner by the window, he remarked, "You can see there's some peeling paint here and there, and there's some stuff that needs to be done." After staring intently at the wood floor, he lifted his head up and seemed surprised to confess, "I'm like, shit, next year, I may just have to walk away from it." Disregarding the health risk already present in the unit, Quinn maintained in a gravelly voice, "So as long as it's not a health issue, or it's not a danger to somebody, I'm just gonna pile all that stuff up." Sighing, he added softly, "Because I don't know what else to do."

Quinn and other landlords lamented the obstacles they faced in trying to generate profit by housing tenants with low and unsteady wages—obstacles daunting enough to motivate them to conserve resources by evading housing laws. That motivation was reinforced by these landlords' belief that authorities enforced housing and safety codes inconsistently in the communities where they invested, leading to persistent crime, a crumbling housing stock, and, in turn, stagnating profit in the business. This legal cynicism, based on the belief that city authorities were illegitimate, unresponsive, and ill equipped to protect the interests of the public, further undermined landlords' sense of obligation to adhere to the laws producing these unintended consequences.[8]

"Why is this such a marginalized place?" Quinn wondered with raised hands, indicating the incidents of violent crime and the signs of illegal squatter activity on the streets surrounding his rentals. When I asked if residents ever reported these circumstances to city authorities, he swatted his arm dismissively and remarked, "Oh, the guy across the street reports everything!" What actions did city authorities pursue to remediate the problem? "Nothing," he snapped. With a sigh, he added, "I'm just convinced the whole idea is, 'Hey, we'll leave them alone over here. They can do whatever they want over here. Just don't go into *these* neighborhoods.'" Sounding more convinced than he had in anything else he had said already, Quinn declared, "There's no doubt in my mind that they decided, 'Fuck the East Side.'"

"Walk Away"

Other landlords, like Laurence, were further along in divesting from their rental business as they responded to falling profits. "I'm gonna give you this address," Laurence had first said mysteriously over the phone. He carefully enunciated an address in the city of Cleveland's downtown business district. "Meet me there in ten minutes."

The address led to an old-time kosher-style deli, with dark granite lunch counters, chipped wood tables, and long booths covered in navy blue leather. The restaurant was mostly empty, except for a White man wearing an apron who was studiously cleaning a meat-slicing machine behind the counter. He lit up at the sight of Laurence, who came swiftly through the door, wearing a dark tailored suit, crisp white dress shirt, and brown dress shoes. The two men bantered animatedly for several minutes. Then, wearing a serious expression, Laurence led me and my colleague toward a booth near a window. The sunshine was a welcome change from the fluorescent lighting at his nearby nine-to-five office job.

"How long is this going to take?" Laurence asked with a steely gaze, propping his elbows on the table. "The only reason I talked to you guys today is because I'm thinking, what is it that you can do?" Shaking his head and leaning over the wooden table, he said stonily, "I'm not talking about long-term. I'm talking about now." Because, he insisted, the business had become "a total loss."

After relaxing back in the booth, Laurence gave us a glimpse into his experience in the rental business and explained how it became a "total loss." With his wife, he first purchased a two-family home on the city's West Side in the 1980s. "I rented one part out and I lived in the other, me and my family," he explained. "Just in case we lose our jobs," he figured at the time, "we'll have income." By the mid-1990s, Laurence determined that the property was generating enough cash flow to be a good investment. His face lit up as he recalled thinking, "We might as well invest in something else, right? So I bought a building on the East Side." As he recalled, "I bought it for $25,000, and I put about maybe thirty-five [$35,000] more in it." Shaking his head slowly, he emphasized, "All sweat equity, no freebies."

For a while that investment paid off as well. "I had good tenants," Laurence remembered longingly, scratching his goatee. "You know, I had bus drivers, schoolteachers, all of that. And after 9/11, all of that went sour." As the East Side communities where he bought most of his single-family and multi-unit buildings became increasingly impoverished and rife with dilapidated properties and crime, he struggled to attract tenants who held jobs enabling them to pay rent consistently. "You get lucky and get a tenant that pays rent every now and then, but for the most part, people are not working here. There's no jobs," he observed gravely. Earlier in the day, three prospective tenants had called in response to the advertisement for his vacant one-bedroom apartment, with an asking rent of $350 per month. None of the callers were employed, Laurence noted disappointedly. Then his silver cell phone on the table rang with several more calls from interested tenants.

"Hello? Yeah, the one-bedroom?" The caller, a young woman, asked Laurence to describe the apartment and the surrounding neighbor-hood. After taking a sip of soda, he told her politely, in one fell swoop, "I can tell you it's nice and clean, it's not in the best area, but it's a nice, clean one-bedroom apartment, it's only $350." Laurence's face clouded with suspicion when the caller insisted that she was interested in seeing the apartment. "Yes, okay, well, you know the area?" His mouth twitched impatiently while he listened to her response. Laurence then interjected, enunciating slowly, "Where do you live now, ma'am?" After hearing her response, he erupted, with a laugh and a wave of his hand, "Oh, hell, you ain't that much different." Slouching down in the booth, he reflected in a more serious tone, "Yeah. Yeah, you're not that much different." This was good news to Laurence; he and other landlords who rented properties on streets peppered with deteriorating properties noted that some prospective tenants who showed interest in the advertised unit over the phone balked upon seeing the downtrodden community where it was located.

"Tell me about your finances, sir," Laurence calmly instructed the next caller. He switched the phone to speaker mode so that we could listen. "I just got approved for disability for SSI," the man responded in a flat, mechanical tone, as though he had given the same speech numer-ous times before. "I'm making on a fixed income. I'm making $720 a month. I get $200 worth of food stamps." Laurence remained silent, taking small sips of soda out of his tall red cup. "So, if you don't have a problem with that," the man continued haltingly, "I also have an agency that's going to pay my first month's rent and the deposit, once they inspect the place."

"How old are you, sir?" Laurence suddenly wondered. "I'm fifty-four years old," the man answered, starting to sound less deferential and more guarded. "You're fifty-four," Laurence repeated, then continued with a slow, dubious "Okaay." After some back-and-forth conversation, Laurence jotted down the man's phone number on a paper napkin. He explained to the caller that the part-time maintenance man would get in touch to arrange a time to show the apartment. "If you like it, then you can contact me. Okay?" he concluded. Once the call ended, Laurence set the phone down on the table. "As you see," he said, extending his arm toward it, "not working." He wondered, "Why is a fifty-four-year-old on SSI? That's the question." Then he insisted knowingly, with a wave of his hand, "Guarantee, guarantee . . . drugs."

Despite his dissatisfaction with the prospective tenants he had spoken to about the apartment, Laurence insisted that it was imperative to select one soon to fill the vacancy. He had experienced over half a dozen incidents of property vandalism of a vacant unit in the marginalized East Side communities where most of his rentals were located. Using an eerily calm, schoolteacher-like tone, he began to instruct us on the fate of vacant properties in those struggling communities. "People are going to go in." Plunking a finger down on the table, and wearing a fiery gaze, he continued methodically, "They're going to tear your place apart. I'm talking about the furnace, hot water tank, the wiring. They'll sell anything." He stared intently at us. "Everything you worked for, everything you've done," he continued calmly, shaking his head in wonder. "It's going to get demolished."

Growing more despondent, Laurence recounted the "no win" situation in which he found himself: whether to incur losses through evicting, or through not evicting. Some of his tenants were several months behind on rent, yet he had not yet filed to evict. "I'm afraid to file," he confessed, tugging uneasily at his shirt collar. "Because if I leave them vacant, [vandals] are going to go tear them up." He added dejectedly, with a slow head shake, "If I don't file, these tenants are going to stay there forever and I'm never going to get anything."

"There's no new revenue to put back in the house because you're not getting a dime off 'em," Laurence finally uttered matter-of-factly, glancing around the restaurant. The tables and booths had begun to empty out. "There are still a lot of bills that I can't pay because a lot of people don't pay." The bills he referred to included thousands of dollars in property tax debt and unpaid tickets the city had issued for not mowing tall grass at several of his East Side properties.

Having determined that the business had become a total loss, Laurence considered abandoning his properties, if necessary. "Selling would be great," he remarked. A smile briefly flashed across his face, but then his expression grew dark. He reminded us of the numerous obstacles to selling his low-valued properties, which included securing an interested buyer who could satisfy lenders' criteria. "The banks appraise your property so low that [buyers] got to have a 700-plus credit score," he explained, adding, in wonder, "But now [buyers] got to meet all these criteria, and the banks don't give money under $50,000 anymore."

Beginning to sound more agitated, with his nostrils flaring, Laurence demanded, "You got to buy in cash, so if I got to sell my stuff for cash, what's the likelihood of me selling it?" He held our gaze intently, seemingly waiting for a response. Laurence did not miss a beat when he was asked what he would do next if his search for a buyer was unsuccessful. "Walk away," he declared. "If I can't sell them, walk away." He said that he had done it before and was ready to do it again.

Several laws fueled landlords' financial anxieties and mounting mistrust toward authorities, believing as they did that these laws unfairly penalized the small-time landlords who rented properties to lower-income tenants in struggling communities.

Landlords were most rattled by laws pertaining to the eviction process, which, in contrast to housing quality codes, were enforced consistently. Laurence began to list the costs of eviction for the landlord. "You got to pay to move out. You got to pay your attorney, and you're not getting any of the rent." Unlike Quinn, who also struggled to attract tenants who earned stable wages that could be garnished in court, Laurence didn't attempt to sue tenants to recoup what they owed him. "You can't get money from them because they don't have nothing to give you," he said, then raised his voice to add, "You risk a chance of taking a day off work to go to court, for what?"

Quinn spoke about the requirement to hire legal counsel to represent him at a court hearing because his property was registered as an LLC; all of the landlords in this chapter, and nearly all across the sample, had done the same. "I cannot step into a courtroom, I cannot do anything legally, without a lawyer," he mused. "So now I've gone from an eviction costing me $125 to minimally [costing] me $300." He paused. "I can see if it's an honest to God corporation, and it's multiple people, okay, we need a lawyer." But revving up, he asked, "Why do I need a lawyer? I can represent [myself]." If he didn't prevail in a case without legal representation, he insisted, he would "pay for the consequences."

Still other laws led landlords to believe that city authorities were indifferent to the plight of small-time landlords. For instance, the city of Cleveland fines the owner $75 (and higher if the business is registered as an LLC) if the property's tall green trash containers are set out earlier than the prescribed time, if they are left on the curb too long after pickup, or if they are not fully closed. Since 2009, the city has substantially increased the number of fines it doled out for violations of its waste collection ordinances.[9]

Laurence clunked down his red cup on the wood table. "Okay, with the garbage thing, they concocted that rule," he began with an incredulous grin, leaning casually on his elbow, "that's something that was voted on, put in—you got a few people to vote on it, oh, this is an ordinance now." He shook his head and looked perplexed. "Well, you don't think about how it's going to affect other people." Holding an arm out courteously, he added, "I can't come over to your house and say, 'Hey, you know what? You got to put your garbage out. You know, a couple of hours before.'" Turning more serious, Laurence muttered, "We got to change some of these stupid rules, because they all hurt the landlord."

According to Housing Court staff, it was common for landlords to complain that local laws contributed to weak or unpredictable profit in the business. They said that landlords justified their poor property maintenance by assigning blame to authorities, who they believed unjustly neglected the communities where they had invested in rental properties and did not look out for the interests of landlords. In these interviews, court staff did not dispute that the rental business was full of uncertainties and that landlords could easily dip into the red.

Regardless, court staff firmly believed that these circumstances did not absolve landlords of their responsibility to tenants, the community, and the city. "It may not be your fault," a staff member routinely told investors who complained in court that crime, vandalism, and eviction costs made it difficult to generate sufficient revenue to maintain their properties. "But," he'd remind them stoically, "it is still your obligation." Then he would warn them: "If you don't want to be a landlord, you don't have to be. But if you're going to be one, you better have the money."

Importantly, changes in the larger economy, both national and regional, created additional sources of financial precarity for these landlords. The city hospitals where Quinn worked shut down, one after another, as the region lost population and residents' financial resources declined. Currently Laurence had been seeking, without success, a different job with higher wages, whether locally or outside of the region altogether. "I had some really good job interviews," he began brightly, but then added forlornly, "Today [the employer] called me, you know, they said they were looking for somebody with a little less experience." Employers looking to conserve resources sought employees who could be paid lower wages, he surmised. Other landlords wondered how much longer they could endure their exceedingly long work hours. All of these financial factors fueled landlords' dissatisfaction with the income they earned through their rentals and increased their uncertainty about whether it was financially plausible, or rational, to invest any further in a flailing rental business.

The dissatisfied landlords who relied on their rental business as their primary source of revenue faced even stronger financial incentives to pursue illegitimate practices. Their sense of urgency when it seemed that tenant behavior could harm their bottom line—for instance, not paying rent or threatening to complain to authorities about property conditions—culminated in even more blatant landlord violations, as shown in this chapter and throughout the book.

"I Took *My* Door, Off *My* House!"

Herman was a tall, lanky forty-something Black man with a playful smile and easygoing gait. "Yeah, let's go to my office. After my son's basketball practice," he instructed over the phone. The address he provided led to a basement office in a narrow office building, located in a struggling East Side community not far from his eight rental properties. The office walls were decorated with posters of the local basketball legend LeBron James, and his desk was piled with stacks of papers and unopened mail. Relaxing back in his office chair, wearing a red paint-splattered jersey, Herman talked about entering the business nearly two decades earlier, in his midtwenties.

"Just came out of college and I want to get this rental property," Herman began energetically. His father, also a landlord, showed him how to find low-cost properties through sheriff sale listings. The first property he purchased, through a sheriff's sale, was a bust. Laws associated with sheriff's sales prohibited interested investors from entering the property prior to a purchase. Only after the purchase did Herman discover the abysmal interior conditions. "It had mushrooms about four inches big," he said in wonder, stretching his fingers out. "All on the basement wall." Lowering his head, he continued, somewhat abashed. "So the foundation had cracked. The walls were bowed."

After unloading the property, he purchased several rentals in lower-income, predominantly Black communities on the city's East Side, while attempting to secure a job with his university degree. To earn cash in the short term, he worked as a plumber and carpenter. Having little success in securing a steady job, Herman finally decided to invest enough to become a full-time landlord: he purchased eight low-cost properties in the years surrounding the housing market crash.

"Landlording is stressful," Herman reflected slowly, wearing a curious grin. "I get calls every day, tenant issue, or they're going to pay late. Or, they're not *going* to pay!" It was challenging to attract tenants with stable employment to his rentals, which were located on streets with boarded-up, vacant properties with broken windows and overgrown grass.

To stay competitive among other landlords in attracting working tenants, Herman invested in upgrades that were primarily cosmetic. "Patios, fences, and landscaping," he offered. With a thump on the desk, he continued, "People see an upgraded house, they figure the landlord's *got* some money." He imagined a tenant enthusiastically thinking, *I want to live here because the guy's gonna take care.* Despite the upgrades, Herman noted drearily, "it's not really profitable. I break even most of the time." Local market conditions had stymied his goal to sell some or all of his properties for a profit. Herman observed, "There are so many houses that are cheap to compete with," and added with a laugh, "If you want to buy one, let me know."

The tenuous employment of the working tenants he could attract culminated in losses for Herman through missed rent payments and the costs to evict tenants. Occasionally, if tenants explained that they fell behind as a result of an emergency situation—"I broke my foot," or "My cousin died"—he was lenient about the rent payment. Yet relying on his tenants' rent payments as his primary source of revenue—he worked carpentry and plumbing jobs on the side—led him to grow unduly agitated about tenants' late rent payments, particularly in light of the court costs involved in evicting tenants.

"Every time you face the judge, you're going into debt as a landlord," Herman announced. He counted up the court filing fees, lawyer costs, and moving costs on his fingers and then, with his arms straight out, burst out incredulously, "You're always paying! Whether you win or lose the case!" Citing the length of the court eviction process, which can last approximately five weeks, Herman concluded, "I guess, they don't want to see a tenant out in the cold. They don't care about the landlord not getting no money. They want to make sure the tenant is secure."

To evade what he believed was an unfairly lengthy and costly court eviction process, Herman occasionally employed informal eviction tactics. For instance, one time "a young lady moved in. Right? She could not pay the rent. So, I literally told her, 'You've got fifteen days to move your stuff out, or I'll move it out.'" When this tenant left quickly and without alerting authorities, he saw that there were few risks in pursuing informal evictions to compel tenants to pay rent or vacate the property or to intimidate them into not complaining to authorities.

"I took the door off this lady's house one time," he said nonchalantly, tilting back in the chair. "She wasn't going to pay me because I didn't repair this and that. And I threatened her by taking her door off." Tapping at his red jersey, he continued, "I took *my* door, off *my* house! It wasn't your door. My door." In extreme circumstances such as these, landlords reported, tenants did reach out to police. Indeed, Monica Bell has shown that despite their general mistrust toward the police, Black residents will seek police assistance in emergency situations.[10] Herman lit up with surprise as he recalled the tenant doing just that. "She called the police guy!"

A police officer arrived and, according to Herman, warned him about what might happen if he removed another door: "We're going to take you in." Herman bristled and sat up more stiffly in the chair. "You can't take me in, because it's *my* door on *my* house," he said staunchly, wrinkling his forehead. Twisting awkwardly in the chair, he fell silent. "Just the argument, of him having to tell me that's illegal, which I already *knew* was illegal!" he called out, staring up at the ceiling.

The officer's informal warning stung, but it didn't dissuade Herman from contemplating, and even using, other threatening tactics to keep tenants in line. He recognized that his marginalized tenants faced financial disincentives to hold their landlords accountable by, for instance, taking legal action. "The good thing," Herman remarked, "is you already know most tenants won't sue you because they don't have the money."

Tenants' social and financial marginalization is clearly important to this story of the unintended consequences of laws meant to protect them. Although landlords protested that the system was unfairly "pro tenant," they also recognized its limited surveillance over landlords' business practices, for reasons that pertained to tenants' economic and social status. As Herman explained, tenants lacked the resources to hold landlords accountable for illegitimate behavior. Furthermore, as reported in chapter 2, low-income tenants' limited housing options made them "incredibly fearful" about complaining to authorities about housing conditions, out of concern that they could lose their housing if the landlord retaliated through an eviction, as the representative from the Cleveland Tenants Organization explained.

Tenants' marginalized status mattered for other reasons as well. In line with a "culture of poverty" argument, landlords of all racial backgrounds invoked myths about their marginalized tenants' personal characteristics, including their irresponsibility, immorality, and untrustworthiness. These beliefs served to neutralize landlords' distress in failing to adhere to codes meant to protect tenants' access to safe, affordable housing.[11]

Tenants' lack of stable employment in particular stoked landlords' aggrievement toward them and toward the system more generally. Laurence was incredulous that unemployed tenants who fell behind on rent called to complain to him—although not to city authorities—about some of his properties' subpar conditions. "You get calls every night," he marveled, his jaw hanging down, from "the nonpaying tenant, someone who's not working? They screaming!" Indeed, Laurence and other landlords frequently invoked tenants' unstable employment and missed rent payments to demonstrate that the system, they believed, was particularly unfair to landlords who housed poor tenants. With a look of disbelief, Laurence told us, "You work hard for everything you have, and you got to sit back and watch people that's *not* working, that's trying to get everything for free." He continued in a low, coarse tone, "Just drain you. Just be like a towel in the bathroom, squeezing all the water out of it. It's the people squeezing you, the city officials squeezing you."

That his tenants were marked by extreme stigma, including criminal convictions, no doubt fueled Quinn's mistrust toward them. When first asked to describe his tenants, Quinn did not proceed as most other landlords did. Instead of mentioning his tenants' family status ("most of my tenants are single mothers," other landlords would say) or employment status and occasionally offering vague pleasantries ("I have nice tenants," some offered), Quinn remarked matter-of-factly, without blinking, "I think probably 30 percent of them are just dirtbags." Then he ducked his head and added more softly, "The other ones are just folks that just can't get their shit together. . . . They have some sort of substance abuse problems. I think, sometimes, they have some sort of mental health problems."

Low-income renters burdened by extreme stigma—for instance, those with criminal convictions for serious criminal offenses—face steep obstacles to securing housing with landlords who will adhere to laws meant to protect them. The following case is extreme and serves to warn us about the consequences of trusting the private market to house residents whose stigma renders them ineligible for government-subsidized housing.

"It Is a Very Dark Picture"

Curtis and Terrence, Black cousins in their midforties with bullish expressions, inherited an apartment building from their uncle in the mid-2000s. Both had recently earned a degree from a local university but struggled to find work, a reflection of the flailing local economy. Entering the landlord business therefore appealed to them. It was not until the two cousins became landlords, however, that they learned what their uncle had hidden all along: the business of renting to very low-income tenants, at $400 per month for a small one-bedroom apartment, did not generate sustainable profit.

Missed rent payments became even more common among their predominantly lower-income, Black tenants as the local economy continued to struggle and shed more jobs. The pair began to invest less and less in their properties, all but ensuring that they would not be able to fill the units with tenants who had financial resources and "clean" records and could therefore secure better-quality housing. They had little choice but to rent to tenants who had typically been turned away by most other landlords, whether because of criminal convictions for homicide or sexual assault or because their record was dinged with multiple evictions.

Over lunch at a bustling family restaurant, the cousins explained that their profits in the business had hit rock bottom. "We're operating on a shoestring budget," Curtis said and then began to fume about the court costs to evict a tenant for nonpayment of rent. "Why should I pay for my own demise?" he challenged tensely. With a furrowed brow, he then described the illegal informal measures that he and Terrence used to remove a tenant.

The first time they used such measures they removed a tenant's door after her rent was a month late. Unlike Herman's tenant, who called the police after her landlord took off the front door, the woman grabbed what belongings she could and quickly vacated the apartment. Removing the door had the desired outcome—to quickly remove a tenant without paying the costs associated with a court eviction. Since they experienced no financial or legal consequences of the illegal door removal, the pair did it again when another tenant fell behind on rent. And then with another tenant. They also used illegal door removal at the single-family homes that they had purchased at low prices in struggling East Side communities.

Viewing their tenants as unrespectable members of society—they described them as "thugs" and "parasites"—the pair justified the increasingly callous measures they used to remove tenants or to house them under poor conditions. Tenants who fell behind on rent or threatened to complain to authorities about property conditions might discover that their door had been removed, that the locks had been changed, or that the electrical service had been shut off. Curtis described playing "Scrooge" one Christmas morning: he cut off the electricity in one of their single-family homes because the tenant, a woman with young children, fell behind on rent. Standing by the window, he heard the tenant's despair when the house fell dark while the family opened presents. Clearly, Curtis meant it when he warned us, before sitting down to talk, that "it is a very dark picture."

Conditions set in motion by macro-level economic shifts, exacerbated by local market conditions and ordinances, created a "perfect storm" of circumstances to motivate and enable landlords to violate important housing codes. A few landlords did, however, demonstrate that it was possible to earn satisfactory profit in the business of renting to marginalized tenants in struggling communities while also adhering to laws and norms of decency. Doing so, however, required being strategic as well as having a business plan that minimized financial uncertainty so as to avoid developing legal cynicism and mistrust toward tenants.

Economies of scale were important to the success of landlords who reported a moderate-to-healthy profit in the business, as demonstrated by the large-scale landlords who rented properties to very low-income tenants and are featured in Matthew Desmond's *Evicted: Poverty and Profit in the American City*.[12] Collecting revenue from more than just a few properties smoothed profits when an unexpected loss occurred, whether through missed rent or unanticipated property repairs. Having more than a handful of properties deterred landlords' excessive scrutiny of particular tenants and subsequent harassment of them for what they perceived as irresponsible behavior.

Next, owning several dozen or more rental properties provided landlords with sufficient revenue to support full-time staff. With a staff, these landlords could run their business smoothly and efficiently, whether by addressing property repairs in a timely manner or by keeping up with maintenance tasks so as to avoid city fines for small violations, including overgrown grass. With staff also serving as "middle men" between tenants and the landlord, some of the emotional burnout and "compassion fatigue" seen among the landlords who handled all interpersonal interactions with tenants was minimized.

These landlords' presence in the local community also contributed to the success of their business model. Although they did not reside in the communities where they rented properties, they maintained a consistent presence there, often with an office or centralized work space. Being visible in the community enabled them to build connections with local residents who looked out for their interests—for example, by warning them about suspicious activity on the property, such as a break-in or a water leak.

This subset of landlords who, in these ways, earned satisfactory profit in the business and maintained a good attitude toward their tenants even appeared to gain a slight edge in the market.

"The Biggest Thing Is, You Can't Let It Get to Ya"

All of these factors that are conducive to running a legitimate, profitable rental business in marginalized communities were seen in Nelson, a forty-something White man who rented thirty properties in a struggling community on the city's East Side. The air was thick and hot in Nelson's dusty workroom, which was centrally located in relation to his properties. The room was packed with vacuums, brooms, TVs, and microwaves—remnants of tenants' lives that had been left behind after an eviction, nearly always because of nonpayment of rent. Periodically Nelson pulled a dark blue baseball cap off his head to fan his pale cheeks or run his fingers through his dark hair.

He had pursued the rental business since he was a young boy, inspired by advice from a family friend who was a real estate agent:

"'That's a great thing, if you buy a double, you can live in half and rent the other half, and live pretty much for free.'" Straightening his posture, Nelson added, "And ever since then I was like, man, that's a good idea." He remarked affably, "I like houses, I like remodeling them. When I was a kid, I mean, my grandfather took me in, we always built stuff."

Soon after graduating from college in the early 2000s, Nelson took out mortgages to purchase several duplex properties on the city's West Side. Then he shifted his business model in response to the precipitous drop in property sale prices on the city's East Side in the mid-2000s. Nelson sold off the duplexes to purchase a cluster of single-family homes in one predominantly Black community on the city's East Side. "I have like, ten houses on this street, and like, five or six on that street, and then ten on that street," he said as he pointed in each direction. The dusty workroom became the central headquarters for his full-time staff of tenants who "paid" him by doing painting, carpentry, and plumbing work. This arrangement kept his maintenance costs low and city inspectors at bay and also enabled him to sweat less when tenants missed a rent payment. It was an important strategy to deploy in a community where cash had become scarce for several reasons, including the disappearance of the government cash safety net.[13]

As we spoke, several Black men trudged in and out of the workroom to pick up supplies. "I have quite a few people work for me," Nelson nodded at them. "My main guy, Jarrod, is four blocks away, and then my other guy, Rick, is right back there," Nelson said pointing to his right. "So those guys, they're like the main fix-it guys." As he pointed in the direction of a small, tan structure behind the house, he said, "Patty lives upstairs. She paints and cleans; she lives upstairs in the back." Nelson marveled, "I collect the rent and get supplies for these guys. And just manage all that part. I do very little actual work on the property, because I just don't have time to do it." As he explained, he worked long days and nights at his full-time job in the health care industry. Staring upward, he remarked in wonder, "Actually, yesterday was like, the first day that I was really doing a lot of work." Tilting his head to the side, he added wearily, "I'm like, 'Man.'"

"I don't understand some of these landlords," Nelson mumbled as he scratched his head. He recounted some of the stories he had heard from his tenants about their former "slumlords." "Like, the furnace doesn't work for months, or like, some people have a carbon monoxide leak and like, they have no gas, the gas is shut off for a month." Squinting in disbelief, he wondered, "How do you do that?" He added, "I mean, I'm bad, where people will call me and I make my guys go do it right now, whereas I could probably let it wait until tomorrow."

The properties needed to be free of hazards, but not luxurious. In his early years in the business, Nelson explained, "I used to put [down] carpet. I used to paint the walls off-white and make the trim white." Then he toured another investor's property, which he was interested in purchasing, and was stricken by the stark decor. "Wood floors, painted brown. All-white walls," he recalled with a grimace. "I walked in and I'm like, 'Man this looks like crap.'" Nevertheless, the other investor had carefully instructed him, "This is the way you do it and save money." Nelson admitted to us that, "Man, that old man was right," and he had taken his advice several years after they met. "Damn, if I would have just listened to him in the beginning, I would have been so much better off," Nelson chuckled and slapped the knee of his faded jeans. Now all of his properties had white walls and brown paint on the floors, like many other properties at the lower end of the market. Holding his arm out, he assured us, "It looks decent."

Maintaining his properties with uniform, serviceable paint jobs not only helped Nelson's bottom line through the cost and efficiency of buying cheap paint in bulk to have on hand for touch-ups but also kept him from becoming emotionally attached to his properties; such an attachment does not necessarily serve the interests of landlords who provide low-cost housing. For instance, Quinn glowed with pride in talking about the yellow walls and mottled wood floors in his duplex and about all of the work he and his father put into renovating the property. But an emotional connection built through "sweat equity" can lead landlords like Quinn to become unduly agitated if they believe that a tenant's behavior was responsible for any damages. Quinn was steamed when a tenant, he believed, damaged a cabinet in one of his duplex apartments, and he subsequently sued the tenant at a second-cause court hearing to collect on the cost to repair it.

Nelson, in contrast, was nearly unflappable when asked about property damage that could result from tenants' behavior. "You kind of have to just have the mentality, 'just fix it,'" he said with a shrug. "I don't care, you know, if they put holes in the walls or whatever. I mean, that's stuff we can fix," he explained, referring to his staff who perform repair work in exchange for rent forgiveness. He added matter-of-factly, "Obviously, I'd rather they didn't. As long as it's not costing me any money, specifically, you know?" As an example, he offered, "Okay, the cabinet's broken, I tell [staff], 'Take some two-by-fours and screw it back together, and just get it to work and throw a coat of paint on it, and call it a day.'"

Exclusively renting single-family homes was another strategy that set Nelson apart from other landlords described in this chapter; this strategy enabled him to generate satisfactory profit in the business.

"It's just *so* much better with a single," he said, breathing out a sigh of relief. "They're solid and they're easy." Nelson nodded toward a tenant "worker" who was hustling in and out of the workroom to retrieve tools. "We're in and out, running plumbing, and you know, when you get to the colonials and stuff, it's a little more complicated." Then he leaned over to confide quietly, "You just can't find a decent tenant to move into those doubles." With the single-family properties, he insisted enthusiastically, "you could really be selective." Nelson shook his head and continued, "But the doubles, you know. It's hard. They just don't want them." He continued brightly, "The singles, yeah, I mean if I put an ad on Craigslist, I'll get one hundred calls."

Filling vacant units quickly was key to staying afloat in the business of renting single-family properties in struggling communities. "If you leave a single vacant for any amount of time, it's going to get vandalized," Nelson observed. "So then you spend all this money to fix it up, and then it's destroyed and then you've got to fix it again and again." It didn't take long for him to fill a vacancy, he reported with relief. Whenever one of his units became available to rent, "my phone rings all day long," Nelson said nonchalantly. "I don't even advertise. I just have people callin' me. Because I have so many houses in this tight area. You know, just word of mouth." Gesturing down the street toward a small, beige bungalow house, he said assuredly, "They just moved out on Sunday. I'll have a new tenant in there by the end of the week."

"I think I have a good reputation, people tell me all the time. Like, 'Oh, yeah, I heard you're a good landlord,'" Nelson remarked, then assured us, "I don't do anything special." Yet clearly he did, not only by adequately maintaining his properties but also through his willingness to be lenient in regard to rent payment. Despite his reported goal to become more stringent in collecting rent on time, Nelson related story after story of permitting tenants to pay late. "I've been lied to so many times," he said lightly, pulling at the visor of his baseball cap. "Hilarious, anytime there's some major event in the news. . . . 'You know that guy that got shot in the news? Oh, that was my nephew, and I had to help pay for the funeral.'" He held his palms up in a disarming stance and continued good-naturedly, "Just say, 'I don't have the rent.' Just say, 'I don't have it, and I'll have it on this date,' and that's fine." Sometimes he would tell tenants, "You've got to have it by this date, or I'm going to file the eviction." It was rare for him to attempt to collect on missed rent in court. "I don't think it's worth it," Nelson concluded, shaking his head. "You know, I just don't see ever getting the money."

"People all the time are like, 'Oh, how do you do that, how can you stand it?'" Nelson said, speaking of the landlord business. "I mean, there's worse ways to make money," he said, glancing around the cluttered workroom. "The biggest thing is, you can't let it get to ya." He remembered being sure that "I was going to make a lot more money, I'll tell you that." After estimating his net take-home profit from renting thirty single-family homes (slightly above $100,000), he admitted that his primary gauge of profitability in the business was the balance of his bank account. "If you have plenty of money to pay the bills, and there's still more money than there was last month, then all is well," he said jauntily, and added, "To me, it's more a financial investment, you know, for now I'm making money to survive and maintain them. Hopefully, I either leave them to my kids, or sell them and do something else."

Some landlords in this sample had identified a model to earn a profit in providing affordable rental housing in struggling communities, using a strategy that included geographic concentration, economies of scale, a full-time maintenance staff, strategic investment in properties that generated sufficient tenant interest to avoid the risk of vacancy, and perhaps even a good attitude toward tenants. Yet as long as compliance with laws meant to protect renters remains largely "voluntary" and the system of housing code enforcement is mostly driven by tenants' and residents' complaints, there is little guarantee that landlords who play by the rules will continue to do so if their financial goals change or their revenue is disrupted. Ordinances are simply words on paper; they do not come alive until they are enforced through either formal or informal mechanisms.

City officials proved unwilling to take formal steps to enforce housing codes on the books, citing unintended consequences for vulnerable tenants and communities. "If you hammer landlords too much," a senior housing code enforcement official warned me, "they'll walk away from their properties. Which could contribute to more blight." City housing inspectors report "going easy" in doling out citations to property owners in struggling communities in order to shield them from the costs to remediate violations.[14]

Cleveland's longtime mayor, Frank Jackson, cited the risk of losing low-cost rental housing as a reason for flexibility in code enforcement. He warned local reporters that systematic code enforcement could uncover a groundswell of hazards in the rental stock, including lead paint and faulty wiring, and that landlords might subsequently abandon their properties instead of paying for necessary repairs. Overly zealous enforcement, the mayor predicted gravely, could lead to "clos[ing] down half, or three-quarters of all the rental properties in the city of Cleveland that's not Public Housing." He added, for emphasis, "Which means the number of units that are available for low-income people to rent in the city of Cleveland, it'll be substantially reduced. Believe me."

Unfortunately, research on the benefits and limitations of strict code enforcement in poor communities is scarce and fragmented. The mayor of Cleveland's fear of the consequences of strictly enforcing codes in marginalized communities was perhaps understandable. As this chapter has demonstrated, however, hidden mechanisms cause the current system of laws pertaining to landlords, housing, and public safety to undermine access to affordable rental housing for poor and Black residents and also deepen community decline.

Chapter 4

"If I Got Him Paranoid Enough, I Knew He Would Go"

Renters nationwide are increasingly facing a new kind of scrutiny as criminal activity nuisance ordinances (CANOs) become more widespread. These ordinances enlist landlords in efforts to curtail activities on private property that could contribute to criminal activity, undermine quality of life, reduce property values, or put a strain on city resources, including police departments. Through CANO legislation, landlords are coerced into monitoring tenants' behavior on their property and helping to abate "nuisance activity" through the threat of financial or criminal sanctions for failing to do so.[1]

The spread of these laws reflects what David Garland has called the "responsibilization" of crime control: rather than drawing on police officers to investigate or respond to criminal behavior, private citizens are increasingly tasked with monitoring others' behavior.[2] As shown here, responsibilization in the context of nuisance laws ultimately penalizes tenants—by increasing landlords' financial precarity and straining their relationships with their tenants, as well as with city authorities.

Criminal activity nuisance ordinance legislation first emerged in the 1950s, when the fear of crime in urban areas began to spike. In the mid-1980s, municipalities across the nation began to hasten their implementation of CANOs. The War on Drugs, which took off in the 1980s, accelerated the pace at which cities passed ordinances to control what they deemed undesirable or illegal behavior. As part of the War on Drugs, Congress passed the Anti–Drug Abuse Act of 1988. One of the act's provisions, the "one-strike" policy, required public housing authorities to evict tenants for drug-related activity on or near the property. In 1996, as part of the HOPE VI Act, PHAs began to hold tenants accountable when family members or guests engaged in criminal or nuisance activity on the property. That same year, President Bill Clinton signed the Housing Opportunity Program Extension Act, which permitted a PHA to deny occupancy to a tenant based on a record of drug activity or criminal behavior.[3]

The passage of CANOs across the Cleveland metropolitan region coincided with the fallout from the housing market crash and the Great Recession. Population loss as a result of foreclosures undermined the local tax base, which funds essential services, including police.[4] At the same time, dilapidated and abandoned properties and violent crime spread through the city of Cleveland and in its inner- and outer-ring suburbs, which had largely evaded these "central city problems."[5] These shifts incentivize municipalities either to secure new sources of money to fund the police or to curtail the behavior that requires their assistance.

As seen in the Cleveland metropolitan region and others across the nation, CANOs have burgeoned most rapidly in suburbs and communities where rates of homeownership are high and where rental units make up a small portion of the housing stock.[6] Indeed, in Cuyahoga County, CANOs first emerged in affluent inner-ring suburban communities, including Cleveland Heights (2003), Shaker Heights (2004), and Lakewood (2004).[7] This was a time when these municipalities were also seeing upticks in the share of residents who were lower-income, who were Black, or who held housing vouchers.[8] Importantly, a concentration of Black residents in a community leads residents to perceive more community problems.[9] This is another mechanism by which growing racial diversity can trigger residents' and authorities' concerns about safety and property values.

Despite some variation among municipalities—across both Cuyahoga County and the nation—CANOs share some striking similarities. First, properties are designated a nuisance based on the number of calls for assistance received over a given time period, including calls for help with domestic violence. The definition of nuisance behavior then expands into a catchall category that also includes littering, noise, drug use and distribution, and fighting.[10] Finally, these laws require property owners to abate the nuisance or else face fines or criminal sanctions. Unpaid nuisance fines may become attached to the property as tax debt, and the city may place a lien on the property and ultimately take possession of it.

There is even direct evidence that race- and class-based biases have motivated some municipalities to enact laws that extend the scope of civil law to monitor and control residents' behavior. Bedford, an inner-ring suburb of Cleveland to the east, first implemented its CANO in 2005. Around that time the number of Bedford residents who were lower-income, Black, and renters was growing.[11] On the evening when the Bedford city council met to vote on the proposed CANO, the mayor reassured community members in the audience that the ordinance would protect "middle-class values." "We believe in those middle-class values of neighborhoods where people can go home, and their home is their castle and feel safe," he stated. "We believe in neighborhoods, not 'hoods. We will do everything we can to maintain those quality-of-life issues. . . . That is one of the reasons we passed that nuisance law tonight." Indeed, the ordinance passed with a unanimous vote from the council.

Despite the potential financial strain these laws put on landlords—and relatedly, their tenants—there is little research on the firsthand experiences of landlords who were tasked by a CANO with preventing undesirable or illegal activity.[12] As shown here, CANOs motivate landlords to pursue business practices that disadvantage renters, including illegal informal evictions and discriminatory screening. These laws disproportionately affect renters' access to decent, affordable housing in communities with lower rates of poverty and racial segregation. Black renters and survivors of domestic violence, who are disproportionately women, are most sharply affected by these laws because landlords assume that they are more likely to engage in "nuisance activity" on the property. Notably, in disadvantaging tenants, these laws may trigger crime and bolster demand for more emergency services, such as homeless shelters—unintended consequences that further strain city resources.

Landlords' decisions about whether to evict a tenant depended on a range of factors. Some were willing to accept late rent payment, rather than evict for nonpayment, to evade the costs and losses associated with eviction: filing fees, lawyer, bailiff, and mover fees, the costs to turn the unit over to a new tenant, and the risk of vandalism of a vacant unit. Further, landlords were typically more willing to be lenient regarding rent payment from long-term tenants. They were also more likely to offer tenants a grace period before filing for eviction for nonpayment of rent if they believed that tenants' financial struggles were due to reasons outside of their control—an illness or job loss—as opposed to "irresponsible" behavior, such as poor budgeting.

CANOs, however, disrupted landlords' calculus about whether to evict a tenant. Typically, the nuisance notice motivates landlords to evict a tenant by informing them that commencing eviction proceedings can exempt them from paying the fines associated with their tenant's nuisance activity.[13] This practice denies tenants due process: with notices mailed directly to the landlord, tenants are left unaware of an impending eviction filing and sometimes have no right to appeal the decision.[14]

The threat of CANO-related sanctions takes away landlords' ability to use discretion in dealing with their tenants, even when they had established a pattern of doing so. As a result, tenants are at risk of losing their housing on the basis of laws that add strain to the landlord-tenant relationship.

Playing by the Rules: "I Had to Evict Them"

In middle-income Lakewood, a predominantly White suburb to the west of Cleveland, homeowners are subject to fines after three or more "nuisance" activities on their property in a twelve-month period. Lakewood's nuisance legislation was passed in 2008, a time when renters and Blacks began to occupy a slightly larger share of its residential population. Upon the first instance of police assistance as a result of nuisance activity, the Lakewood property owner receives a notice in the mail.

One such notice arrived for Katie, a White woman with a kind and friendly smile and long blond hair. She and her husband had entered the rental business in the early 2000s, first purchasing several single-family and small multi-unit properties in lower-income communities in the city of Cleveland, before property values took a dramatic nose-dive. Several years later, they purchased several small apartment buildings on the city's West Side and in several inner-ring suburbs to the west, including Lakewood, before property values there also declined precipitously.

Seated in a mostly empty Lakewood café, Katie reflected, "Initially, I was just going to do it on the side to help supplement our income." She sought flexible work hours in order to raise the couple's young children and care for a family member with special needs. With a wry smile, Katie confessed that she realized, a few years into the business, that "this might not be the way to do that." While pouring milk into her second mug of coffee, she remembered, "Those first couple of years were good. And then I really started learning what you can't really read in books. It's just kind of one of those things that you just have to do." She stared dully down at the blue mug. "Some years we didn't make anything. Or we lost."

Typically, she looked to work with a tenant who breached the lease, usually for nonpayment of rent, rather than immediately file to evict. "Eviction's the last place I want to be," Katie remarked with a shudder, citing the financial costs, plus a harried morning schedule that made it difficult to arrive at the courthouse in time for a 9:00 AM eviction hearing. "There's been times where I have to get my daughter on the bus, you know, so I'm like, I'm not going to be there till literally five [minutes] to nine," she remarked. "I'm going to skate in by the skin of my teeth." Her willingness to work with tenants for a breach of lease rather than evict them shifted, however, when she received a CANO warning from Lakewood authorities.

The notice that came from the city informed her that the police had recently responded to reports of noise and fighting among several tenants in one of the Lakewood buildings. "If we have to come there again, we're going to start fining you," she recalled an officer instructing her over the phone. After a sigh, Katie continued wearily, "So I'm telling my tenants, no more. You know, knock it off. These cops cannot be back here again. You know?" She tilted her head and added flatly, "And lo and behold, I have two more reports."

As a result of more tenant calls to the police for assistance with disputes, Katie received another notice from the city. It warned that she would incur a fine if the police had to provide any further emergency assistance at the building over the course of the next year. "Not huge," Katie remembered thinking about the fine at the time, which was several hundred dollars, "but enough to make it a pain," she added, especially because it came during a period when the business had become a financial loss for the couple, given their tenants' increasing struggles to pay rent as the regional economy declined. Lakewood's CANO notice informed her that landlords could avoid incurring nuisance-related costs by commencing the eviction process, so as to demonstrate that they had taken action to abate the nuisance. Given this information, Katie was certain that "I had to evict them." Upon filing to evict and presenting police records at the court hearing, she received a judgment in her favor.

Formal court eviction is but one measure that the landlords in the sample pursued in order to alleviate the financial concerns created by CANOs. In an attempt to minimize the risk of incurring fines, criminal charges, or property loss as a result of unpaid nuisance fines, landlords also engaged in excessive tenant monitoring and harassment—behavior that often amounted to informal eviction. This was most evident among landlords who rented properties in the inner- and outer-ring suburban communities, where it seemed to them that authorities aggressively enforced nuisance laws.

"Bluff Him Out"

Antwan, a Black man in his midforties, was breathless when he arrived to meet with me one the evening after a long shift at his company day job as an electrician. Alternating between bites of a glazed doughnut and sips of coffee, he told me why he entered the rental business in the mid-2000s. The local economy had begun to plummet, and he had lost his full-time electrician job. "It's tough being laid off the first time," Antwan confessed with a sheepish grin. "I was praying I would find something, income-wise." To make ends meet until he could secure new employment, he turned to the rental business. For $15,000, he purchased his first rental property, a small multi-unit building in the city of Cleveland.

With a laugh, Antwan recalled learning the hard way about entering the business with little background knowledge. Upon purchasing the property, he excitedly told a friend, who was also a landlord, "Hey, come look at my house." With a crestfallen expression, he recalled his friend's response upon seeing the deteriorated condition of the building: "Let me get two sticks of dynamite and blow it up." Antwan continued, ducking his head: "He was like, 'Man, you got a lot of work here to do.'" After investing an additional $25,000 to repair the property, Antwan decided it was "just about right" and began to rent it out.

After regaining employment as an electrician several years later, Antwan paid cash for eleven more properties, including single-family and small multifamily properties, in the city of Cleveland and in suburban Euclid, a previously White community to the east of the city whose population became majority-Black by around 2010. "The suburbs are easy," he said brightly of the Euclid property. But, he added darkly, with a wince, "I've had drug dealers."

It was the tenant at the Euclid property who made Antwan grow anxious at the possibility that he had a tenant who, he came to believe, was using illegal drugs. His suspicion about the tenant's illegal behavior began with reports from homeowners on the street, whom Antwan had made it a point to get to know. "They're kinda gonna look out for me a little bit," he reasoned. "Because I can't see that person every day." He exclaimed, "I can't go over there and sit and watch. I'm not a cop or a stakeout guy or whatever." Sparked by the neighbors' suspicions about the tenant's illegal drugs on the single-family property, "I kinda looked into it a little bit," Antwan explained nonchalantly. His anxiety mounted when he thought about the police scrutiny that could result from the tenant's alleged nuisance behavior. "I don't need the police coming in my house and tearing it up because he's doing something wrong!" Antwan exclaimed with his hands out. Accordingly, he followed the neighbors' advice: "Bluff him out. See if he moves."

In reenacting his attempt to "bluff out" the tenant, Antwan puffed up his chest and said authoritatively, "Police are calling me about the property." He ducked and added under his breath, "It was a lie." Straightening up to resume his reconstruction of the conversation with the tenant, he continued, "If you're doing anything wrong, let me *know*. Because they're asking questions." To convey that he was looking out for the man's interests, Antwan even informed the tenant, "I'm not supposed to tell you!" Soon after this conversation, the tenant informed Antwan that he'd need to move out the following month. With a look of suspicion, Antwan told me slowly and satisfactorily, "Good." Holding his arm out as if swinging a door open, he added coarsely, "Get out."

There were other local authorities besides the police whom landlords invoked to warn tenants that authorities were scrutinizing their behavior on the property. Threats of surveillance by housing code inspectors, who performed systematic inspections in many of the region's suburban communities, including Cleveland Heights, also accomplished this goal of convincing tenants that they were being watched.

Dottie, a soft-spoken White woman with thick eyeglasses and wavy silver-gray hair, wanted to meet at a café in Cleveland Heights, an inner-ring suburban community to the east where she owned several properties. "I had some money and I wanted to invest it, and I bought a house," she recalled, reminiscing on entering the rental business several decades earlier. "My dad had a rental, and I got the idea from him." Now, however, she was struggling to pay off what she described as "pretty steep" mortgages she'd taken out to purchase her handful of small multifamily buildings in the area. "I'm trying to get them paid off so I can retire," she said dismally as she took off her glasses to rub her eyes.

The monthly mortgage payment for her three-unit property in Cleveland Heights equaled the combined rent collected from tenants in the first- and second-floor apartments. "If I've got the third floor rented, then I'm making money, okay," she said haltingly. "So, it's not great, but again, once I pay the properties off, I'll be okay. And that's what I'm shooting for. Hopefully I'll live long enough to benefit from it." She rubbed her temples and sighed, "I've wondered many times, why even do it, because I could have just taken my salary, stuck it in the bank, put it in stocks, and been done with it—a lot cleaner, a lot simpler." Then she broke into a hesitant smile. "I'll blame it on my dad."

Dottie grew anxious after hearing that a tenant in one of her apartment buildings suspected that a downstairs tenant's live-in boyfriend sold drugs there. "I had no concrete evidence, nothing," Dottie confessed bluntly. Although the boyfriend denied the charge, Dottie took the word of the neighbor who accused him. At the time, she was well aware of efforts by the Cleveland Heights Police Department to enforce its anti-drug laws. She feared that police would discover evidence of drug-related activity on the property. Yet, she said disappointedly, "I had no way of legally getting him out." The tenant was current on rent payment, and therefore Dottie could not evict the tenant and her boyfriend on the basis of nonpayment, the most cut-and-dry breach of lease for which a judgment in the landlord's favor would be issued at an eviction hearing. Dottie therefore looked for other ways to persuade the tenants to leave on their own accord, figuring that, "if I got him paranoid enough, I knew he would go. Nobody wants to get arrested for stuff."

Together with her husband, she devised a story to make the tenant fearful about scrutiny from the community's building department, which mandated rental property inspections every three years. "You know, you better watch out. Cleveland Heights is looking for something," Dottie instructed her husband to inform the tenant when he visited the property to perform repair work. To lend legitimacy to his claim, Dottie contacted the building department to arrange for an inspector to come by the property several days afterwards. Believing it would legitimize her story about the city's looming scrutiny, "I didn't give any warning, so it would seem like it was a surprise inspection," she explained. "They were out of that apartment within a week."

These acts to "bluff out" tenants amount to informal eviction—the removal of a tenant without due process, typically by creating an unsafe or unsustainable living environment that compels them to leave. The prevalence and techniques of informal evictions are not well documented, as there are no legal records of them that could be reviewed, and surveys do not typically ask about them. The most comprehensive survey to assess the prevalence of informal evictions is the Milwaukee Area Rental Study (MARS), which uses multiple questions to measure the prevalence of evictions, including informal evictions, among Milwaukee renters. The survey asks respondents to indicate whether they have experienced specific circumstances that could compel a move, for example, "because the landlord wouldn't fix anything and the place was getting run down."[15] Yet a threat about institutional scrutiny made by a landlord in order to make tenants feel unsafe enough that they decide to move out appears to be another form of informal eviction, and one that has not been studied.

Informal eviction is important to study as a form of involuntary mobility, as it may have disastrous consequences for tenants, even though it does not leave the stigma of a formal eviction through legal proceedings on their record. First, involuntary mobility, whether in response to overt eviction, threats, or unsafe property conditions, typically leads tenants to accept less desirable housing. Under duress and a looming threat of homelessness, tenants, and especially marginalized tenants, find it difficult to be selective in the housing search.[16] Second, a hasty move can also lead to the loss of belongings, including government-issued IDs or birth certificates. Such documentation is instrumental in securing housing, employment, and social services, including health care.[17] Finally, the emotional trauma of a hasty forced move can also linger and even pose challenges to performing well on a job.[18]

The threat of institutional scrutiny to remove a tenant may be most potent in the lower end of the rental market, where there is a greater concentration of renters who are Black and who, relatedly, mistrust authorities.[19] In fact, tenants' mistrust toward authorities may well have been essential to these landlords' execution of an off-the-official-radar plan to remove them.

Importantly, when landlords saw how tenants responded to their threats, their beliefs about their tenants' deviance were reinforced and perpetuated. Landlords attributed tenants' hasty departures to the (fabricated) threat of law enforcement attention to their illegal activity. "I knew he was doing something illegal," Antwan remarked knowingly, in reflecting on his tenant's announcement of an impending move. "Some people, you mention the police, they're gone!" he bellowed with a clap and a huge laugh, then added, "They're living wrong." Her tenants' hasty departure also confirmed Dottie's belief that the couple was engaged in illegal activity.

Laws that fostered landlords' financial precarity and mistrust toward authorities on the basis of tenants' potentially undesirable or illegal activity also disadvantaged tenants through the screening process. An applicant's criminal conviction or experience of incarceration was a "red flag" for landlords.[20] The reasoning behind landlords' inclination to turn away applicants with criminal records has not been made altogether clear in previous research. Did fear about their own personal safety lead landlords to reject tenants with criminal backgrounds? Some landlords indicated as much. As shown here, however, their perception of the risk in housing tenants with criminal records had another source: citations from the city.

"Drugs? . . . They Take Your Property for That"

Seated at a quiet McDonald's restaurant late in the evening, Betty, a petite sixty-something White woman with short brown hair, and her husband Jack, a tall, lanky White man with curly gray hair, recounted how they got into the landlord business. Leaning back in the booth, Jack wrinkled his forehead and slowly reminisced, "Maybe thirty, thirty-plus years ago . . ." Betty, in a more upbeat tone, chimed in, "For me since '93, when we got married."

On weekdays both worked in the Cleveland public schools. On nights and weekends, Jack worked at the buildings, which were mostly located in lower-income, predominantly Black communities on the city's East Side. "The biggest thing I think I did was I did a lot of ceramic flooring. I did that for some of the kitchens and stuff," he said proudly. Now retired, Jack made daily trips to the properties to perform repair work. "He does all the work, so thank God," Betty remarked, wide-eyed. "If he didn't do it, we'd be in big trouble."

"If I had to pay skilled labor, plumbers and electricians . . . I wouldn't be able to survive," Jack said grimly, adding, in reference to profit, "There would be nothing there." On an even glummer note, he said, "There's nothing there now. And I'm doing a lot of the work." Betty jumped in, sounding disappointed. "We don't buy anything new." Tugging at his paint-splattered blue polo shirt, Jack jokingly retorted, "These are good clothes!"

Jack and Betty were among other longtime landlords who had lost the safety net they believed they had built for themselves for their retirement years, owing to the sharp decline of the once-vital neighborhoods where they had purchased properties years earlier. Jack remarked in wonder, "I was doing all this stuff, and I'd be losing money here and there, and just trying to make ends meet and figuring, 'Well, but when I sell them, I'm going to be selling them for twice as much as what I bought them for.' But that isn't going to happen now."

Betty teared up as she watched her husband's face grow dark. "Twenty, thirty years of your life you put into this." Slowly shaking his head, he declared, "That was the plan. That's how I was going to make my money, and retirement, and be able to do whatever I wanted to do."

For the next several hours, the two took turns getting up, to make an order at the counter or take a phone call. Each left the table with an anxious expression and returned with a look of relief. After Jack stood up to order ice cream and fries at the counter, Betty huddled over the table to confess in a hushed tone, "If it were up to me, I would sell it off." In recent tax seasons, she said, their accountant always commented, "When are you going to sell these things? You're losing every year." Betty whispered more fervently as she glanced at Jack standing at the counter. "He had to take money out of his retirement account just to pay [property] insurance, and that's not, just not right."

The couple used a screening bureau to perform background checks, which was uncommon for small-time landlords who housed low-income tenants, owing to the cost. Yet they had been motivated to screen tenants more closely when authorities discovered tenants' illegal activity in their buildings. "We've had cases where a couple times, drugs. Really bad stuff. Drugs," Betty said, grasping at her throat. Nodding enthusiastically, Jack insisted that the cost of using the screening bureau was "definitely worth it," adding that applicants themselves were "not going to tell you if they've got a police record." Re-creating what she considered a commonplace interaction with prospective tenants, Betty asked, "Have you ever been arrested?" and answered plainly, as the tenant, "'No.'" Sighing, she added, "And then here comes a stack of stuff for, you name it. Drug trafficking . . . I mean, drugs?" She flinched and pushed her hands straight out. "We don't want any. They take your property for that."

Fear of drug-related nuisance sanctions was not widespread among the landlords who rented properties in marginalized communities in the central city. Those landlords expressed the starkest legal cynicism; from their perspective, authorities, including police, were not invested in effectively enforcing laws. Yet, as a result of a local crackdown as early as 2007 on violent crime and drug sales, which was launched by the councilman who represented the community where their buildings were primarily located, Betty and Jack were distinctly afraid of illegal activity in their properties. Betty exclaimed, "We've had the Strike Force involved!"

The councilman, whose name Betty uttered with a look of fear, gave bold statements to the local press about the crackdowns, which were meant to rid the community of drug distributors. "My position is that we should get every one of these two-legged rats," Councilman Mike Polensek, a White man, insisted to local press in 2012. "That's just what they are. Rats. They destroy the soul of a community, and I don't want them destroying mine."[21] In a 2007 letter he sent to a teenage offender who pleaded guilty to two counts of drug trafficking in his ward, Polensek described him as an "idiot" and "dumber than mud."[22] The letter, which was written on city letterhead, also informed the recipient: "There are only two places you will end up, at the rate you are going—that is prison or the nearest funeral home. Quite frankly, I don't care which you get to first." The letter went viral, but it was not an outlier for the councilman, who told reporters, "Hell, I write those kind of notes twice a week," adding, "That one just got a lot of notoriety."

In some municipalities, both in Cuyahoga County and nationwide, tenants' repeated calls for police assistance with domestic violence are considered a nuisance. Landlords who rent properties in these communities therefore are motivated to threaten tenants or move to evict them if the tenants have called the police for help with a domestic dispute.[23] Yet, as shown here, these landlords use other tools of exclusion besides eviction or the threat of it to evade nuisance-related penalties they are assessed when tenants seek police assistance with domestic disputes. Screening is but another tactic that landlords employ to reduce the risk of authorities scrutinizing their tenants' nuisance activity. These practices disproportionately disadvantage women, who are markedly more likely than men to experience domestic abuse.[24]

"Domestic Violence One Time, You Will Be Kicked Out"

Gabriel, a tall, lanky, middle-aged Asian Indian man, arrived at our first meeting at a busy café wearing a lightweight tan suit jacket and carrying a worn cognac leather briefcase. With a snap, he opened it to reveal stacks of documents that related to his primary work as a land-lord for over thirty rental properties and also as a part-time contractor. Most of his rentals were located in inner-ring suburbs to the east, including Garfield Heights, Maple Heights, and Bedford. Property values in all of these communities declined after the housing market crash in 2008, and the population of residents who were lower-income, Black, and renters significantly increased.[25]

Nevertheless, his business was lucrative, Gabriel explained proudly, owing in part to the benefits accrued through economies of scale. He calculated: "$850 a month [rent] for each house, times thirty. And total cost, 40 percent. And I make over $160,000, $175,000 a year." Despite his success, Gabriel's belief that housing laws were unfair to landlords and that city authorities treated landlords disrespectfully sparked his sense of being justified in evading those laws. He reported, incredulously, that a Maple Heights administrator had informed him, "You investors destroy the city," and in support of his claim cited tenants housed by Gabriel who "don't work and they don't pay taxes." "I do not destroy the city," Gabriel insisted defensively, tugging at his suit jacket. "I'm here for twenty-seven years, and I work hard. I work six days a week, twelve hours a day, to make a living."

On the subject of CANOs, Gabriel adamantly insisted that "[tenants] are your problem, I will tell you." He explained, "That's why we tell the neighbors, 'If you see [drug use on the property] going on, please call us.'" He continued urgently, "We can find out if there is any drug [use] going on." Instead of following prescribed courtroom procedures to remove a tenant on the basis of confirmed "nuisance activity," Gabriel sought to handle the matter off the radar of authorities. "Easier to just kick them out," he stated matter-of-factly. "Not pay the court cost, get stuck with the city."

Then Gabriel voiced grievances about the nuisance-related penalties that landlords could incur in Bedford, which is one of the municipalities in Cuyahoga County (along with Lakewood) that designated calls for emergency assistance with domestic disputes as "nuisance activity." "Domestic violence," Gabriel explained, "can be very costly for the landlord," then went on to describe the proactive measures he took to reduce his risk of incurring penalties.

During the screening process, he sought clues that applicants had experienced domestic violence. In his interviews with prospective tenants, Gabriel explained, "we ask two things." Raising a finger, he began, "Number one, if you have eviction on your background." Lifting a second finger, he finished, "Or if you have any domestic violence." Yet he acknowledged that applicants could be wary about revealing any experience with domestic violence. Moreover, unlike evictions or criminal convictions, a search of legal records would not readily reveal whether an applicant had experienced domestic violence. Accordingly, Gabriel designed a practice to compel an applicant to reveal what legal records could not.

As part of the process to determine whether an applicant had experienced a domestic dispute, Gabriel required them to complete a questionnaire asking about their employment, residential history, criminal convictions, and any incidents of domestic violence. Applicants also were required to submit a $100 fee to reimburse Gabriel for the cost to perform a formal background check. The $100 would be returned, he told applicants, if the information they provided matched what he discovered during the background check. If it did not match, he warned applicants, "then the deposit you pay, I am not returning back to you." Occasionally, Gabriel had observed, tenants withdrew their application upon hearing about the penalty, leading him to believe that he had honed a successful strategy to retrieve applicant information to which he otherwise would not have access.

In another attempt to deter the potential costs associated with tenants' calls for police assistance, Gabriel issued a warning to current tenants. "If [tenants] have domestic violence one time, you will be kicked out," he noted flatly. The threat puts tenants' safety at risk by forcing them to make a choice: protecting their physical safety during a domestic dispute by calling the police, or avoiding the risk of eviction and protecting their access to housing by not requesting assistance.

Researchers who have spoken directly with women who experienced domestic violence describe multiple pathways by which their safety is jeopardized by laws that penalize landlords for tenants' repeated calls to police for assistance with domestic disputes. Lower-income, predominantly Black women who experienced domestic violence in St. Louis—another municipality where a call for assistance during a domestic dispute constitutes a "nuisance," with sanctions for the landlord—reported their reluctance to call the police for help with a dispute out of fear that it could lead to an eviction.[26] Furthermore, the women told researchers, the law contributed to their sense of being unsafe in their day-to-day life because their abusers, recognizing their partner's fear that a call to the police could trigger an eviction, were emboldened to act violently, they believed. The women explained that CANOs, by dissuading them from calling the police, incentivized them to respond to their partner's violence with violence—with the unintended consequence of escalating their abuser's violence.

As with tenants' drug-related nuisance activity, landlords who rented properties in the city of Cleveland were less concerned than their suburban counterparts about tenants' experiences with domestic violence. This lack of concern largely reflected the provisions of Cleveland's CANO, which did not designate calls for help with domestic violence as a nuisance. As a result, landlords who rented properties in the city were not unduly agitated about the possibility of their tenants getting involved in domestic disputes.

Instead, some expressed indifference, simply noting that domestic violence was a common experience among their tenant population. John, a middle-aged Asian man who rented several properties in a struggling community in the city of Cleveland, remarked casually, "As far as I understand, the neighbor tells me that the police were here the other day." He surmised, blankly, that "it could have been domestic violence. I don't know. I have no clue. I'd ask, but no one says anything."

Still other landlords who rented properties in the city showed interest in helping their tenants who experienced domestic violence. Rather than discouraging tenants from calling the police about it, these landlords even did so on their behalf, whether in the midst of a dispute or after later learning about it.

"I'm Gonna Call the Police to Do the Job"

Antwan, the landlord who "bluffed out" his tenant in Euclid based on suspicions of illegal drug use on the property, grew aware of domestic disputes between the couple who lived in the upstairs apartment in one of his duplexes located in the city. While performing repair work in the property's downstairs unit, he overheard loud noise and shouting; later he remembered, with a shudder, that "the guy was hittin' on her." The downstairs neighbors confirmed to him that the upstairs disputes had become frequent. At a subsequent visit to the property, Antwan warned the man upstairs, "When I'm working here, I don't want to be hearing it."

Weeks later, the neighbors downstairs informed Antwan that the disputes upstairs were continuing unabated, despite his warning. He grew worried about the safety of his other tenants, and his own. "I don't want to get in the middle of it, because they could turn bad on me!" he exclaimed to me. So he decided, "I'm gonna call the police to do the job." The police arrived at the property several times in response to Antwan's calls about the disputes, but the tenants upstairs turned them away.

Unfortunately, the situation was not resolved well. "Sad story," he began morosely, looking down into his empty coffee cup. "He got killed a month later. He was mentally wound up. Someone killed him." He confessed to feeling puzzled when, soon after hearing the news, he witnessed the tenant burst into tears about the loss of her partner.

"She should be happy," Antwan pleaded, holding his hands up in wonder. Then he admitted quietly, "But that's me looking at it."

Other Cleveland landlords and property owners were even more sympathetic and protective toward tenants who experienced domestic violence in their units. Angel, a Black woman in her thirties with a warm smile, managed a midsized apartment building located in an East Side community in the city of Cleveland. Five days a week she worked from a spacious office decorated with photos of tenants, primarily Black women, who were smiling with family members at a picnic or a high school graduation. She interacted with tenants frequently enough to understand their personalities. "You have your 'bubbly outgoings,'" Angel giggled. "You have your 'quiets to yourselves.'" At times tenants settled in the chairs in front of her large wooden desk to discuss personal matters. "I try to sit and listen and give my advice that I could on the situation," Angel said congenially. "Sometimes I just sit and listen, let them vent, and then they say, 'Thanks for listening,' and walk back out."

"The most major problem I have in here is domestic disputes," Angel sighed, cupping her cheeks with her hands. "Which is sad," she said slowly and gravely. "That is probably the worst problem I have." In her two years as a property manager, Angel carefully estimated, "I've had to call the police at least three or four times about domestic disputes." In several instances, tenants had urged her to call the police on behalf of another tenant who, they believed, was in danger during a dispute. "They don't want to get involved, so they'll call and ask me to call the police. So, I mean, I tell them, 'You can remain anonymous,'" Angel explained gently, "but I'll still call anyway, just so they don't have to be involved." One time, she recalled, "one tenant's sister called because she couldn't get here. But her sister was getting beat up on, so she told me to call the police for her." Blinking rapidly, Angel remembered, "It was like, a silent warning," then added softly, "It was like, crazy."

Angel's eyebrows shot up high in surprise when I asked whether a tenant who called the police for help with domestic violence could subsequently face eviction from the building. She frowned and fell silent, twirling the silver cross necklace she wore. Staring down intently at the desk, she answered in a low, curious voice, "I've never even thought of that."

It is unlikely that homeowners would lose access to their housing, or otherwise face obstacles to housing, as a result of nuisance activity on their property. It is renters who are disproportionately disadvantaged by criminal activity nuisance ordinances.[27] Indeed, CANOs pose a direct threat to renters' access to housing, in particular through landlords' decision-making regarding tenant screening and eviction.

Whether or not CANOs were directly intended to target renters or marginalized populations, their implementation clearly puts these residents at a disadvantage. Joseph Mead and colleagues discuss the undue scrutiny of renters as a result of CANOs in four Cuyahoga County suburbs—Lakewood, Euclid, Bedford, and Parma.[28] They looked at whether renters were excessively targeted by CANOs in their examination of whether the percentage of nuisance tickets issued to rental properties aligned with the percentage of rental units in the community's housing stock. Their study showed that rental properties appear to be disproportionately targeted by these laws.

In Euclid, the suburb where Antwan "bluffed out" his tenant, close to 80 percent of CANO notices were sent to rental properties, although rental properties comprise only slightly over 20 percent of its residential housing stock. Meanwhile, in Lakewood, the suburb where Katie evicted tenants from her building after a nuisance notice from police, and where slightly less than half of the residential properties are rentals, close to 90 percent of all nuisance notices were sent to rental properties. In Bedford, the suburb where Gabriel threatened his tenants about calling police for help with domestic violence, close to 60 percent of all nuisance violation notices were sent to rental properties, though just under 40 percent of Bedford residential properties are rentals.

In disproportionately disadvantaging renters, these laws also disadvantage racial minorities, who are more likely to rent than own their homes.[29] These laws are especially disadvantageous to racial minorities, especially Black Americans, for other reasons as well, including their greater likelihood of being marked by a criminal conviction or incarceration.[30] Among the reasons that a criminal conviction or incarceration raised red flags in landlords' screening process was the common and faulty presumption of an association with nuisance activity that would provoke a CANO notice.

Through their disparate impact on Black Americans, as well as on women, CANOs also violate the Fair Housing Act. The vast majority of domestic violence survivors are women, and being female is the most significant predictor of being a survivor of domestic violence.[31] Accordingly, nuisance laws disproportionately pose obstacles to women's access to stable rental housing.

The city of Bedford repealed its CANO in 2020 after it was sued by a tenant. Beverly Somai had faced eviction after the city warned her landlord about her multiple calls for police assistance with a downstairs neighbor's noise and intimidating behavior. The American Civil Liberties Union and the Legal Aid Society of Cleveland successfully litigated the case, demonstrating that Bedford's CANO did indeed violate the Fair Housing Act in disproportionately targeting women and people of color.[32]

Acknowledging the risk that female renters face as a result of nuisance laws, the 2005 Violence Against Women Act (VAWA) moved to protect residents in government-subsidized housing from an eviction as a result of domestic violence in their unit. The VAWA protects tenants in subsidized private housing as well by making it unlawful for a landlord to evict a subsidized tenant on the basis of domestic violence, except if the landlord can prove that other tenants and staff face "actual and imminent threat" if the tenant is not removed.[33] Notably, the law does not address the practice by some private landlords of turning away applicants, whether subsidized or not, on the basis of having experienced domestic violence. Nor does it shield unsubsidized tenants from landlords' informal eviction tactics undertaken to abate a "nuisance." Accordingly, tenants in private-sector housing who have no government subsidy face the starkest disadvantage from CANOs that would sanction their landlord if they communicated with police in order to protect their safety.

For several reasons, CANOs also seem to be counterproductive to their stated goals of deterring undesirable activity that could undermine safety or quality of life or drain municipal resources. First, they may inadvertently lead to an increase in crime by exacerbating situations that are conducive to deviant or criminal behavior. It is typical for tenants' financial resources to fall into decline after an eviction.[34] In line with Robert Merton's strain theory, individuals who face obstacles to getting by financially through legitimate means become motivated to pursue illegitimate means instead.[35] Nuisance laws can also inadvertently trigger more criminal behavior through the "chilling effect" of disincentivizing landlords and tenants from calling police when necessary.[36] Furthermore, the financial and emotional trauma of an eviction can trigger illegal substance abuse, particularly among people who struggle with addiction.[37] For all these reasons, CANOs not only fail to address the issues that may lead to crime but may even create motivation or opportunities for illegal activity.

In yet more evidence of a counterproductive effect, ordinances meant to protect a declining municipal budget may inadvertently strain it by adding the costs to pay for homeless support services, emergency room visits, policing, court hearings, and other services that assist renters with the fallout from evictions and housing insecurity. Although it is essential that cities provide these services, they do not provide long-term solutions to the factors that may contribute to "nuisance" behavior, including poverty and mental health issues. Nuisance laws can in fact deepen these problems.

Finally, CANOs are another case of local laws that encourage landlords, however unintentionally, to treat and see their tenants as disposable.

By incentivizing landlords to address tenants' nuisance activity through eviction and other harmful measures, these ordinances codify renters' interests as secondary to those of the community. Criminal activity nuisance ordinances block lower-income renters' access to decent, stable, affordable housing in the private market—not only because of landlords' actions in response to them but also because of local authorities' lack of consideration of their consequences for the lives of renters and landlords.

= Chapter 5 =

"What Kills Me Now
Is the Water"

A NEW KIND of housing challenge is emerging in many American
communities. The cost of water is rising dramatically, greatly
outpacing wage increases. One reason for rising water and sewer
bills is the cost to repair the U.S. water delivery system, which, in most
cities, was last updated shortly after World War II. Water infrastructure
repairs are largely funded by local resources, not federal dollars, and the
federal government has been allocating less and less money for water
infrastructure upgrades each year.[1] Accordingly, cities are passing along
to consumers the costs of tearing up their streets and replacing water
pipes—so much so that water bills rose by an average of 40 percent in
cities nationwide between 2010 and 2015.[2] Thousands of households
across the country, and especially in distressed cities, including Detroit,
have lost water service in the past decade as a result of water shutoffs
for failure to pay rising water bills. Water shutoffs for nonpayment are
typically concentrated in lower-income and Black communities.[3]

Rising water bills and regulations about who is ultimately responsible
for paying water bills pose a unique threat to low-income renters' housing security. In Cleveland and numerous cities nationwide—including
Baltimore, New York City, and Seattle—the landlord is responsible for
paying the municipal water bill. Though landlords may arrange for
tenants to pay the bill directly or may reimburse them for the cost, an
unpaid water bill ultimately falls in the lap of the property owner. The
consequences of unpaid water bills can be dire, including the loss of
the property. In the Cleveland metropolitan region, as in many others
nationwide, unpaid water bills are added to property taxes at the end
of the year; as such, they can lead to forfeiture of the property to the
municipality as a result of delinquent property tax payments.

Landlords' sense of financial precarity surrounding water bills is only
deepened by laws found in Ohio and other states that protect tenants'
right to privacy. Landlords are not permitted to enter the property without giving the tenants twenty-four hours' notice, except in emergency

circumstances, such as a water leak. Thus, landlords cannot observe or control the amount of water their tenants use and may not find out about unusually high water usage—whether due to higher consumption or infrastructural problems such as leaks—until they receive an unexpectedly large city water bill.

Financial anxiety over water bills was especially stark among landlords who rented multifamily properties in the Cleveland metropolitan region. Local laws prevent the units in multi-unit properties, unlike single-family homes, from being separately metered by landlords. Without the ability to track individual tenants' water usage in multi-unit buildings, the landlords must pay the bill directly and in full to the water department. Notably, landlords with fewer property holdings also expressed stark financial concerns stemming from water billing regulations: a large and unexpected water bill could cancel out the profit they earned through their handful of rental properties.

Water billing regulations disadvantage tenants by perpetuating, and even amplifying, landlords' preexisting beliefs that tenants are irresponsible or untrustworthy. Expecting or observing higher water usage among tenants with characteristics associated with a "culture of poverty"—lack of employment, larger family size, receipt of a housing subsidy—served to reinforce landlords' beliefs about tenants' untrustworthiness and carelessness. Their mistrust of tenants combined with rising water costs and their financial precarity cast tenants' mundane domestic activities, such as doing laundry or watering the lawn, as additional evidence of tenants' irresponsibility.

Taken together, the rising cost of water, the multitude of ways in which tenants could use water, landlords' inability to observe tenants' water use or legally shut it off, and the legal sanctions associated with delinquent water bills sparked for landlords an outsized sense of risk and mistrust toward tenants that was not seen with respect to other utility bills—for heat or electricity, for example. Landlords, and especially small-sized landlords, responded to this sense of risk by tamping down water costs in ways that sometimes violated federal, state, and local laws.

Concerned about water bills, landlords screened out tenants based on "red flags" that they associated with higher water usage, turning away applicants who had larger households, lacked current employment, or held housing vouchers (based on the unfounded assumption that voucher holders lacked employment). Such practices disproportionately disadvantaged Black Americans, who faced the steepest obstacles to securing steady employment and who made up the vast majority of the region's voucher population.[4] In disproportionately undermining access to housing on the basis of racial background and family status, such practices also constitute a violation of the Fair Housing Act. Landlords' methods of intimidation to minimize current tenants' water usage was also a violation of state laws meant to prohibit harassment and tenants' subsequent involuntary moves.

This chapter demonstrates the risk of reliance on the private market to provide essential services and commodities—including municipal measures that enlist private corporations to collect on residents' unpaid water bills. Cuyahoga County and other municipalities nationwide contract with private corporations that reimburse them for homeowners' delinquent water and tax bills in exchange for the right to collect on the debt from the owner and add on astronomical interest fees. Owners who cannot pay off their debt to the corporate tax lien purchaser lose their home to foreclosure. Black owners and communities face the greatest fallout from this practice, as discussed later in this chapter.

Water billing regulations and municipal measures to collect on delinquent water bills provide still more examples of laws that appear race-neutral on paper but, by disproportionately penalizing communities of color, are far from it in practice.

Financial precarity as a result of water bills was widespread among the landlords studied here. They walked us through their operating costs, including water bills, on the backs of napkins and pointed to the scarce profit left over after all of the costs were accounted for. Landlords with small property holdings in particular expressed a potent sense of risk regarding water bills and were keen to share their concern about them as soon as possible.

"It Is Very Tight"

"Yep, I'll meet you," Sid, an Asian Indian man in his fifties, said over the phone. "Nine o'clock. After work. There's a Burger King on Carnegie. Quiet. We can talk there."

Wearing a plaid button-down shirt and khaki pants, Sid was pacing outside the Burger King and stretching his legs after a long shift at his job in the health care industry. He admitted that he was tired but welcomed the chance to talk. After settling into a booth, he leaned across the table and, with urgency in his voice, declared, "The water bills are terrible for the landlord. It is the biggest problem now."

After some back-and-forth discussion on water bills, Sid agreed to briefly switch the topic to his entrance into the business a decade earlier. The first rental he purchased was a small duplex in Brook Park, a quiet inner-ring suburb to the west of the central city. "I paid a pretty high price for that duplex because the economy was pretty good at the time," he remembered with a fleeting smile. The value of the property had declined by 20 percent since then, though Sid shook off the loss because the property generated profit. "You can rent it pretty easily," he said affably. Lower-income renters were drawn to the property because of its low rent—a reflection of the small square footage—and the low crime rates in the surrounding community.

Despite holding a full-time job in the health care industry, Sid decided to expand his rental business by purchasing more rentals after home prices declined in the years surrounding the housing market crash. Since Sid was "building my social security, pension," he became more strategic in his real estate purchases. "Now, I usually buy the single homes, actually the brick ranches." Though brick-exterior properties command a higher price, his decision to purchase them was strategic in the long run. Brick exteriors are less susceptible to deterioration than aluminum, vinyl, or wood siding, and so, with "less outside mainte-nance for me," Sid was willing to pay more for them upfront. He also rented several ranch houses in working-class and middle-income sub-urban communities on the West Side, but the most profit was generated by his two ranch houses in Solon, a middle-income suburban commu-nity to the east. Typically, after a tenant moved out of a Solon property, "it doesn't even stay vacant for one week," Sid beamed. "The school is number one in Ohio."

Nine minutes into the conversation, Sid raised the topic of water bills again. "That's the nightmare for [landlords], water and sewer." He paused for emphasis, then slowly enunciated, "It's a *nightmare*," while gripping the plastic table. It was even a nightmare in his single-family homes, though he required that tenants pay the water and sewer bill and even insisted that they register the account in their name. "If they don't pay, the government comes after you," he said incredulously, adding, "If you don't pay, that bill comes as a lien [on your property]!"

Water bills were also a "killer" for Dennis, a forty-something Black man with a guarded but serene demeanor. The day we first met he arrived breathless, wearing a green soccer jersey with blades of grass stuck to it. Earlier that morning, Dennis had mowed the lawns and tended to the yards at the two duplex properties he purchased a decade earlier; they were located in struggling communities on the city's East Side. Half of the properties on the street where he bought the duplexes had since fallen vacant and been abandoned over the course of that decade. Because he lived an hour away, near the office where he worked as an accountant, Dennis used to pay the "boys down the street" to mow the lawns to ensure that the properties were up to city health codes. But every dollar seemed to matter now. "You hardly break even by the time you do everything," Dennis reported morosely. "I don't see how any-body can be profitable except if the tenant paid the water."

Using a pencil and a white paper napkin, Dennis started to jot down the operating costs for just one of the duplexes. Each of the units in the duplexes commanded $450 per month in rent. "The water bill, at least about on an average $350, $400 a month," he began, scribbling on the napkin. Next he turned to property insurance costs. "On an average, insurance is about 100 bucks a month on one house. And you know, they adjust and go up every year," he sighed as he wrote. "The property tax is about the same thing, about $120 a month." After updating the tally on the napkin, he added in the $650 monthly mortgage payment for the property, which he had purchased for $60,000. Glancing down at his calculations, he estimated, "So when you add all of that, your expenses every month is over $1,000. And if you have two families, and you rent $450, you're only getting $900." Dennis breathed in deeply. After slowly exhaling, he admitted with a grimace, "It is very tight."

Unlike some landlords who justified lowering the quality of their rentals when profits turned sour, Dennis insisted, with a wave of his arm, "I'm not a slum landlord. I'm the kind of guy that walks into the house, and if the kitchen is old, I don't mind doing a little bit of updates to make the tenant happy, so that way they don't move." Like other landlords who rented properties in distressed communities, he had a deep fear of vandalism from leaving a property vacant. As he explained, that fear motivated him to keep his current tenants satisfied with their housing and not wanting to leave. "My wife always tells me," Dennis said with a grin, "'Happy home is a happy wife.' So a happy home is a happy tenant. If they like it, they'll do anything to keep it."

To avoid becoming a "slum landlord," despite waning profit, Dennis cut costs when possible by doing repair and maintenance work himself. That kept him spending Saturdays cutting grass and performing odd jobs, like painting, instead of spending time with his wife and young children. It was a "sacrifice," he admitted, but "that's okay," he said stoically, wearing a deadpan expression.

Dennis contemplated getting out of the business but foresaw obstacles to selling the properties. "You owe more than what the house is worth," he said glumly, dropping his shoulders. "The house next to you [is] boarded up. It's just so terrible. Nobody would buy." He fell silent and looked down, picking at some bits of grass on his shirt. After looking up again, he asked solemnly, "Pretty sad, ain't it?" Unlike owners who abandoned properties that became financial losses, Dennis remained adamant that walking away was not an attractive option for him. "I love my credit," he said wistfully. "So I'm just hanging on to something that is hard to keep hanging on to."

The stress of large water bills did, however, have some other land-lords still thinking about leaving the business of providing afford-able rental housing. Abe, a dark-haired, middle-aged White man, was another landlord who called water bills a "killer." He brought up water bills early on in our first conversation over the phone. He agreed to meet in person later that week at his office job in the finance industry, figuring, "I may as well talk to you during lunch. Because I'd be work-ing on this stuff anyway." Typically, his lunch hour was dedicated to managing his eight rental properties, most of which were multi-units—duplexes and fourplexes—located in lower-income communities on the city's East Side.

Seated in the glass-walled conference room at his workplace and wearing a white button-down shirt, pale blue tie, and dark pants, Abe reminisced fondly on his early childhood interest in investing in real estate. He first entered the market as a "flipper": someone who rehabbed properties and sold them for a profit. "For a while, I was making a lot of money," he said longingly. "In the early 2000s, I was buying a house, 10 percent down. I ended up getting a credit line, and I would pretty much have the house sold before it closed."

The housing market crash led Abe to leave the flipping business, which was no longer profitable to him. Instead, he began to invest in low-cost real estate to rent out, hoping to expand his landlord business enough to be able to leave his day job. "I'd like to grow big enough where I could leave this job and have some control over my time. While you're always running from property to property, you can't control . . ." He trailed off with a wince, then glanced around the spacious confer-ence room. "The nine-to-five grind I'd like to get rid of. I've been doing it many, many years."

"I didn't finance heavily. I wasn't going to get into big debt payments," Abe explained about his investment strategy, citing his children's steep college tuition costs. "I'm always looking for a value property. I don't care where it's at. I try to find a property that's low because I don't have a lot of money, so I'm trying to buy them cheap," he reasoned. He added, with outstretched hands, "I still try to keep them, you know, nice." For example, he explained, "I rehabbed this new property, and you know, I went and bought low-end Home Depot cabinets. I could have gone to the resale store and bought used cabinets that didn't match and, you know, probably saved myself, you know, a thousand dollars." He shrugged and insisted that he tries "to find a middle ground where I'm doing it right."

Then he grew eager to discuss water bills again. "What kills me now is the water," Abe said humorlessly. "It's gone up significantly. I want to say it's gone up 40 percent to 50 percent in the last couple of years."

Sighing, he continued: "A toilet running . . . that's a big one. That happens every now and then." Tugging on his tie to loosen it, he frowned. "If the toilet's running, I don't know about it, and the tenant really doesn't care. It doesn't affect them directly, so there's no impact on them and they don't care." Then his voice softened and he nodded: "I will say, sometimes [tenants] don't understand that it's that significant. And a lot of times when you do [tell them], they will tell you." Abe smiled and playfully remarked, "I have one woman, she's like, 'My toilet's been running for about half an hour.'" With a sigh of relief, he relaxed his shoulders and added, "I'm like, 'Thank you.'"

Like other landlords, Abe was aggrieved by his inability to separately meter water usage in his multi-unit properties. "It doesn't make sense," he wondered, wrinkling his brow. "With the electric, I can go to the electric company, and I can have four separate meters put in, and I can say to the tenant, 'Okay, here's your meter. Call the electric company, set the bill up in your name, and pay your bill.' Water, you can't do that." Waving a finger, he continued animatedly, "The electric company is not giving us a gift when we separately meter. We pay for the meter. We pay for it to be installed." Sounding more exasperated, he insisted, "I'm not asking [the water department] to pay for that." What he wanted most, Abe insisted, was to have the ability to instruct tenants in the multi-units, "Okay, this is your water bill, and you're going to pay that."

The water bills led Abe and other small-sized landlords to consider leaving the business of providing affordable rental housing altogether. "It's almost to the point where, you know, [bills] go up a little bit more, I'm done," Abe said curtly. "I'm not getting rich off of these properties. I still have a full-time job for a reason." He explained that he collected $2,000 per month in rent from the four units in the fourplex—when all of the tenants were current on rent—and received a water bill of $800 per quarter. Anticipating that water bills could soon reach $1,000 per quarter, he said tensely, "You know, $1,000 a quarter for a water bill when you're only making $6,000 [in rent per quarter], you know, then you got taxes, and you got insurance, and you got upkeep, you know. It doesn't leave enough to put in your pocket." Tapping the table in thought, he continued: "Rents have gone up a little bit the last couple of years, but they haven't gone up as much as the bills have." Abe had begun to envision leaving the business because, he said with a tight jaw, "It's not worth the risk."

For some landlords, it was primarily the size of exceedingly large water bills that evoked precarity and suspicion toward tenants. Though such bills were rare—reported by just a few landlords—their potential consequences were huge enough to make water billing a salient issue for all landlords. The prospect of an atrocious water bill deepened land-lords' mistrust toward tenants—and especially those they perceived as stereotypically irresponsible or untrustworthy.

"We're Going to Go Bankrupt"

When we met Max, a White forty-something man with sandy blond hair, he was relaxing in his lush green backyard, wearing a faded T-shirt and sporty sunglasses. His wife, Kendra, a White woman with wavy blond hair and a bright smile, sat alongside him, watching their young children playing softball. Until a few years earlier, Max had worked a double shift at his job on the workroom floor; now he mar-veled when he remembered the hustle it took to maintain the prop-erties and also find time for his family. After a full day at work, he recalled, "I would come home, I'd eat dinner, and at 6:00 I'd leave [to work on the properties]. And then I'd be back at 11:00. Then I'd get up and go to work." Kendra chimed in incredulously, "It was crazy," and Max wholeheartedly agreed, cackling, "It was insane." Looking over at his young children, he explained, with a grin, "I wanted to see them once in a while."

The middle-income suburban communities on the West Side, where Max and Kendra owned several small apartment buildings, experienced some decline after they purchased them at the height of the housing bubble. One building generated decent profit, Max said, but another, a fourteen-unit apartment building, had become a loss. "I paid too much for it," Max said dully, slumped down in the chair. "I was at the top of the market when I bought everything, and everything crashed." With a shrug, he conceded, "We get a nice fat tax return, but we're losing money hand over fist, and I'm locked into this loan, so I can't even sell the thing without taking a huge prepayment pounding. So we're trying to hang on for another two years and see if we can unload it without losing too, too much money."

The couple attributed some of their losses to their lower- and moderate-income tenants' struggles to pay rent. "Part of the problem is," Kendra explained, with a halting smile, "you get someone in there, they sign a lease and stuff, and then they don't pay their rent. Then we have to pay to evict them, but then we never get any of that money back. They don't have any money to go after them, it's not worth the court cost."

But water, Max declared unwaveringly, "is the biggest enemy. It's the highest expense, it does the most damage." Citing the skyrocketing water bills, Max wondered, "I don't know what [the county] is think-ing," adding, "People aren't going to be to afford to live in Cleveland is what's going to happen." With a big laugh and outstretched hands,

Max exclaimed, "Every three months, I go, 'Oh crap, how am I going to pay the water bill?'"

The costs of tenants' routine water usage put Max on edge, but it was one astronomical water bill at the small apartment building that instigated his undue anxiety about the cost of water. Immediately before the birth of his youngest son, he received a $10,000 municipal water and sewer bill—more than three times the typical amount for the building. Right after opening the bill, he remembered grimly thinking, "We're going to go bankrupt." Looking down at the grass, he admitted, "I literally sat on the couch and cried. I was crying."

Max discovered the source of the excessive water bill—one tenant's running faucet—during a subsequent visit to the building. The tenant, who received a federal housing subsidy for formerly homeless people with mental illness, Shelter Plus Care, informed Max, "I've got a problem with my sink," and led him into the apartment. "He had nothing in his apartment, except a chair and a weight set in the living room. And a Bible," Max remembered. Kendra anxiously placed her hands in front of her face in anticipation of what Max was about to describe. "He tore the handle off the faucet in the kitchen, and the water had been running and running and running," Max remembered miserably, rolling his head to the side. "How long has this been going on?" he had shouted at the tenant, who replied that he did not know. "I flipped my lid," Max roared. "Because I knew damn well, that's where all my money was."

Max was aggrieved not just by the cost of the water bill but also by his interaction with the tenant's caseworker. His interactions with the tenant over time had led Max to believe that the tenant's mental health was steadily in decline. "He would tell me stories, about squirrels crawling under his skin and aliens calling him," Max recalled with a twitch. "This guy needs help," he informed the tenant's caseworker, who said that there was little she could do. Max contacted several of the tenant's family members, in search of help for him. "Called his ex-wife, she wanted nothing to do with him. I called his sister, she didn't want anything to do with him," he remembered, counting on his fingers. "So you became a social worker," Kendra remarked to Max, leading him to nod and add somberly, "I ended up having to babysit this guy, and finally, I had to throw him out." Max grimaced and added, "Then I saw him wandering the streets for about a month, and then I haven't seen him since."

Because they were accountable for paying water bills, landlords began to suspect that tenants might take advantage of water billing arrangements for self-serving purposes—whether for financial gain, such as washing nonresidents' laundry in exchange for cash, or as an emotional outlet, such as in response to eviction.

"My Big Fear . . . That They Just Turned the Faucets On and Walked Away"

The tale of the tenant who used water excessively to retaliate for an eviction was passed around and retold among landlords. This fear of a mythical water-wasting tenant loomed large and deepened landlords' mistrust toward all tenants—even landlords who had never experienced it firsthand.[5] The myth clearly rattled Quinn, the White landlord who, as recounted in chapter 3, struggled to glean satisfactory profit from renting properties on streets with decaying properties in a community on the city's East Side. Blinking rapidly, Quinn described the anxiety he experienced before entering a unit for the first time after a recently evicted tenant moved out. "My big fear, every time I go into a vacant apartment," he remarked flatly, "is that they just turned the faucets on and walked away."

A year after we first met, I joined Quinn again at the same upstairs apartment in the tall gray duplex property, which had again fallen vacant. The tenant he had eventually selected to fill the unit, a young woman with a job and several evictions on her record, had fallen a month behind on rent, leading Quinn to evict her. Unlike most other landlords who rented to lower-income tenants, Quinn pursued the debt in second-cause court. The magistrate rendered a verdict in his favor, because the tenant earned wages that could be garnished.

His expression pinched, Quinn stood in the gravel driveway in his usual outfit of a white T-shirt, faded blue jeans, and white sneakers. He bolted up the duplex's interior stairs and stopped short in front of the upstairs door. Seeming unusually distracted, he flipped through a large ring of silver and brass keys clipped to his jeans in search of the right key. "Ah, there it is!" He twisted the lock open and took several steps into the empty apartment. Standing with his hands on his hips, he glanced around with a perplexed look.

Silver foil wrappers, pennies, and what appeared to be small glass marbles were scattered haphazardly across the apartment's wood floors. His brow furrowed, Quinn kneeled down to inspect them. "I wonder what that is," he pondered, spinning a marble between his fingers. He brought one closer to his face. "It's just a stone," he determined nonchalantly and set it back down on the floor. Slowly wandering around the apartment with a yellow pad, he began to jot notes about damages that he insisted were caused by the tenant, including torn window blinds and a broken mirror. "What in the world happened here?" Quinn mused, standing over an inch-wide hole in one of the small bedroom's wood floors. Crouching down to skim the floor with a finger, he remarked lightly, "I think this is going to be a pain in the ass." He recalled that, "when Dad did this, he had to actually sand this thing down to make that fit."

Quinn seemed mostly unfazed by the damages. His calm, even placid, demeanor was a departure from his occasionally feisty persona. He seemed only relieved upon discovering that the tenant had not left the water running. In his thirty years as a landlord, had a tenant ever purposefully turned on the faucets to retaliate after an eviction? "Never, ever," he answered immediately.

The rising cost of water, alongside water billing regulations that made landlords accountable for paying bills associated with tenants' water usage, over which they felt they had little control, caused these landlords to develop an acute sense of uncertainty and mistrust. In an attempt to minimize the risk of financial losses through water bills, landlords turned to business practices that ultimately undermined renters' access to decent, stable, affordable housing, including discriminatory screening, extreme monitoring, and even harassment.

"It Is to My Advantage to Have Them Working"

Without direct control over tenants' water usage, landlords attempted to minimize the risk of high water bills by screening out tenants who they presumed would use more water—and who also happened to face some of the greatest barriers to housing.

Tenants' employment status was especially salient to landlords' screening process, for reasons beyond its perceived association with the ability to pay rent: being unemployed was correlated, landlords assumed, with more time spent on the property and subsequently higher water usage and bills. Unemployment therefore exacted a "double penalty" on disadvantaged households that further blocked their access to stable housing: landlords perceived them as less desirable as prospective tenants not only because they assumed that the unemployed had less capacity to pay rent or have their wages garnished, but also because of their assumptions about the lifestyle of the unemployed.

Layla, a petite Black woman in her late forties, wearing a light blue denim jacket, owned forty properties, mostly duplexes. They were concentrated in what she described as "working-class neighborhoods" on Cleveland's East Side and in nearby inner-ring suburbs, including Cleveland Heights. Layla entered the real estate trade at a younger age than most other landlords. When she was seventeen, "my mom and I, we just started looking for other places to live, and I just realized that

I probably would be the one that would need to secure the financing, because she was not employed at the time," Layla explained. "So it sort of started from there." Upon earning a bachelor's degree and obtaining a real estate license, then holding various administrative positions, Layla became a full-time landlord. She was grateful that the properties generated enough revenue to support full-time staff. "I have plumber, electrical, and carpenter, all full-time," she tallied. "I have a couple painters too, that only do painting."

Although the business generated satisfactory profit overall, Layla lamented that water bills could determine the profitability of a particular property. "Most of them I do [earn a profit] on," she said, but not on others, "because sometimes the water bill absorbs the profit." She added smoothly, "To me it still balances, because it's never going to be sometimes a perfect situation. So as long as you get a balance there, I think you don't need to beat yourself up about it."

Applicants' employment status was salient to Layla and numerous other landlords, however, because of its presumed correlation with water usage. Layla turned away tenants who did not hold a steady job. "I would prefer to have someone working, because they're not there all day, running water, which I'm responsible for, the water bill," she said matter-of-factly. "So it is to my advantage to have them working."

Antwan, the Black landlord who "bluffed out" his tenant whom he suspected of illegal drug use on the property (see chapter 4), paid close attention to prospective tenants' employment status out of concern about water bills. He was wary of accepting unemployed applicants, particularly if they did not provide a socially approved reason for not working. "If you're not working, you're supposed to say, 'I'm in school,' or, 'Stay[ing] at home with the kids,'" Antwan mulled. "If you don't have a story . . ." Shaking his head, he maintained, "I have to look out for myself, for the benefit of my property."

Tenants without jobs could add to the wear-and-tear on the property, he reasoned, including through higher water usage. "You shouldn't even be up in my property twenty-four hours a day!" Antwan exclaimed. "I'll get somebody who go to work for eight [hours] and got to go pick up the kids and go grocery shopping and have some type of life." Otherwise, he insisted, "that's eight to sixteen hours just sitting, beating the property up." Tapping his temple, he gave a knowing look. "You have to *think* like that."

Landlords' differing levels of aggravation and suspicion about tenants' water usage indeed reflected their judgments about why tenants spent time on the property. Tenants with "socially approved" reasons for spending more time on the property, such as advanced age, were spared the judgmental gaze of the landlord. Yet tenants who received government assistance on the basis of low income—many of whom were erroneously presumed by landlords to be unemployed—most strongly triggered landlords' beliefs about tenants' immorality for using water they had not "earned."

"I'm a Little Discriminatory"

"Be there at 3:45. Sharp," Donald had instructed over the phone. His penchant for timeliness and deadlines was a holdover from his ten years in the corporate world, which he had left behind six years earlier to become a real estate mogul. "I was really just kind of getting tired of corporate America," he explained excitedly at our 3:45 meeting at a café located in bustling Ohio City, near the central city's downtown district. From the beginning, Donald, a tall Black man in his midforties, radiated excitement in talking about his transition into the landlord industry.

Over a glass of iced tea, Donald explained that he mostly looked to invest in what he believed were low-risk properties in the city of Cleveland—ones that were located in B- or C-graded neighborhoods on "nice" streets and required little rehab work. "I even prefer to buy houses with tenants in them," Donald said. He reasoned: "I know it's functional. I know the water is running." With a shrug, he added, "[Tenants] wouldn't be living there if it were that dilapidated."

"I really got a vision," Donald continued animatedly, tapping on the wooden table. "I really wanted to be the first person to brand homes in Cleveland." He planned to create a well-regarded brand that could attract financially stable tenants—or even potential buyers if he decided later to sell the properties. As part of the process of building a brand, Donald invested in new floors and roofs for the dozen single-family and duplex properties he owned, which he had purchased for approximately $20,000 each in the wake of the housing market crash. The properties were managed by a man whom Donald considered "a hybrid type of a property manager/handyman."

Despite culling modest profit in the business, Donald also expressed a sense of precarity. "Just the fact that you're a landlord," he observed, "it's perceived that you have money." He continued, saying sternly, "Do not perceive that. I'm waiting for you to pay me so I can pay these bills." Tapping at the shiny silver watch on his wrist, Donald insisted, "I'm very strict. You have to pay on time. I'm not lenient about that."

Donald brought that sense of financial precarity to his screening practices as well. Early on in the business, he recalled, he received an $800 water bill for one of his properties—more than three times the usual amount for that property. "It's part of the business," he reasoned calmly, lifting a shoulder. "I have to pay it." The shock of receiving a large water bill led him to adjust his lease and screening practices so as to avoid the risk of having to pay tenants' water bills. Instead of entering into yearlong leases with tenants, Donald switched to month-to-month leases. After receiving the $800 water bill, "that's the big thing I learned right away," he reported. Short-term leases may be desirable to renters seeking flexibility, but they may disadvantage renters who seek more stable housing conditions by allowing landlords to terminate leases without cause, typically with thirty days' notice, and to increase rent amounts more frequently.

Donald explained that his approach to screening also evolved over time in the rental business. "I've changed in terms of who I look for," he noted. "I'm a little discriminatory." Specifically, he chose not to rent to tenants who paid rent using government assistance they received on the basis of earning low or no income. "You know what SSI is?" he asked, referring to Supplemental Security Income (SSI), the federal program providing funds for the low-income elderly or disabled. "If you're solely getting your income off [SSI], you're not for me," Donald insisted adamantly, stiffening his posture. "This is a little biased, but it says that you don't work, and so that trend is really . . ." After thumping his fingers on the wooden table in search of words, he blurted out, "You're home all day, more wear-and-tear on the home."

Donald further demonstrated his belief that tenants' "deservingness" of housing was contingent on their work history when he showed enthusiasm for housing elderly tenants. Although they presumably spent more time on the property, they paid rent with Social Security benefits, which were delivered to them for "socially approved" reasons—having reached an advanced age or having accumulated funds through former employment. "Now, if there is an elderly person on Social Security," Donald added brightly, "I have no problem with that."

With water bills in mind, landlords were also wary about renting to applicants who had large families. Landlords' reluctance on this score is thus yet another obstacle, for these families, to access to affordable rental housing.[6] Nelson, the nonchalant White landlord featured in chapter 3 who rented several dozen single-family homes in a struggling East Side community, remarked that small family size was an important consideration for him in selecting a new tenant. Seated in his dusty workroom, he maintained that profit in the business was decent, "as long as the water bills are okay." He explained that "you have to try to find the people that you think aren't gonna have a bunch of people." He preferred to house older tenants, believing that they would not have dependent children living with them and also using water. With a laugh, Nelson admitted that this logic had proven faulty as more and more households "doubled up"—having one or more adults in the household, such as an adult child, in addition to the household head in order to alleviate a high housing cost burden.[7] "You think, 'Oh great, older couple,'" he began good-naturedly, pretending to scan over a tenant's application. With a wary grin, he pointed toward one of his bungalow rental properties across the street. "You go there, and they're like, 'Oh, my daughter is gonna be stayin' here for a few weeks. Oh, here's her son, and her boyfriend. She's got ten kids.'" He added comically, "You're like, 'Oh shit,' you know?" Then his voice dropped low. "And now you're sunk."

One of Nelson's single-family properties had recently experienced an unexpected growth in household size, with a corresponding rise in water costs. "She ended up having like, five kids, and they each had their girlfriends, and they had kids. The water bills were high," Nelson remembered. "In their lease, they're supposed to pay anything over $200 in a quarter, but I don't enforce that." He shook his head. "So that's one of the things I'm workin' on, enforcing that," he noted, though "it's hard," he admitted. Citing the difficulty of collecting additional money from his struggling tenants, he shrugged, "As long as they know, you know, then hopefully, they'll start to pay attention more."

Water bills evoked a greater sense of financial precarity among these small and midsized landlords than any other local policy. Yet the financial anxiety over water bills among those landlords who rented more than a handful of units was not so stark. The steady revenue generated by their properties "smoothed" their losses, whether through the unexpected shock of a high overall water bill or an elevated bill at a particular property. Layla had explained coolly that, in gleaning sufficient profit from her several dozen rental properties, "you don't need to beat yourself up" about receiving higher water bills at one or two properties. Nelson said, with little conviction, that he was "working on" collecting more money from tenants when water bills spiked above the amount noted in the lease. Donald conceded matter-of-factly that water bills were "part of the business."

Tenant screening was the primary business tactic used by landlords with midsized property holdings to lessen the risk of high and unpredictable water bills. "You have to try to find the people that you think aren't gonna have a bunch of people," Nelson had remarked. In screening tenants, Donald had admitted, "I'm a little discriminatory." Yet the landlords with midsized property holdings did not use extreme surveillance tactics to curtail their tenants' water usage. Nelson found it amusing that some landlords micro-managed tenants about their water usage, a practice whose financial rewards he questioned. "I know a lot of people who won't let [tenants] have their own washer machine, washer and dryer, 'cause of water bills," he nodded.

He tilted his head. "But then they wash their clothes in the bathtub." After glancing toward his crew of tenants who performed maintenance work in exchange for rent forgiveness, he leaned forward to whisper teasingly, "So then they're fillin' up a bathtub how many times to wash a load of clothes in their bathtub?" He straightened up and added good-naturedly, "Well, you're better off just letting them have a washing machine!"

For several reasons, it was small-time landlords who expressed the greatest financial anxiety in regard to water bills and who took more extreme measures beyond screening, including excess scrutiny and even harassment, to limit tenants' water usage. First, small-time landlords typically spent more time on their properties than landlords whose larger property holdings generated sufficient revenue to enable them to hire staff who could oversee routine tasks, such as coordinating property repairs and attending inspections for their subsidized units. To conserve resources, small-time landlords performed repairs and attended inspections themselves and so were able to observe what seemed to them to be tenants' "irresponsible' or "excessive" water use. Accordingly, the stage was set for these landlords to grow particularly aggrieved about tenants' routine water usage. That small-time landlords typically generated less revenue overall also contributed to their distress about unpredictable water costs.

"We Caught Him Red-Handed"

In an attempt to curtail water usage at his duplex property, Dennis chided tenants, "Listen, I know you've got to wash. At least, you can't wash your car." Wagging a finger, he added, "That's a no-no." Other observable outdoor uses of water were also fair game for Dennis's comments. "Don't worry about putting the water on the grass," he instructed tenants. "You let the rain do that." Tenants mostly went along with these requests, perhaps out of fear that he would raise rents to compensate for rising water bills. One low-income tenant who had paid exactly $450 per month for the past fourteen years was "so afraid I'm going to raise the rent," Dennis knowingly observed.

Sarah and her husband Eric, both White and in their early forties, showed up at a wine bar in Tremont, a historic West Side community in the city of Cleveland brimming with art galleries, craft breweries, and indie boutiques. Sarah, a petite woman with long dark hair and a warm smile, explained that she bought her first rental property in 2000, in Ohio City. She made the purchase before meeting Eric, a soft-spoken man with blond hair who worked as a building inspector. "I renovated it myself, and it was a total learning project," Sarah confessed as she glanced slyly at Eric. "He could tell that I did it myself, and I didn't know what I was doing quite yet."

Sarah bought several more rentals in the early 2000s in predominantly White, working-class communities on the city's West Side, while maintaining a career in the real estate industry. Unlike the first property, the properties she later purchased were already renovated. She bought them at the top of the market, hoping to eventually "flip" them. Sarah described her business plan: "Rent them out, and look for ones that have cash flow. Keep them like, five years or so, and then just, then sell them at that point." Then the housing market crashed, destroying her plan to flip the properties at a profit. The day we met Sarah still owned all seven of the single-family and small multifamily homes she had purchased nearly a decade earlier and had intended to sell.

"We're stuck," Sarah admitted after taking a gulp of red wine. "Can't get out. Like, I owe more than what the home is worth. Or if I don't, I've already put so much in, I just can't." She shook her head vigorously. "I can't do it for that. I can't just give it away." She gazed at her empty wineglass. "I'll just keep it, and eventually it'll come around." Looking at Eric, she remarked softly, "He was suckered in from me. He wouldn't have chosen [the business] by any means." The couple locked eyes and she pressed, "Right?" Without pause, Eric stoically replied, "No. I would not."

"Water bills," Sarah began with a deep sigh. "They've more than doubled." Despite rising costs for water service, insurance, and taxes, it was impossible to raise rents, she said. "Well, I can raise the rent, but then can't get the rent," Sarah maintained. "Nobody will [move in], it'll be vacant forever." Instead, she instructed tenants to use less water. "We've said that to people, like, if you know, 'Maybe you want to go to a laundromat if you can't afford the water bill.'" Sarah continued, "'Cause every time you go to the house the washing machine's running." She nudged Eric and prodded, "Like, we do two loads a week, you know?"

"Tell 'em your story of, 'No, I never wash my car,'" Sarah instructed Eric, tapping at his wrist. "Oh, yeah," Eric perked up. "We had a tenant that was, we knew he was washing his car, because we'd go over there, and it would be like a big, you know, the driveway would be wet and it hadn't rained for a few days." Sarah chimed in enthusiastically, "And the water bills were outrageous." The tenant insisted that he didn't wash his car on the property. Sarah and Eric searched Google Street View for images of the property and discovered a picture that showed him washing the car. "There he was, washing his car in Google Street View," Eric remarked. "We caught him red-handed," Sarah added with satisfaction, noting, "Every time the new Street View pictures come out, I always go around to all the properties just to check them."

Other landlords used more overt threats to control what they perceived as tenants' self-serving water usage. Gary, a burly, animated, sixty-something White man wearing a faded blue T-shirt, rented eleven single-family and duplex properties in a struggling community on the city's East Side. Inspired to invest in the rental business after he became dissatisfied with the routine of a nine-to-five job, Gary had purchased these properties after local housing prices fell dramatically. "With a job, your employer has this invisible chain around your neck, and he starts rattling it about an hour or two before you're scheduled to come into work," he complained. "And then he lets up on Friday and gives you some slack, but then he starts rattling again come Sunday night. And then the rattling gets stronger and stronger come Monday, when it's in full force and effect." As a result of becoming a full-time investor, Gary said proudly, "you're in business for yourself, or not dependent upon other people for money, health insurance, benefits, things like that—you don't have that rattle."

Slowly walking us through the community where his rentals were concentrated, Gary discussed the strategies he developed to become a successful landlord in the "inner city." "The card that I play is, power perceived is power achieved. If [tenants] think that they have something to fear, they're apt not to mess with you," he observed. "And if they perceive you as being weak and wishy-washy, and think that they can run over you, they'll do that too."

When Gary received atypically large water bills for one property on several occasions, he came to believe that the tenant had brought in washing machines—a violation of his lease terms—to wash other people's clothing in exchange for money. "You've got to take that washing machine out. Or I'm going to cut your water supply to the point where it's next to nothing, or raise your rent through the roof," he warned the tenant after discovering a washing machine in the unit. He punctuated his threat with a commentary on the tenant's morality. "If you want to wash clothes every day and invite everybody in the neighborhood to come over and wash clothes, I'm not going to pay for it. See, I already pay for your welfare, your food stamps, your Section 8, your Medicaid. All right? That's enough."

Following through on a threat to cut tenants' water service or raise rents in order to curtail their water usage constitutes a clear violation of state and local laws meant to protect renters. Harassing tenants over water usage, as Gary and other landlords did, also violates laws that are meant to protect renters' housing security. Since harassment typically occurs behind closed doors, off the radar of city or court officials, tenants must report it to authorities in order to benefit from these protections. Lower-income tenants with few alternative affordable housing options are the most likely to withhold reports of landlord harassment, out of fear of retaliatory actions by the landlord, such as an eviction or a slow response to requests for repairs.

That small-time landlords scrutinized tenants' water usage to the point, in some cases, of overt and illegal harassment raises questions about their suitability as providers of decent, stable housing for marginalized tenants. Their limited cash flow and, relatedly, their time spent on the property to perform necessary work ensured that they had more opportunities to observe the routine tenant behaviors that put them on edge. An important part of this story is the unique set of financial and legal circumstances that transformed some of the most routine and essential human behaviors—drinking water, bathing, and cleaning—into evidence of carelessness or deviance. In line with "confirmation bias"—which holds that individuals pay more attention to observations that confirm their preexisting beliefs—these landlords became fixated on evidence of tenants' "irresponsible" behavior, including their water usage, that ultimately reinforced their preexisting belief that marginalized tenants were irresponsible.[8]

Small-time landlords do, however, provide their struggling tenants with opportunities that larger-scale landlords typically would not. In contrast with larger-scale landlords, small-time landlords are able to interact and form personal relationships with their tenants, which may prompt them to be lenient in rent collection and screening.[9] For instance, information gleaned through conversations with prospective tenants during the screening process can cause a stigmatized experience, such as an eviction, to lose its salience for the landlord.

For Abe, the landlord for whom water bills were a "killer," an eviction was a "red flag" that usually made him turn away a prospective tenant. Yet learning about the eviction through conversation occasionally changed his stance. "There's always a story," he explained with a shrug. Learning, for instance, that the eviction came about through a sudden economic shock, such as an illness or divorce, rather than poor money management could persuade him to give an applicant a chance. The time frame of the eviction mattered as well. "It happened eight years ago," Abe said about one applicant, adding affably, "If I look and see they have a pretty clean record after that, no problem."

Clearly, there may not be an "ideal" private landlord to house the most marginalized renters. Despite landlords' legitimate intentions in the business, their pursuit of profit makes renters' interests secondary and motivates them to engage in disadvantageous practices for the sake of financial gain, including discriminatory screening, extreme tenant surveillance and harassment, and property disinvestment.

Transferring responsibility to private-sector actors for work previously undertaken by government authorities comes with extreme risk for marginalized populations. Further evidence of this risk can be seen in the measures taken by municipalities, apart from raising water rates, to gather resources to fund costly water infrastructure upgrades.

Cuyahoga County and other municipalities nationwide have looked to corporate investors to recoup the losses associated with delinquent water bills. At the end of 2014, the county's delinquent property tax balance—which included delinquent water bills—was a staggering $578 million.[10] To collect much-needed cash to fund essential services, Ohio permits its municipalities, including counties, to place a lien on a property that is delinquent on water bills or property taxes. The county then turns the lien into cash by bundling and selling property liens to private corporations that act essentially as debt collectors: they pay the property's debt to the city and obtain the right to collect payment from the homeowner for the amount of the delinquency, plus *18 percent* in interest fees. If a tax-delinquent homeowner fails to pay the private corporation the full amount owed, including interest fees, within the allotted time frame (typically three years), they lose their home through foreclosure.[11]

The practice is not limited to Ohio. Tax lien sales can be found in Alabama, Arizona, Colorado, Florida, Illinois, Indiana, Iowa, Kentucky, Maryland, Mississippi, Missouri, Montana, Nebraska, Nevada, New Jersey, New York, North Dakota, South Carolina, South Dakota, Vermont, West Virginia, and Wyoming. The District of Columbia also allows municipalities to collect on tax debt by working with private corporations. Tax lien sales are more successful in recouping unpaid tax and water bills in strong markets, like Washington, D.C., where home-owners have more resources to pay the debt and are motivated to avoid losing their valuable asset to foreclosure.[12] Motivation to pay the debt for homeowners in Cuyahoga County, however, is more problematic, since they struggle with fewer resources.

The Cuyahoga County Water Department has grown more aggres-sive with each passing year in placing liens on properties with delin-quent water bills (and eventually delinquent tax bills). Between 2013 and 2015, the rate at which the water department placed liens on tax-delinquent properties tripled: it turned over nearly 8,000 water customers to the county auditor, leading to liens on their properties.[13] Indeed, the lien process recouped $8 million for the water department during that time period. But the short-term cash infusion came with long-term negative consequences for the county's residents and communities. Among the 3,651 water tax liens issued in 2015 alone, one in ten culmi-nated in a foreclosure, and one in three properties fell vacant.[14] Most foreclosures triggered by this process were concentrated in low-income and predominantly Black communities on the city's East Side, where subprime lending practices targeting their communities had burdened homeowners with higher housing costs.[15]

Inez, a middle-aged Black woman with neatly coiffed rust-colored hair, a raspy voice, and dark eyes that sometimes appeared bright and lively, but often appeared deeply sad or dazed, is a landlord who eventually experienced the loss of property through overdue tax and water bills. Inez collapsed into the seat at the wine bar where we first met. She had just finished a long shift as a community outreach specialist, helping residents with mental illness live independently in their communities. "One of these days I'm going to treat myself to their steak," she said wistfully while looking at the menu. After flipping it closed, she explained, "They say it's good, and I want to treat myself to a couple of things that's over—out of my income."

In describing her motivation to enter the landlord business, Inez recalled, "I was kind of interested in obtaining property to rent because I decided to get a hold of my retirement." Eight years earlier, she had purchased a tan, colonial-style, single-family home in a predominantly Black community on the city's East Side. She bought it at the top of the market, for $86,000; its current assessed value had fallen to one-third of that.

"That was a perfect rental property," Inez reminisced with a faraway look in her eyes. "It was completely rehabbed. It had ceramic floors in the kitchen and in the bathroom, and everything in there was new." She added softly, "The street that it's on is very close-knit. Every Memorial Day they have a block party with—they have activities for the kids. The food is free. Since I had the property for eight years, I've never had an opportunity to enjoy it." She sipped her martini and said dreamily, "This year I'm going to be able to experience it."

Inez grew somber, even despondent, as she described the decline of the rental property after she lost her health care job and remained unemployed for several years before obtaining her current position a year earlier. "It takes so much strength to, just to survive the unemployment angle. And now that I'm employed and trying to get financially stable, I'm exhausted. Literally exhausted." She stared down at her empty soup bowl with a glazed expression.

With no revenue coming in from a job, Inez fell behind on her obligations as an investor, including property maintenance and water bill payments to the city. The property's water bill delinquency exceeded $1,000, and she worried that the water service would get shut off. To quell her worry Inez decided to get caught up financially by securing a new tenant for the rental property, which was vacant. Finding a tenant for the property, which had fallen into decline, had not been easy. The carpet needed cleaning, and so did the gutters. The bathroom Inez had fallen in love with earlier was now in pieces. She lacked the capital and the time to finish repairing the damage to the bathroom floor after a water leak. "I started the bathroom, but I ran out of tile," she said dismally. With a furrowed brow, she pleaded, unconvincingly, "But it still looks good, you know?"

Inez then confessed that the county had placed a lien on the property because of the delinquent water bill and several thousand dollars in unpaid property taxes. She had two more years to pay the accumulated debt plus 18 percent interest to the company that had purchased the lien, or else lose possession of the property.

As she talked about the business, Inez's face remained pinched with worry. She only began to breathe out deeply and begin to relax when she talked about her son, an engineering major at a state university. He had told her on the phone the night before that, "you know, there's hardly, there's no African Americans in the engineering [school] that graduated." He told his mother, "I want to graduate." Clutching the edge of the wooden table, Inez recalled how she responded. "I said, 'Jordan, I hope you do, because this is a hard major. You know, we come from the inner city, and they don't really teach us how to take tests.'" She squeezed her eyes tightly together. "I got to pray for him. That's what I got to do." When Inez eventually stood up to leave, she walked toward the door with an uneven, lilting gait. She dropped her faded black purse on the floor, scooped it up by the straps, and then hurried out. The next day she reassured me over the phone, "I'm fine. It's, you know, it'll be fine."

A year later, we met again at the same wine bar. Inez still hadn't tried the steak. The tenant she had secured a month after we met had just served her a thirty-day notice of her intent to vacate. Inez had not followed through on her promise to the tenant to make some necessary repairs. Nonetheless, she was stung at receiving the notice, having divulged her financial struggles to the tenant. "I thought she could sympathize with me," she said sullenly, gazing at the floor. But then Inez reported happily that she had finally attended the cozy street's Memorial Day party, and her joy spilled over as she recounted how much free food there was, the different games for the children, and how friendly the neighbors were. Inez had one more year to attend the party as a property owner in the neighborhood. Then, a year and a half later, she lost possession of the house as a result of a $6,000 unpaid debt to the corporate tax lien purchaser.

Tax lien sales impose a double penalty on Black communities: not only do they deepen the racial wealth gap through individual home-owners' loss of equity, but they also perpetuate more disadvantage in poor Black communities, which have already suffered the disastrous economic and social consequences of long-term divestment on the part of federal and local authorities.[16] Corporate tax lien buyers make little financial or social investment in the communities where they obtain properties, and although they are obliged to follow the same housing codes as ordinary homeowners, in practice few do—and especially not those who own properties in distressed communities. Property negligence further destabilizes marginalized communities and deepens the racial wealth gap.[17]

Taken together, municipalities' measures to generate resources to fund essential water systems systematically disadvantage marginalized communities. The fallout for marginalized renters often falls off the radar of authorities, particularly given their limited knowledge of landlords' business practices. Yet the consequences of water lien sales for marginalized owners and communities are predictable and readily observable. Indeed, a federal judge ruled in 2021 that the NAACP Legal Defense Fund's class action lawsuit against the Cleveland Water Department alleging that its practices disproportionately harmed Black residents and violated the Fair Housing Act could move forward.[18]

In the meantime, Cuyahoga County and other municipalities across the country continue to collect fast cash in exchange for tax-liened properties in struggling communities—a practice that, as a city official remarked to me, is akin to making "a deal with the devil."

= Chapter 6 =

"You Said You're Section 8 . . . That's *Why* I Don't Want to Get in Touch with You"

O NE AGENCY, perhaps above all others, has the most important role in ensuring that the poorest citizens in the Cleveland metropolitan area have access to decent, stable housing. The Cuyahoga Metropolitan Housing Authority (CMHA), as the primary public housing authority (PHA) in Cuyahoga County, administers the federal Housing Choice Voucher Program (HCVP). The HCVP is intended to address many of the struggles that landlords and their low-income tenants face in the rental market.

The voucher program—colloquially called "Section 8"—looks to prevent households from experiencing too great a housing cost burden by requiring that no more than 30 percent of their gross household income will go toward rent. The government subsidizes the remainder of the rent amount, which is set according to the fair market rent (FMR) for the region. According to the voucher program's payment structure, most landlords do collect some rent payment from voucher tenants each month, though a substantial portion of the rent is paid directly by the government. Continued government rent payment is contingent on whether the rental unit passes an initial quality inspection and then subsequent annual inspections, both performed by inspectors who work for the local PHA. According to these rules, a "slum" property and its landlord should not be eligible to receive steady rent payment from the government by housing a subsidized tenant.[1]

The voucher program has not met its goal of providing decent, affordable rental housing to lower-income families. As seen in the Cleveland metropolitan area and in other U.S. metropolitan areas, subsidized tenants struggle to find landlords who will accept their voucher. Cuyahoga County's voucher holders, who are predominantly Black and very low-income, face stark obstacles to securing housing in racially and economically diverse "high-opportunity" neighborhoods, despite their preferences for living in these communities.[2]

Prior to the housing market crash and the Great Recession, the region's voucher holders primarily secured rental housing in the city of Cleveland's lower-income and predominantly Black communities on the East Side. Lower-income households faced obstacles to securing affordable rental housing in the region's inner- and outer-ring suburbs, given the limited supply of rental properties and the high cost of rent in those communities. Yet market changes that began in the mid-2000s enabled lower-income renters, including subsidized renters, to gain access to the suburbs. Foreclosures rippled through the inner-ring suburbs to the east and led to the conversion of owner-occupied units to rentals, as well as to falling rents.[3] By 2014, slightly more than half (53 percent) of Cuyahoga County's 14,565 vouchers (which represented 7 percent of all renter-occupied units in the region) were used in suburban communities.[4]

According to a senior administrator at CMHA, the vast majority of their subsidized tenants secure housing with both landlords who own just a handful of properties and some who own up to several dozen—they are not large-scale corporate landlords. In light of how important they are to the HCVP, it is important to understand the factors that lead these small and midsized landlords to make business decisions that impact subsidized tenants' access to decent, affordable rental housing. This chapter looks in particular at the social and structural factors in landlords' decisions as to whether, where, and under what quality conditions they will house voucher holders.

The sociologist Eva Rosen has examined landlords' financial incentives to rent to subsidized tenants, and she discusses the consequences for the perpetuation of racial segregation.[5] Specifically, reliable rent payment from the PHA is a powerful incentive to landlords to house a subsidized tenant, particularly landlords who rent properties in disadvantaged communities and struggle to attract tenants who can pay rent consistently. Another way in which landlords' practices perpetuate racial segregation is their preference for steering Black voucher holders toward their rentals located in predominantly Black communities and White voucher holders toward their rentals located in more advantaged communities with larger White populations.

This chapter delves into the landlord characteristics that factor into a decision to house a subsidized tenant—including their motivation to enter and persist in the rental business and the profit they earn in it—and under what circumstances. The chapter also shows the importance of considering the conditions under which landlords house voucher holders and the impact of local regulations and market conditions on those decisions. These findings reinforce that when the HCVP fails to consider landlords' business motivations and how they are driven by market and regulatory factors, it can perpetuate the deeply entrenched disadvantage and spatial inequality that federal and local policies created in the first place.[6]

A family that qualifies for a housing voucher on the basis of low income must go through an extensive process to secure rental housing with it. Notably, just one out of four eligible families receive one. Once applicants are selected from the wait-list—which is several years, or even decades, long in some cities—voucher holders have a limited period of time to secure rental housing.[7] In Cuyahoga County, the median time on the wait-list was 21 months, and voucher holders had 120 days after being selected to secure housing with their subsidy.[8] A family that failed to use the voucher in the allotted time frame could lose it.[9]

Notably, most HCVP wait-lists across the nation are closed, to the point that, especially in declining cities, renters cannot enlist at all.[10] In 2015, CMHA's 95 percent lease-up rate—the percentage of a PHA's authorized housing vouchers that tenants are using to lease units—ensured that it could remain eligible to receive new voucher allocations and be rated a "high performer" by the U.S. Department of Housing and Urban Development (HUD).[11]

Before a subsidized tenant can sign a lease and move into a property, an inspector who works for the PHA administering the subsidy must inspect the property. The inspectors who work for the PHA perform inspections that are far more rigorous than those performed by inspectors who work for the city of Cleveland or even its more affluent suburbs.

The program's comprehensive inspection process was explained by Luther, a lanky, good-natured, forty-something Black man who had performed inspections for the local PHA for well over a decade. "Safety is first and foremost," he said squarely. "We just notice the condition on the surfaces throughout the house. Lead-based paint, chipping paint, defective paint. Areas of hazard, railways, in and out the house, handrails. Smoke detectors. Make sure the utilities are working properly." Luther chuckled and added, "Suffice to say, you can run into about one hundred minor, but important, violations."

A failed first inspection leads to a follow-up inspection several weeks later to determine whether the landlord made the necessary repairs. Upon passing the first inspection, the landlord is told the rent determination for the unit, which is based on the fair market rent set by HUD, which is typically the fortieth percentile rent for all comparable units in the entire metropolitan area, primarily on the basis of the number of bedrooms. Altogether, it can take several weeks or months for the landlord to learn of the rent determination and for the tenant they have selected to move into the unit.

Annual PHA inspections are meant to ensure that the landlord maintains the property in safe and habitable condition. If the unit fails its annual inspection, the landlord must make necessary repairs before the follow-up inspection to ensure that the rent payment is not stopped, or "abated." After a failed second inspection, the PHA schedules a third and final inspection. A failed third inspection has serious consequences for the landlord and tenant: the voucher contract is terminated, and the tenant is forced to secure housing with a different landlord who will accept their voucher.

Two-thirds of the landlords in this study participated in the voucher program. Preexisting beliefs about the program's bureaucracy and about voucher holders' supposed irresponsibility deterred some landlords from housing a subsidized renter. Concerns about programmatic bureaucracy and tenants' lifestyles were found across the landlord sample—but most of those who chose not to participate in the voucher program were landlords who did not look to the rental business for immediate cash flow but rather for the personal gratification of investing in real estate, and particularly in moderate- and middle-income communities.

"I Just Can't Spend That Much Time Doing That Stuff"

Dustin, an easygoing Asian man in his thirties, explained over dinner after a long workday that he had entered the landlord business two years earlier in pursuit of the thrill that came with investing in real estate. Indeed, profit was not his primary business goal; he earned what he called "a healthy living" in his job in the financial sector. "It doesn't matter how much you make," Dustin said lightheartedly. "The rental income's just fun money for me."

His first purchase was what he described with a chuckle as "a pretty rough property" in Lakewood, a predominantly White, middle-income suburb to the west of the city. The Lakewood Building Department mandated that Dustin fix over eighty code violations that its inspectors discovered during a point-of-sale inspection, to ensure that the property was safe and habitable. Investing to repair the property was financially worthwhile because, as Dustin said with a grin, the "renters you get in Lakewood are outrageously good." The fact that he had not yet been compelled to file to evict a Lakewood tenant reflected both his limited time in the business and the economic resources of the tenants he could secure.

With unsubsidized tenants, the property generated steady profit for Dustin. Accordingly, he didn't look forward to the bureaucracy that he expected would accompany housing a voucher tenant. "It looks great on paper," Dustin remarked brightly about the voucher program, but he lamented the hassles of the yearly inspection process. It was important to Dustin to make clear that his concern about participating in the voucher program centered on the program's bureaucracy, not on its tenants. "I'm not against it because of the renters," he insisted adamantly, shaking his head. "I'm against it because of the administration." His face clouded over as he continued: "Once you look into how often they do inspections and all that, it's going to take a lot of my time out." He put his soda cup down on the table and again insisted, "I wouldn't mind the renters at all, but I just can't spend that much time doing that stuff."

Dustin then also admitted to a concern that renting to a subsidized tenant could strain his relationships with Lakewood neighbors and city authorities. In fact, he remarked with a nervous laugh, "my neighbors would revolt to kick me out of there." Then his smile faded, and he added somberly, "The city really does not like renters." He hunched over the table and said, his voice low, that Lakewood city officials had warned him about housing low-income renters. "They said that it's a source of their crime. It's a source of low school performance. And they like to have higher-income folks have single-family homes."

Other landlords who entered the business primarily as a hobby, not as a profit generator, and refused to participate in the voucher program cited their beliefs about the lifestyle of subsidized tenants—or "Section 8" tenants, as most landlords called them, a term with stigmatized connotations. Landlords invoked "culture of poverty" arguments to defend turning away voucher holders, reciting the myths about their irresponsibility and even fraudulence that politicians and the media began to promulgate widely beginning in the 1970s.[12] That landlords could easily invoke such biases about subsidized tenants without having ever housed one—or even having had a positive experience in doing so—indicated just how deeply entrenched these biases are.

Sipping coffee at a quiet coffee shop, Paul, a middle-aged White investor, recounted his entrance into the business with the purchase of a handful of single-family and duplex properties in inner-ring suburbs to the east, including Maple Heights and Bedford, at a low cost after the housing market crash. "This is more of a hobby on the side that I do," he explained with a shrug, admitting, "I don't know that I really have a vision." Sounding more stoical, he continued: "I make a little bit of money, it's not a lot honestly, the spread between the mortgage and what [tenants] pay in rent after expenses." Although Paul was disappointed in the profit the properties were generating, he held on to them out of a hope that the market would eventually recover. "I'm holding them, hoping that inflation comes back and the appreciation of houses' values goes back." Paul crossed his fingers tightly. "That's the bet that I'm making."

Paul described the qualities he looked for in a prospective tenant. "Somebody who would treat the house as if it's theirs, is the ideal tenant," he remarked plainly. Subsidized tenants didn't meet that criterion. "Those people are not invested in the house," Paul explained, shaking his head. "The tenant doesn't have any ownership of the property, because it's not their money. They have no respect for the property." In meticulous detail, he went on to describe how subsidized tenants behave on the property. "The tenant moves in, they don't care about the house, they are not paying rent, they don't clean it, they don't take care of it," he remarked rotely. "The area around the oven is all greasy and terrible-smelling, they barely even clean the toilet, or their bedroom's never vacuumed." Sounding increasingly weary, Paul continued, "Carpeting is all ruined. They smoke in the house. The whole house smells like smoke." It was surprising, then, that upon being asked whether he had ever housed a voucher holder, Paul conceded matter-of-factly: "I have not done it."

"Guaranteed Headache"

As further evidence of the deeply ingrained societal biases about subsidized tenants' lifestyle, there were landlords who, despite having positive experiences in housing a subsidized tenant, retained an unflinching belief that they were "risky" to house. Donald, the Black investor mentioned in chapter 5, had left the corporate world to build a real estate "brand" by renovating and renting properties on "nice" streets on the East Side. "I'm in this for the next fifteen, twenty years, so I want to take a little bit more care of my homes," Donald said enthusiastically, seated at the café where we first met. "You know, turning a house over once somebody moves out. Putting down new carpet." He grinned, "It's expensive as hell, but I don't mind not making a profit right now and getting it together if that's going to last for the next fifteen to twenty years."

A few years earlier, Donald had purchased a duplex that housed a longtime subsidized tenant. Despite his wariness about renting to subsidized tenants, Donald allowed the tenant to stay. "I was like, 'All right. She must be a good tenant if she's been there for seventeen years,'" he remembered affably, relaxing back in the booth.

But Donald felt that it would be risky to rent to any additional subsidized tenants, despite having gathered positive firsthand experience with his current voucher tenant. Indeed, he remarked that his subsidized tenant was a "good tenant" who paid rent on time and took good care of the property. Donald looked perplexed as he slowly observed, "You know, Section 8 always gets this bad rap of, 'Oh, your people are going to tear up the house.'" He marveled, "I've had one person on Section 8, and she's nice. And I've had tons of people [not on Section 8] tear up my houses!"

That the court process to evict a subsidized tenant is lengthier also increased the risk that Donald and other landlords perceived in housing them. As he and Housing Court officials explained, there were additional bureaucratic hurdles to evicting a subsidized tenant in court, especially when the breach of lease pertained to problematic tenant behavior, such as nuisance activity or excessive wear-and-tear on the unit. "Let's say this [subsidized] tenant is a bad tenant, and they're tearing everything up," Donald began, casually leaning across the table on his elbow. "You're going to have to jump through more hoops [to evict]." Raising his brow, he continued, "You can't just evict them like that," with a snap of his fingers. "You've got to go through another round, so *that* kills Section 8." Shaking his head, he insisted that "nobody wants to get stuck. You can say, 'Okay, you're guaranteed money.' More than likely a guaranteed headache that you can't get rid of."

The landlords who sought short-term cash flow from the rental business had more financial incentives to house subsidized tenants. Yet landlords seeking immediate cash flow from renting properties in middle-income communities, in particular, experienced disincentives to participate in the HCVP, for reasons pertaining to the rent amounts they could receive and the administrative burden they experienced.

Landlords who rented properties in resource-rich communities expressed dissatisfaction with the rent payment they could collect from the PHA, based on HUD's FMR calculation. The FMR calculation incorporates rents from all communities across Cuyahoga County—from its impoverished central-city communities to its middle-income suburbs. In 2015, landlords in the Cleveland metropolitan region could receive an FMR payment of $764 from the PHA to rent a two-bedroom unit to a voucher holder—almost $100 higher than the region's median gross rent of $674.[13] But landlords who rented properties in more economically advantaged communities where rents typically exceeded the FMR effectively took a pay cut in housing a subsidized tenant. By contrast, landlords who typically commanded rent amounts from their unsubsidized tenants that fell below the FMR could receive a rent boost in housing a voucher holder.

These patterns are found in other metropolitan areas, including Baltimore, where landlords must accept an even steeper cut in the rent they collect in housing a subsidized tenant because of an FMR calculation that incorporates rent amounts from nearby affluent suburbs in the Washington, D.C., area. The FMR for a two-bedroom unit in Baltimore is $1,232, whereas the city's median gross rent for a two-bedroom unit is $1,038.[14]

The FMR calculation thus creates financial disincentives to house voucher holders, who are lower-income and predominantly Black, for landlords who provide housing in resource-rich communities, which typically have larger White populations. Relatedly, it creates financial incentives for landlords to secure voucher holders for their properties in struggling communities, which typically have larger Black populations. In this way, the program's payment standards inadvertently perpetuate racial segregation and the concentration of poverty.[15]

"I'll Get a Market Tenant for That"

Shia, a middle-aged White investor with dark hair, met us at a café wearing a black-and-white button-down shirt and black dress pants. Talking animatedly with his hands, he began to explain how he had built a full-time career in renting out "blue-collar, simple apartments" in University Heights and South Euclid, both racially integrated, low-poverty inner-ring suburbs to the east. "My market is people that are, you know, just making it," Shia explained cordially. "I'm more hand-to-mouth people, more living on a paycheck-to-paycheck. And because of that, my apartments are not going to have dishwashers and, you know, central air." Shia noted that the quality of services in the suburbs helped to attract cash-paying tenants who could stay current on rent payment. "They've got a very, very good school district," he said enthusiastically of South Euclid, which, he observed, attracted renters with children. "I want an address in South Euclid because I want to be able to get my kid into the schools," applicants often told him.

Like other landlords, Shia observed that the rental business required far more people skills than meets the eye. "You have to be a people's person," he insisted. "I've had ladies come to me and cry on my shoulder, and say she's just diagnosed with breast cancer." In such emergency cases, he looked to offer tenants leniency in rent payment. "Let's work something out," he said congenially and shrugged, "I try."

Unsubsidized tenants' inconsistent rent payment, owing in part to the flailing local economy, motivated Shia to fill some of his units with subsidized tenants to ensure a steadier cash flow. Yet he was currently divesting from participation in the voucher program. "It's getting more and more difficult for me to rent Section 8," Shia remarked, drumming on the table with his fingers. "I haven't rented to a new Section 8 in a long time. I'm less inclined to rent to them." He held out both hands and turned up his palms. "If I have two people in front of me, and one's a Section 8, one's not a Section 8," he deliberated, looking back and forth at his hands, "I would probably say, 'Hey, let me go with the person who is not a Section 8.'" Then he explained why.

Like other landlords who rented properties in moderate- or middle-income communities, Shia was dissatisfied with the housing authority's rent determination. "I have to fight them to get a rent to market," he complained. "I can do better with a market tenant." Some landlords who rented properties in more economically advantaged communities insisted that they collected less rent than they otherwise would from cash-paying tenants because voucher holders sometimes struggled to pay the tenant portion of the PHA's rent determination (set at 30 percent of their income). "Even Section 8 tenants have portions that they have to pay," Shia explained. Speaking of one of his subsidized tenants who struggled to pay the rent on time, he said, flicking his wrists around as though he were the tenant, "I'll pay you here, I'll pay you there."

Shia spoke spiritedly about the programmatic factors that created "administrative burden" for landlords, contributing to their sense of financial uncertainty and even psychological distress. The quality inspection process in particular fueled landlords' frustration and undermined the autonomy they valued from being in the rental business.[16] Shia lamented having to make adjustments to the units in response to an inspector's mandate rather than tenants' preferences. "Let's talk about those toilet bowl caps," Shia began animatedly. He and other landlords buzzed about the PHA's recent update to its quality standards: it now required a plastic cover over the bolts connecting a toilet bowl to the floor so as to protect young children from injuries if they fell on an uncovered bolt. Landlords who typically made sure that their units passed the first inspection reported that the new standard was not communicated by the PHA well in advance of its enforcement, causing their units to fail an inspection. "They changed the rules in the middle. Right?" Shia pressed. "Somebody could have been in there for three years, not had a problem with the toilet bowl." He sighed, "But they made it a point. So it's making it difficult." Shaking his head, he noted that, "if I have a tenant that's a market tenant, he's not complaining about toilet bowl caps." In fact, "I don't think I have toilet bowl caps in my own home," he added.

"It's not uniform!" Shia further complained about the inspection process, an issue raised by numerous other landlords. "You deal with one inspector and you have this," he said, holding a hand out, "and with another inspector, you have that." He held the other hand out. "Some people are very, very particular about electrical issues, some people are very particular about plumbing issues." He shook his head. "It all depends who your inspector's going to be," he said, "if he had his coffee that morning."

Landlords' grievances about the voucher program also stemmed from a belief that it was unfair to sanction them for violations caused by tenants' behavior on the property. "The hard part is, once they've moved in, they have these entitlements," Shia said about his subsidized tenants. "'You've got to fix my apartment because I'm bringing you a Section 8, and you want that money, and you need to fix this up,'" Shia said as he impersonated a tenant, waving his finger around. "And basically," he added, "they can destroy an apartment. Then [tenants] say to you, [*speaking in a singsong voice*], 'You've got to fix it up, or you're not going to get paid.'"

A belief among landlords that subsidized tenants do not necessarily deserve high-quality housing is an important part of this story.[17] Shia described a recent PHA inspector's discovery of violations in one of his apartment units, including damaged carpet and torn window blinds, which, he insisted, the tenant had caused. He estimated that it would cost several thousand dollars to make the necessary repairs so the unit could pass the upcoming follow-up inspection. Although he was currently in the midst of performing the work, Shia did not plan to renew the subsidized tenant's yearlong lease after it expired. "All the carpet's going, but not for her," he said adamantly. "For somebody else. I'll get a market tenant for that."

"Not too long ago, I think in Cuyahoga County, a bunch of vouchers went out," Shia slowly recalled. "And sure enough, I was getting calls every other day! Section 8, Section 8, Section 8," he exclaimed incredulously, waving his arms around. "These people are calling that, 'Hey, I won the lottery. *You* want to get in touch with me. I've got a Section 8 voucher.'" Shia wrinkled his brow and looked at us in awe. "And I'm saying to myself, 'You said you're Section 8. I *don't* want to get in touch with you. That's *why* I don't want to get in touch with you.'"

Other landlords interested in the business for short-term cash flow housed voucher holders in some or all of their units located in middle-income suburban communities, despite concerns about rent determinations, quality inspections, and voucher tenants' lifestyle. Yet they did so under select conditions, which included taking measures to ensure that they could command satisfactory rents and that voucher tenants would treat their properties responsibly—sometimes to the disadvantage of the tenant.

"The Tenant Is Stuck"

Gabriel, the Asian Indian landlord mentioned in chapter 4, housed some subsidized tenants in his nearly three dozen rental properties located in inner-ring suburban communities to the east, despite his complaints about the PHA's low rent payments. The rent determination typically fell $100 below the amount that Gabriel insisted he could command from cash-paying tenants. Rather than turn away subsidized tenants and forgo the benefits of consistent rent payment, he devised several practices to collect the rent amounts that he believed his units deserved—violating PHA policies in the process.

Gabriel and most other landlords firmly believed that the PHA inspection process was subjective and capricious, and some felt justified in finding ways to manipulate inspection outcomes to their benefit.[18] Gabriel believed that the gifts and flattery he offered PHA inspectors during the unit's first inspection led them to rate the unit more highly, which led in turn to a higher rent determination. "Inspector says the condition is excellent, then they pay more. The house condition is poor, [the rent determination] will be less," Gabriel surmised. "This is why we offer lunch to most of the inspector. Saying condition is excellent. Save you more."

In another tactic to garner higher rent payment from the PHA, Gabriel requested that tenants remit additional rent money, above the "tenant portion" of the rent they were expected to pay him. The request violated the program's policies meant to ensure that renters didn't spend more than 30 percent of their income on housing costs. "Side deal, you cannot make," Gabriel admitted, noting that his request was illegal, but then added that it was something "we do with our tenants." After a prospective tenant met his screening criteria and agreed to pay him an additional $100 in rent each month, Gabriel would say: "You can move in."

Other landlords also attempted to collect side money from subsidized tenants, yet noted that the agreement was difficult to enforce after tenants moved into the unit. Since the request for side money violated the voucher program's rules, landlords could not seek assistance from the PHA if the tenant didn't pay it. For this reason, Gabriel asked tenants to remit the side money as a lump sum prior to moving in. "He pay upfront for the whole year, he can move in," Gabriel plainly explained, adding, "You don't pay, then you can find a new place."

Facilitating Gabriel's collection of more rent from some voucher tenants was the desirable suburban location of his units and the limited time frame in which voucher holders could use their subsidy. If they declined Gabriel's request for extra rent money, a prospective tenant would have to restart their housing search, and with even less time to use the voucher. A harried housing search can lead tenants to move into lower-quality housing, as demonstrated in research on tenants' housing outcomes after they experience an "involuntary move" such as a court eviction or an informal eviction.[19] Indeed, Gabriel recognized subsidized tenants' disincentives to turn down the request, knowingly observing, "The tenant is stuck."

"I've Got to Come to Your House — Especially for Section 8 People"

In select cases, landlords housed subsidized tenants in well-maintained properties in some of the region's more affluent suburbs, and without hassling tenants for more rent money. The voucher tenants who eventually filled these landlords' units, however, were subject to extreme scrutiny and surveillance of their lifestyle—both when the prospective landlord visited their current residence and when the landlord visited the property once they moved in. These tactics are reminiscent of early practices by welfare caseworkers, who assessed low-income families' home environment to determine their moral character, lifestyle, and, relatedly, deservingness of means-tested government assistance. During informal "white glove tests," caseworkers would run their gloved fingers across a fireplace mantle or windowsill to check for dust.[20]

Landlords' extreme surveillance over voucher tenants served several purposes. First, believing that voucher holders engaged in more destructive behavior on a property than unsubsidized tenants, they kept an eye on tenants to ensure that they were treating their well-maintained properties with care. Furthermore, landlords believed that voucher holders were more likely to engage in unruly or deviant behavior, and they justified their strong surveillance as a way to ensure that tenants adhered to city ordinances—which, as discussed in chapter 4, are enforced more strictly in the region's middle-income suburban communities.

Joanne, a Black retiree with a school teacher–like demeanor, wanted to meet over coffee near her one remaining rental property, a four-unit apartment building in Cleveland Heights, a middle-income, racially integrated suburban community to the east. Over green tea and a scone, Joanne shared that she had been seeking financial security when she entered the rental business—to ensure that she never fell back into the deep poverty she experienced as a child. "I was really poor. Po. Like P-O," she stated boldly, then added for emphasis, "Not P-O-O-R. P-O." Joanne let out a hearty laugh and added softly, "And we lived in public housing." She began to recall childhood memories that had been tucked away for years. "I sold popcorn balls, because I was eight years old," she remarked wistfully. Snapping back to attention, she added curtly, "Long story short: one-parent household, welfare."

"People always have to have a place to stay," Joanne had reasoned in selecting the rental business as a safety net several decades earlier, at a time when she was cycling through various jobs, including as a marketer and an insurance representative. She bought several properties in the city of Cleveland and its inner-ring suburbs and then sold them off upon finding them difficult to manage on her own. Finally, she purchased the four-unit apartment building in Cleveland Heights in the late 1990s, before property values began to fall dramatically throughout the region. The property had become her primary source of revenue.

The property did not generate sufficient profit, Joanne lamented. "I am not making any money on this building, let's put it that way," she announced firmly. She commanded $765 per month in rent from each of the three units and lived in the fourth unit. "The rent's just barely enough to cover the mortgage," she noted glumly. "It's providing me a place to live right now, and it's an asset." She sighed, "Not that great an asset, but it's an asset."

Joanne was motivated to house subsidized tenants by the rising economic struggles of the region's renter population—a reflection of the region's declining economy, which affected even landlords' profits in the suburbs. In earlier years she typically turned down subsidized tenants, citing her dismay about their work ethic. "Nine times out of ten, those people aren't too industrious, or they don't really want to do very much except live off the system," she observed. Nevertheless, Joanne decided to house voucher holders because she needed a short-term cash flow. She remarked smoothly, "The money is guaranteed, and with the economy, I'm like, 'Give me Section 8. I'll take it,' because I know I'll get paid."

Joanne and several other landlords who rented properties in middle-income communities agreed to rent to voucher holders under the condition that they earned wages, which could be garnished in court. "I don't particularly like renting to people that don't have some kind of income other than government assistance," Joanne explained, "because there's no way for me to get my rent if something goes wrong. You can't attach a Social Security or SSI check to your rent." She suddenly looked fearful. "I hope that's not illegal!" It was one of the few moments when a landlord acknowledged—and expressed concern to me—about the dubious legality of one of their business practices. Indeed, turning away a prospective tenant collecting government assistance on the basis of a disability constitutes a violation of the Fair Housing Act. "But," she continued more firmly, "I'm a businessperson. I've got to know how, if I am going to evict you, how I am going to get paid for the damages?"

Besides voucher holders' employment status and source of income, Joanne was concerned about the cleanliness of their home environment, and she inquired about it as part of the screening process. "I screen them on the phone first," she began. "I want to know where you live now, how much rent you pay, do you have roaches or bedbugs?" She would then insist, "'I've got to come to your house'—especially for Section 8 people." After a sip of tea, Joanne continued: "I go to their homes initially to see how they live. And if you're a nasty housekeeper, you're throwing clothes under the bed, I'm not going to cut it." She noted that some prospective tenants withdrew their interest in an advertised unit after she requested the home visit. "A few of them told me 'Well, if you've got to come out, then that's okay.' And I'm like, 'Good luck in your search, and thank you for calling.'"

Tenants could expect close scrutiny from Joanne upon moving into one of her units. "There's a 'no drama' policy here," she would inform new tenants immediately, before telling them what would happen if they violated any community ordinances. "I tell them, 'I will call the police.'" The Cleveland Heights Police Department was "extremely responsive," she told us excitedly, boasting, "I know many of them." In one instance, police officers arrived in response to her concern about a tenant who occasionally violated the community's ordinance prohibiting excessive noise before 7:00 AM. The tenant occasionally honked her car horn outside the building around that time to let her children know it was time to go to school, explained Joanne, who asked the police to stop by the property to observe the noise. "They came, they parked, they sat there that morning, they missed her," Joanne began. "The next morning they went back, they got her." Her posture softened, and she added in a low, raspy voice, "I felt kind of sorry for her." Then she perked up, noting that the intervention served its purpose of ending the early morning noise.

Landlords' excessive monitoring can disadvantage tenants in multiple ways. If tenants come to experience their home space as a "carceral environment," emotional distress may be triggered and they may even make a hasty move in response. Further, tenants can struggle financially if landlords assess fees or even elect to evict tenants who violate their strictly enforced codes.[21]

Other landlords who rented properties in desirable suburban communities also held their subsidized tenants to higher standards than landlords in lower-income communities. They insisted that their subsidized tenants be currently employed, scrutinized prospective tenants' housekeeping, and sometimes "trained" tenants in maintaining their properties.

"Just Pop Up on Them, Check for Cleanliness"

Isaac, a sturdy, forty-something Black man wearing a tan button-down shirt and a disarmingly bright smile, first met us at a café on a Sunday afternoon. The wood-paneled café was located in Shaker Heights, one of the region's more affluent inner-ring suburbs, and one with a legacy of racial integration. The predominantly Black staff lit up when they spotted Isaac. Line cooks working the grill in the back shouted out to him, and a woman darting between tables to distribute menus and take orders nodded at him. "I come here all the time," Isaac explained to us. He didn't need a menu to order the plate piled high with eggs and toast that soon appeared in front of him.

The café was located near his first rental property—a twelve-unit, century-old apartment building with tall ceilings and crown moldings. The declining availability of mid-tier jobs for college-educated professionals in the early 2000s had made it difficult for Isaac to secure a job with the business degree he had earned at a local university. He grew interested in the rental business, which was a short leap for him given the plumbing and carpentry skills he had learned from his father, who was once a landlord himself.

Importantly, Isaac remarked over and over that he sought to build a rental business in the suburbs where he could provide the elusive "full package" for lower- and moderate-income renters: well-maintained, affordable housing in a community with high-performing schools and safe streets. His modestly priced units—$650 to $750 per month for a one- or two-bedroom apartment in the building—did just that.

"For this area," he remarked, "it's probably one of the cheapest places that you could rent." Then he chuckled as he noted that the road to get there was not easy.

The building was rife with code violations at the time of his purchase. Its longtime owner had struggled financially and fell behind on necessary repairs. Isaac purchased the building for what he described as a "below market" price—$110,000—knowing that significant investment would be required to bring the building up to code upon transfer. Indeed, the city's building department produced an extensive list of violations during the building's point-of-sale inspection. "Came down on it hard," Isaac recounted with a wry smile. The total cost for all of the repair work—which included reinforcing the foundation, reconfiguring the electrical work, painting, and repaving the parking lot—was approximately equal to the building's purchase price. Yet the costs were financially justifiable, Isaac believed, because he expected the building's desirable quality and location to draw the interest of prospective tenants who could remit timely rent payments.

"My phone is ringing off the hook," Isaac marveled. He was taking calls from prospective tenants inquiring about an advertised vacancy in the building and another in one of the six single-family properties in nearby suburbs he had purchased after housing prices dropped in the region. Regardless, he insisted that profit in the business wasn't as high as he had hoped, or as high as what anyone outside the rental business presumed. "I mean, it's not the greatest hit. It isn't," Isaac remarked cautiously of the business. But "the sentiment about landlords is that we're rich," he remarked playfully. "[Landlords] are the bad guys, look at him. He owns that house, oh, he's got to be rich, he's got to be loaded." Isaac sighed. "You're not taking that five hundred bucks [in rent payment] and saying, 'Oh, let me go shopping.'" Looking surprised, he added with a laugh, "No, some of that is lights, some of that is gas, some of that is property taxes. If you do it on a breakdown basis, that $500 rent, maybe $300 of it is what you'll probably put in your pocket."

"The biggest thing that hurts a landlord is turnover," Isaac insisted. He typically was lenient with his tenants regarding rent collection and often waited until tax refunds were issued before filing to evict a tenant who had fallen behind on rent. "If you let them go throughout the year in a hole, so to speak," Isaac observed good-naturedly, "most of the time, tax time, a lot of them are able to catch up." His lower- and moderate-income tenants—whom he screened to ensure that they were employed—often received payments through the Earned Income Tax Credit (EITC) program. In a somber tone, he recalled a recent eviction after one of his tenants fell too far "in the hole" to catch up. "They had lost their jobs and they got behind, but I tried to work with them," Isaac explained softly. The tenants struggled to pay rent despite receiving a tax refund, and he eventually filed to evict them.

To illustrate his belief that "the biggest thing that hurts a landlord is turnover," he brought us to see the recently vacated apartment, which his staff were working around the clock to repair. "You have got to see the condition it was left in," Isaac urged, leading us up the building's polished granite stairs to the second floor. His property manager, Cynthia, a middle-aged Black woman with a bullish demeanor that broke down easily when she laughed, was leaning against the apartment's door frame. "Still a ways to go!" she called out.

Fabric couches, small wooden tables, and chairs were heaped inside the apartment. The building's full-time repairman, Rob, a slim Black man in his fifties, was fixated on a small hole in the wall, wondering aloud if he could patch it back to the condition it was in when the tenant first moved in. As Cynthia and Rob bantered good-naturedly about fixing the hole, Isaac charged past them into the kitchen. "Look at that sink dripping! Why do people not tell us about this?" he exclaimed, stretching his hand toward the faucet. "When that water bill comes, that drip will cost you a lot."

Subsidized tenants had to meet Isaac's high standards in order to qualify for one of his units. He sought what he described as "elite participants"—renters with full-time jobs. "People who are working, are

striving, are trying to better themselves, they just need a little help,"
Isaac said enthusiastically. "If they say they don't work, I don't want
them. I don't want nobody that doesn't work, that just want to sit
around all day and watch TV. And tear up the place." Isaac's concerns
about unemployed tenants' wear-and-tear on the property also pertained to water usage; he had received several atypically large water
bills at the apartment building. Rising water costs and water billing
regulations that prevented landlords from billing tenants separately
for water usage in multifamily properties (see chapter 5) had motivated Isaac to invest primarily in single-family homes after he purchased the building.

To ensure that voucher tenants treated his properties with care,
Isaac assigned Cynthia to assess the housekeeping and parenting
skills of both applicants and current tenants. Isaac's instructions were:
"Go out to where they are presently staying and just pop up on them,
check for cleanliness. Check for control of their kids, that's a big one
for us." Cynthia later demonstrated how she arranged a home visit
with an applicant. Typically, she began with an impromptu phone
call to ask if she could drop by. In a bright, friendly tone, she said,
"I be like, 'Hey, Ms. Sally. This Cynthia, and I'm right around the
corner! You know that home visit? Since I'm in the area, can I just stop
on through?'" This way, she explained to us, "they don't even have
time to prepare."

Applicants who did not pass the "home economics" test could
remain eligible to fill Isaac's unit if they satisfied his most important
criteria, notably current employment and a willingness to be coached by
Cynthia on housekeeping after moving into the unit. "She's very good
at that," Isaac said. "She will go in there and say, 'Look, you know, you
need to do this to your stove once a week, you need to do this on your
floors once a week.' And she would kind of coach them, train them, and
it's been successful." Isaac continued affably, "Usually, they are very
compliant."

Cynthia brought us to several of Isaac's single-family properties that
housed subsidized tenants. The two-story homes had handsome brick
exteriors, well-manicured lawns, and colorful flower gardens. One
property's tenant, a forty-something Black woman wearing an elegant
green head scarf, led us through the home where she and her teenage
son had lived for the past year. Smiling warmly, she led us to a bright
and spacious modern kitchen with a smooth beige tiled floor, tan-and-
dark-brown-tiled backsplash above the stove, and light wood cabinets
finished with modern dark steel handles. Next, she walked us through
the living room and several bedrooms, which had gleaming wood floors
and crisp blue and tan paint on the walls. Intricate black-and-white

ceramic tile work danced off the floors in the bathrooms. "We love living here," she glowed.

Landlords in pursuit of immediate cash flow through renting properties in lower-income communities saw more financial benefits of participating in the HCVP. They valued the consistent rent payments from the government in an amount that was modestly higher than what they could typically command from cash-paying tenants.[22] Yet landlords who housed voucher holders did not necessarily garner satisfactory profit. Relatedly, and for several reasons, some were unmotivated to maintain their properties in line with PHA codes year-round.

First, the aging housing stock in the region's lower-income and Black communities required more financial investment to be maintained in safe and habitable condition. Crumbling roofs needed to be repaired, and lead-based paint, which Congress banned for residential use in 1978, had to be remediated. Thus, the higher and more consistent rent payment they received from the PHA, in contrast with the rents they could get from cash-paying tenants, was partly offset by the cost of keeping their units up to PHA standards.

Also, the depressed market conditions in the region's struggling communities—reflected in the low property values regardless of unit quality—undermined landlords' financial incentives to invest substantially enough for units to pass PHA inspections. Harboring these concerns while also doubting whether subsidized tenants "deserved" good-quality housing, some landlords who rented properties in impoverished communities prioritized cost-saving and efficiency rather than safety and quality in their maintenance plan.

"Kids Under Six You Avoid"

Betty and Jack, the retired White couple introduced in chapter 4, began to build a model around housing subsidized tenants. As the city's East Side communities where they rented several small multifamily buildings grew increasingly impoverished and crime-ridden, it became difficult to secure tenants with stable jobs who could stay current on rent payments. When asked about the timeliness of their tenants' rent payments, Betty clutched at her chest. "On time?" she asked teasingly. "It's almost like you have to [accept Section 8] in these neighborhoods," she continued in a hushed voice, huddling over the table. "I mean, don't get me wrong. We have some nice tenants. We do." She winked at Jack. "I mean, we have this one lady . . . she'd give us fruits and vegetables. She cooked for her church and Jack would do things for her." Tossing his head back and laughing, Jack remembered that "she called me her White Son!" He added affably, "Such a sweetie."

In recalling several recent voucher inspections, Betty anxiously began to shred a white paper napkin in her lap. One of their one-bedroom apartments currently sat empty, close to two months after it passed the initial inspection. The couple was waiting to hear from the PHA about the rent determination, so that they could sign the lease and allow the tenant they selected to move in. Sighing, Betty began pulled at the napkin more vigorously. "These tenants, they're calling you five, six times a day. 'Well, have you heard from them yet?'" She grimaced and added, "They think you're going to rent the place to somebody else, so they're worried, so they call often."

Betty and Jack were most rattled by the costs to satisfy the PHA's lead paint safety standards. An inspector's discovery of chipping or peeling paint triggers an order for a lead test if the unit houses a child under age six and was built prior to 1978. Only a certified lead abatement contractor is permitted to remediate lead-based paint when it is discovered in a unit. Several years earlier, a PHA inspector had discovered peeling paint in one of their units, requiring the couple to schedule a lead test. "Cost $500!" Jack exclaimed, though it would have cost them several thousand dollars, he noted, to remediate the unit if the lead test had turned up positive. Betty chimed in vehemently, "So we can't afford that." She held her palms straight out. "We *cannot*. We have some Section 8, but kids under six you avoid."

The PHA's lead safety policy is clearly meant to protect young children from the array of deleterious consequences associated with lead paint exposure, including developmental delays and poor school achievement.[23] The landlords who struggled to earn sufficient profit in the business insisted, however, that they lacked the capital to maintain their aging properties so as to prevent chipping paint or remediate lead-based paint. Their decision to instead exclude subsidized tenants with young children, so as to avoid PHA scrutiny and ensuing costs, adds to the obstacles to housing faced by families with young children.[24] The practice of denying applicants on the basis of young children in the household—to avoid liability for lead poisoning or for any other reason—also violates the Fair Housing Act of 1968, which bans discrimination in rental housing on the basis of factors including race, national origin, and family status.[25]

Betty and Jack's increased interest in housing voucher holders is an example of the extent to which landlords' business goals and business decisions evolve over time. The couple had not looked to the properties for short-term cash flow in the first few decades they were in the business; at that time they were generating full-time income from working for the public school system. The buildings were meant to be an asset that would sustain them during their retirement years after they sold them to another investor at a profit. As Jack reminisced in chapter 4 on the renovations he performed in the units, "I was doing all this stuff, and I'd be losing money here and there, and just trying to make ends meet, and figuring, 'Well, but when I sell them, I'm going to be selling them for twice as much as what I bought them for.'" Yet declines in property values had put that goal out of reach. With renters' increasing struggles to pay rent and cuts to their own monthly income upon retirement, the couple became interested in filling some of their units with voucher holders.

Landlords who entered the rental business to generate short-term cash flow but with fewer resources and less planning were also motivated to house voucher holders—but invested even less to ensure their properties' quality and safety.

"Cracked Walls, Bad Painting"

"I always wanted to be a businessman," explained Boris, a forty-something wisecracking White man who spoke with a thick Russian accent, while seated in a bustling coffee shop. In the mid-2000s, Boris had completed an advanced science degree and hoped to build a business with it. Yet he was thwarted in reaching his goal by the struggling economy, and at the urging of a close friend, also a landlord, he purchased several single-family and duplex properties in a working-class community on the city's West Side and in lower-income, predominantly Black communities to the east. After attending multiple eviction hearings in his first few years in the business as his tenants became increasingly unable to pay rent consistently, he decided it was too risky to rent primarily to unsubsidized tenants. "I changed my model because [eviction] just was too much," Boris remembered, growing serious. "I decided to do Section 8."

Citing what he believed were capricious PHA inspections, Boris looked to maintain the properties just well enough to prevent an inspector's discovery of violations that would require costly remediation work, such as peeling paint. Aside from attending to the paint condition, he reported, "I never even prepare for inspections because I know that they're going to fail me anyway." Boris continued with a shrug. "I don't even go in there. I don't go," adding, "Send me the list [of violations]!" Since he performed most of the repair work himself, Boris rationalized that it was more efficient for him to put off essential repair work until a PHA inspector cited the unit. "I mean, I'm trying to save my time," he remarked bluntly.

Boris's lax approach to property maintenance was reinforced by his belief that subsidized tenants' expectations for housing quality were not very high. "I'm telling you, if you go to a lot of my [Section 8] houses, you wouldn't live there," he claimed. When asked to elaborate, he responded, "Cracked walls, bad painting," adding in wonder, "They could be Section 8 approved." He had observed that prospective tenants with subsidies were not deterred by the quality of the walls and paint, citing their excitement about the properties' large square footage. Boris marveled that prospective tenants would exclaim, "Wow, we love it!" while touring his homes. "You're like, okay . . ." he said dubiously, blinking rapidly. He added matter-of-factly, "They're looking for space. That's what they do."

Boris's observations align with research on the trade-offs that cost-constrained families make in their housing search, such as moving to a distressed community to maximize the amount of living space in the home.[26] The difficulties that voucher holders encountered in trying to use their vouchers to secure housing with qualities they otherwise could not afford—such as desirable neighborhood location and large square footage—enabled landlords to get by in the business while providing lower-quality housing.[27]

"When Are You Going to Fix Something?"

Other landlords expended even fewer resources to provide decent-quality rental housing to their subsidized tenants. In particular, the small-time landlords who entered the business in some of the region's most impoverished communities with little to no financial investment or planning were the least likely to adhere to laws meant to protect subsidized renters.

Recall Trevor, the Black landlord introduced in chapter 1 whose tenant reported the apartment's caving ceiling and splintered floors to the PHA after Trevor failed to follow through on his informal promise to fix them. Trevor was a fast-talking man who enjoyed being a "ham" and putting on a show; vacillating between bursts of energy and looks of exhaustion, he would sprawl across the table as we talked, or lean perilously on his arm. It was late-night TV commercials in the 1980s singing the financial rewards of being a landlord that first drew him to the business. In the 1980s and 1990s, he rented out several properties while earning a living as a mechanic and general contractor. When he decided to become a full-time landlord in the late 2000s, he acquired, at no cost, seven rental properties concentrated in downtrodden communities on the city's East Side.

Over breakfast at a McDonald's located near his rental properties, Trevor explained that the former owner was anxious to transfer them to a new investor who would maintain them adequately, and willing to do so free of charge. The man had struggled in the rental business and lost the properties through foreclosure, but he remained legally responsible for maintaining them because the banks had not yet completed the foreclosure process. Banks' increasingly common practice of stalling the foreclosure process to evade responsibility for property mainte-nance had served to deepen decay in the city's predominantly Black communities, Judge Pianka had lamented to me.

Despite his experiences as a part-time landlord and contractor for other landlords, Trevor discovered that it was challenging to manage his own rental business. When the tenants he attracted to the deteriorat-ing properties could not pay rent consistently, he figured that he could generate more profit in renting to voucher holders. "I don't like to rent cash. No way," he said, shaking his head vigorously. "When they were cash payers, I was in eviction court every month." Yet Trevor lacked the resources and time to maintain his crumbling properties in line with the PHA's quality standards. "There's so many liabilities," he moaned, roll-ing his head to the side. "You know, like the roof goes out. Or the gutter falls off or something." He insisted adamantly, "The only way that you can really make any extra money is to spend less."

"I guess I think I should be making more money," Trevor said dis-appointedly in chapter 1. Yet like other small-time landlords, Trevor was uncertain about how much he earned, owing to both unpredict-able business costs and losses and his informal record-keeping. "I don't even know how much money I'm making. Because I don't keep track." Flicking his wrist out, he remarked, "Cash flow, you know. I got money. The bill collector called. I can pay them." Growing more serious, he hunched over the table and said fervently, "I'm pressed to the nth. I'm pressed to the nth. But I can't . . ." After taking a deep breath, he shook his head and insisted, "I don't see no break in sight. There's always something else happening, and I've got to keep eating."

Trevor didn't express dismay about voucher holders' character or lifestyle, unlike some other landlords. "All tenants are rough," he declared with a grin after taking a sip of watery coffee. "I get along with them all." He waved casually at a young Black woman, a current tenant, when she entered the restaurant. "A few, we just sit around. We sit around and talk," Trevor said with a shrug. He cautioned, however, that spending too much time with tenants was risky. "You sitting around talking," he began, stretching his arms out playfully, and then, he con-tinued, the tenant would ask, "When are you going to fix something?"

Our subsequent visit to Trevor's duplex property to observe a PHA inspection, as discussed in chapter 1, supported his claim that "I'm pressed to the nth." Trevor frantically hammered at the apartment's splintered wood floors on his hands and knees up until a few minutes before the inspector's arrival. He momentarily looked up when the tenant yelped "Damn it!" after a splinter lodged in her bare foot. After hastily rummaging through his metal toolbox, he found metal pliers for her to use to dig out the splinter. She accepted them and sullenly limped to the bathroom.

Later, standing with Trevor in the gravel driveway, he admitted that it wouldn't take him long to perform the long-delayed repair work. Crouching down, he tilted his head back and pushed his arms up to demonstrate. "Go down to the basement. Push the damaged wood panel up. Push a new one in its place." How long would that take? "About twenty minutes," he figured.

The small-time landlords who rented properties in marginalized communities in the Cleveland metropolitan region had financial incentives to house subsidized tenants. Yet they also had numerous disincentives to house them under decent, safe conditions, because landlords' resources and time were stretched thin. Declining market conditions led them to rationalize that investing further in their aging properties would not enable them to secure more financially stable tenants, command higher rents, or see their property value rise. Their belief that lower-income tenants did not seek higher-quality housing, or even deserve it, further justified their slowness in performing repair work to maintain the properties in decent and habitable condition. Their perception of capriciousness in the PHA inspection process provided further justification to withhold intensive repair work until it was mandated.

There were some landlords whose business model for housing subsidized tenants in low-income communities included treating both their properties and their tenants decently. Most importantly, renting more than just a handful of properties enabled them to generate sufficient cash flow to support full-time staff and to take proactive measures to deter losses, whether a failed voucher inspection, a fine from a city inspector, or vandalism at vacant properties. What's more, having staff to "run the show" shielded these landlords from the interpersonal interactions with tenants that appeared to deepen mistrust towards them, as seen among smaller landlords who personally performed most of the necessary maintenance and repair work.

"Just Put an Alarm In"

Dell, a balding, sixty-something White man, motioned for me to join him in the meeting room of his small consulting firm. The firm's office was in the community where most of his rental properties were located on the city's East Side. Dell was wearing a gray tailored suit and light blue button-down shirt—yet no tie. "We joke about it here: if I'm wearing a tie, it's not a good day," he chuckled. Ties were necessary only on the days when Dell appeared in court, most commonly for an eviction case.

Soon after finishing college in the mid-1970s, Dell had decided to follow in the footsteps of other family members and invest in real estate. After rehabbing and selling off properties throughout the city over the course of several decades, he began to invest in properties on the city's East Side in the 1990s and early 2000s, before widespread foreclosures culminated in vacancies and declining property values. Some of the buildings he rehabbed and sold off to other investors decades earlier currently sat empty and boarded up. "It makes me crazy," Dell confessed, his shoulders tightening. "There's a couple right over here I drive by all the time," he said, wincing as he pointed back in the direction of the office's large picture window. "So last year they became empty and [vandals] stripped them and that's it. It's terrible." Kneading his hands together, he quietly mulled, "I have a lot of memories, tenants, and rehabbing those."

"Good overall" is how Dell cheerfully described the business of providing low-cost rental housing, primarily to subsidized tenants. "Overall, they're real nice people," he said of the tenants who filled his twenty-eight properties. "I've got tenants that have been with me for thirty years. I've seen entire families go through," he added in wonder. Several elements of his business model were key to earning sufficient profit to stay afloat. "The key is maintenance and decent tenants, and don't let them stay in there if they don't pay the rent. It's that simple," he said plainly, his hands clasped on the table. "I can do the repairs reasonably, and then if a tenant doesn't pay, I don't fool around. But I tell them right up front when they move in, one month behind [in rent], that's it. I don't listen to any stories."

Occasionally Dell did extend leniency when tenants fell behind on rent payment. "If I've had a tenant that's in the property for a couple, or three years, I'm a little bit easier than if it's a brand-new tenant that I think is just going to mess around on me," Dell explained. "I will listen to someone that's been in there a while, if they run on hard times." Pointing back toward the window again, he continued: "I had one over here, she was behind four or five months, and without a job. She then cashed in a life insurance policy to pay some rent. Now she's working, and she's paying every week and turning it around."

Unlike most landlords in this study, Dell remained serene in discussing his experiences with the voucher program, whether in regard to rent amounts, inspections, or tenants. "They pay pretty decent rent, Section 8, but the check's there on the first of the month, that's the important part," Dell insisted with a nod. "I don't really have a problem with the inspections, because I keep those places up." Referring again to his staff's proactive maintenance plan, he noted, "We do routine visits to the properties in case there's something that needs normal wear-and-tear [repair]. . . . By doing that, we keep the properties in real good shape." Speaking earnestly, he said, "I have good support and a good system in place. My guys are pretty darned talented."

Evading unexpected losses was essential to ensuring profitability in the business, Dell insisted. The proactive measures he took toward that goal were uncommon among most landlords who rented properties in struggling communities. To avoid receiving city tickets for tall grass, at a cost of $250, "I just have a couple of kids that go around once a week [to mow]," Dell explained. He noted flatly that he refuted city tickets when they did arrive. "We have a form letter that we use. It says we have fully staffed property maintenance people. We cut our own grass. It has to be a mistake." With a shrug, Dell added, "And they always rescind it. They wipe it out. I have never paid one." He frowned and wondered, "So, I don't know, I guess there are people who do pay it, though."

Rather than risk vandalism in vacant properties, Dell explained, "I put alarms in all my houses immediately, because you just need electricity to do that." The alarm did not necessarily deter vandals from breaking in, he explained, but "once the alarm goes off, they don't know if the police are coming or not, so they take off. So I rarely have a problem with theft." Drumming his fingers on the tabletop, he conceded, "I may have to fix a door. But once they find out that there is an alarm system, they're not going to keep coming back."

Dell appeared incredulous in response to my mention of landlords who declined to participate in the HCVP out of fear that their properties would be vandalized while sitting vacant during what could be an extensive initial inspection process. "If that's their reasoning," he began carefully, "then just put an alarm in." He blinked several times and gave me another, even more startled look. "Absolutely."

The voucher program's goal is to assist lower-income renters to secure decent, affordable rental housing, ideally in racially and economically integrated communities. Yet it clearly falls short of that goal. Landlords had numerous reasons for turning away voucher holders or for housing them while simultaneously violating PHA or local codes. They expressed dissatisfaction with rent payment standards, concerns about a capricious and unfair inspection process, and beliefs about voucher holders' irresponsibility and undeservingness of good-quality housing. Landlords' attitudes toward the program and its tenants determined whether—and how well—to house voucher holders, as did their motivation for entering the business, the profit they generated in it, the size of their real estate portfolio, and the markets where they operated.

Participation in the HCVP was not an attractive business venture for landlords who primarily pursued the business for reasons besides immediate cash flow. Landlords who entered the business in pursuit of a meaningful hobby or a long-term investment were disinclined to participate because of their beliefs that the program's inspection process was burdensome and its tenants were "headaches" — despite any supporting firsthand experience. Without an urgent need for the business to provide cash, they determined that enduring the hassles they expected to be part and parcel of participating in the voucher program were not worthwhile.

The landlords who looked to their properties for short-term cash flow had more incentives to rent to voucher holders, though the market conditions where they operated determined whether, and under what conditions, they housed them. By and large, the landlords who looked forward to the financial rewards of renting properties in resource-rich communities, where they could attract unsubsidized tenants who had the resources to pay rent consistently, generally saw fewer financial benefits of housing a voucher holder than landlords who rented in struggling communities. Yet some landlords who rented properties in middle-income communities cultivated strategies to house subsidized tenants that quelled their concerns about low rent payments or voucher holders' lifestyles. One such strategy was extracting more money out of their tenants above the FMR, as Gabriel did. Other landlords, including Joanne and Isaac, rented desirable properties to voucher holders but monitored and scrutinized their behavior closely to ensure that these tenants behaved "responsibly."

Landlords seeking short-term financial rewards in the business of renting properties in low-income communities had stronger financial incentives to house voucher holders. These landlords valued the consistent rent payments from the government, yet were able to justify falling short on maintaining their properties up to PHA quality standards. Because they were rarely held accountable by city building code inspectors, these landlords determined that it was not financially pragmatic to invest in maintenance work until a PHA inspector cited the unit. Landlords who housed subsidized tenants in struggling communities and had no significant grievances about the HCVP were those with larger real estate portfolios, which generated enough revenue to fund maintenance staff and other proactive measures to minimize costs and losses associated with housing a subsidized tenant — or any tenant, for that matter.

The social and structural factors driving landlords' business practices that were discussed in other chapters also apply to their decisions pertaining to the voucher program. Their perceptions of the unpredictableness or unfairness of PHA inspections contributed to landlords' cynicism toward the agency, undermining their sense of any need or obligation to adhere to its codes. The possibility that a unit could fail an inspection because of tenants' wear-and-tear, or that the tenant could stop paying rent, fueled landlords' mistrust toward tenants as well as toward the PHA, which they believed held them unfairly accountable for tenants' behavior on the property.

The path to ensuring that the HCVP meets its goals will require strategies to reduce landlords' disincentives to house voucher holders and also to raise incentives to house them in high-opportunity communities and under high-quality conditions. This analysis indicates that relieving the administrative burden that the program places on landlords would go some way toward encouraging them to participate in it—perhaps even more than adjusting the FMR calculation, which has shown promise in some contexts, though not in others.[28] Measures that would remove some of the administrative burden on landlords include, for instance, a streamlined inspection process, are discussed further in chapter 7.

Together these findings show that a program intended to facilitate marginalized renters' access to decent, affordable housing, ideally in high-opportunity communities, can fall short of its goals when it fails to consider the landlord's perspective. Indeed, in failing to account for the range of social and structural factors that drive private landlords' business practices, the HCVP reproduces inequality for marginalized renters and communities.

= Chapter 7 =

Conclusion

THE PURPOSE of *Collateral Damages* has been to uncover the social and structural factors that incentivize landlord behavior that disadvantages tenants—and often violates a multitude of federal, state, and local laws. Understanding these factors have become increasingly relevant as policy shifts have led private landlords to take on more responsibility for housing low-income tenants, who, in turn, have become more vulnerable to disadvantageous landlord practices owing to their growing financial and social marginalization. Through ethnographic observations and interviews with landlords and the authorities who regulate them, this book has revealed a system of laws that perpetuates inequality, perhaps unintentionally, because it fails to account for both landlords' and tenants' social and economic circumstances.

The landlords studied here engaged in a wide range of behaviors that were harmful to tenants, the surrounding community, and the region. They engaged in blatant property neglect, from caving ceilings to splintered floors, bug infestations, and peeling paint. They intimidated tenants by, for example, removing front doors to harass them into paying rent or to discourage them from reporting code violations to authorities. Deleterious and illegal landlord behavior did not end there. Landlords' screening practices blocked marginalized tenants' access to decent, affordable housing. Some screening approaches violated the Fair Housing Act, which bans discrimination on the basis of race, ethnicity, disability, and the presence of children. For instance, landlords turned away applicants with young children because they lacked the capital to satisfy the lead safety laws that apply to households with children under six. Other applicants were turned away on the basis of their source of income, including disability income and housing vouchers. "I can't touch her wages if they tear this frickin' place to pieces," complained Quinn, the White landlord who rented properties in a struggling community on the city's East Side. He explained having turned away a young White woman whose monthly disability income

131

far exceeded his low asking rent—because it could not be garnished in court.

Other landlords' screening practices crossed moral boundaries if not necessarily legal ones, and in ways that especially disadvantaged marginalized tenants. Landlords shared their "tenant blacklists" with other landlords in their social or professional circles. "If I have a tenant I'm kicking out, it goes into the computer, and all those people get it," explained Sid, the Asian Indian landlord who mostly rented properties in a desirable outer-ring suburb. He added nonchalantly, "We try to protect ourselves in that way." Unlike "marks," which tenants are aware of and can have a chance to explain—such as unexpected circumstances that led to an eviction on their record—tenants never know they are on this list and thus have little chance to explain or defend themselves. Even tenants who have met landlords' screening criteria may end up on the list for purely personal reasons they will never know and therefore cannot change, and they will continue to be turned away from properties owned by landlords who share the list.

Subjective, capricious screening practices extended beyond tenant blacklists. Landlords reported dropping by prospective tenants' current residences, often unannounced or with little notice, to assess their lifestyle, the cleanliness of their environment, and their children's behavior. This is but one landlord practice that made tenants' housing search unpredictable. The day that a landlord chose to stop by could make all the difference in whether they secured access to housing. Some landlords insisted that it was especially important to observe voucher holders in their current home prior to renting to them—a reflection of their belief that voucher holders, who were very low-income and also predominantly Black, were generally irresponsible.

Taken together, these landlord behaviors were shocking—perhaps even more so because these were people who otherwise appeared to conform to societal norms of "decency." Many of these landlords currently or previously held professional jobs in the service sectors, including health care, social work, and education. And more often than not, their origin stories indicated a long-held goal to own and rent real estate—in stark contrast to "milkers," who, over the course of a few years, buy properties cheaply, command low rents from marginalized tenants, and then walk away from the properties after they fall into disrepair.[1]

That many of these landlords' origin stories featured a downward trajectory over an extended period of time—toward property divestment, discriminatory practices, and tenant mistrust—underscores that social and systematic factors are at play. As Albert Bandura notes, "It requires conducive social conditions rather than monstrous people to produce atrocious deeds. Given appropriate social conditions, decent, ordinary people can do extraordinarily cruel things."[2]

Both the macro economy and local market conditions played a role in landlords' sense of financial precarity. This was especially true in the Cleveland area's weak housing market, given low rents, the declining economic prospects of renters, and, relatedly, the costs and losses of eviction for the landlord. In housing tenants who struggled to pay rent, these landlords were more likely to repeatedly incur the costs of eviction as a result of nonpayment. These costs included filing fees, the cost of a lawyer when applicable, and payments to the bailiffs and court-approved moving company if the tenant had not vacated the property by the court-ordered eviction date.

Other local practices and laws also increased the sense of financial precarity and legal cynicism among landlords who rented properties in struggling communities. For instance, the central city doled out fines to landlords whose tenants improperly stored their waste containers. Even more aggravating to some landlords was a perception that city authorities were uninterested, or ineffective, in stemming the spread of run-down homes and crime in the communities where they rented properties; these conditions diminished their bottom line through the tenants they could attract and the rents they could command. Together these laws and practices fueled landlords' real and perceived financial precarity as well as their legal cynicism, which weakened their motivation and sense of obligation to adhere to laws.[3]

Landlords were aggrieved by laws that they believed protected the interests of the tenant or the community—but not the landlord. In their perception, for instance, they were not seen by policymakers as constituents whose voices and interests needed to be considered because they had the right, as landlords, to evict a tenant or to collect on debt. At the same time, landlords saw a contrast between their theoretical rights and legal obligations, on the one hand, and what they could reasonably enforce among their tenants, on the other. A landlord could sue a tenant for money owed only if the tenant had sufficient wages to garnish, a process that typically required a lawyer to perform the legwork of tracking down tenants after they moved out and arranging a payment plan with their employer. Additionally, landlords were frustrated by laws that imposed fines on them for violations resulting from a tenant's behavior on their property—money that they rarely, if ever, attempted to collect from their tenants, who struggled to pay rent.

Laurence, the middle-aged Black landlord who rented properties in struggling communities on Cleveland's East Side, remarked, "You work hard for everything you have, and you got to sit back, and watch people that's not working, that's trying to get everything for free, just drain you, just be like a towel in the bathroom, squeezing all the water out of it." Curling his fists together tightly, he continued, "It's the people squeezing you, the city officials squeezing you. You're losing everything."

Laurence wilted back in the booth of the deli where we first met. "I mean, think about it," he pleaded, suddenly leaning over the table. "Who set all these rules for the water department? Who set the rules for the sewage department? Who set the rules for the eviction process? And the costs?" He fell quiet and then took a deep breath. "The horrific part of it is the people are—" he began passionately, holding his hand out. Then he stopped short. "No, no," he continued more calmly, slowly shaking his head. "The horrible part of it is the city is sucking everything out of the working man."

Renters' racial and economic backgrounds are important to this story of the unintended consequences of laws meant to protect vulnerable residents and renters. Stigma and stereotypes about lower-income and Black tenants provided landlords with what they believed was justification for their subpar property maintenance and close tenant surveillance. Importantly, landlords of all racial backgrounds invoked tropes about their marginalized tenants' irresponsibility, immorality, and untrustworthiness. Many of the landlords, whether they were Black, White, or Asian, had discriminatory screening practices, engaged in informal evictions, and let their properties fall into disrepair. The greater salience of tenants' race than that of landlords aligns with findings on other "street-level bureaucrats" who oversee the distribution of valued resources to marginalized Americans. The decisions of welfare caseworkers, for instance, about whether to reward or sanction welfare recipients depend far more on the recipient's racial background than the caseworker's. Indeed, Black welfare recipients are subject to the most punitive measures, regardless of caseworkers' racial identity.[4]

Importantly, local laws and ordinances amplified landlords' race-based stereotyped perceptions of their tenants as irresponsible, untrustworthy, or even deviant. For instance, laws that made landlords financially or legally accountable for tenants' activity on the property—over which they believed they had no control—gave landlords an out-sized sense of risk about tenants' behavior. Water billing regulations and criminal activity nuisance ordinances made landlords unduly agitated about tenant characteristics associated with a "culture of poverty" argument—unemployment, large family size, criminal convictions—and served to confirm their belief in that argument.

Mistrust toward tenants, intensified by local regulations, enabled the spread of myths about retaliatory tenant behavior—for example, stories about tenants who used water excessively to run up the bill in retaliation for an eviction. Though only experienced by a few landlords, such incidents came to be considered widespread, for several reasons. Landlords believed that an unfair and exploitable billing system that made them ultimately accountable for paying the bill also encouraged tenants' careless or retaliatory water use. They also recognized that their marginalized tenants had reasons not to voice their grievances, whether about housing quality or an eviction, and that recognition fueled landlords' belief that tenants were motivated to use water excessively in order to convey their dissatisfaction. These factors combined to make what was a rarity—a tenant's excessive and retaliatory water use—into what landlords believed was a regular occurrence in housing tenants who, in the landlords' view, were motivated to use water excessively without perceiving the financial consequences.

Race also matters in the legal system, particularly for Black Americans, who have disincentives to interact with the legal system so as to benefit from its protections. Cynicism toward "the system," which is most widespread in Black communities, undermines engagement with authorities in seeking assistance, except under emergency circumstances.[5] Marginalized tenants' disincentives to interact with authorities— whether court staff, building department administrators, or inspectors— can diminish the extent to which these laws and procedures in fact protect them.

Notably, some landlords were able, despite renting to struggling tenants and, in some cases, in very marginalized communities, to build legitimate business models that produced sustainable profit without routinely engaging in illegitimate business practices or growing consumed with mistrust toward their tenants. These landlords' business models had several commonalities. First, they rented more than just a handful of properties. Economies of scale enabled them to absorb unexpected losses and to maintain a steadfast belief that the business would continue to be profitable and worthy of ongoing investment. Renting to more than just a few tenants made the behavior of any individual tenant less consequential for these landlords, tamping down any anxiety they might have experienced as a result of unpredictable financial costs.

Economies of scale also allowed some landlords to support full-time staff who did routine maintenance and took care of other routine business obligations. Importantly, because it was their staff who interacted with tenants in working to maintain the properties, these landlords' opportunities to hyperscrutinize tenants and their lifestyle were minimized. Small-scale landlords' close interactions with tenants as a result of "running the show"—doing everything from screening to maintenance to rent collection—enabled them to observe tenant behavior that aligned with their preexisting stereotypes, thereby reinforcing and perpetuating them. Notably, small-scale landlords also provided some benefits to tenants that large-scale landlords typically did not, including leniency in rent collection and eviction filing. Indeed, large-scale landlords have been found to file to evict tenants at a higher rate than small-time landlords do, and in response to smaller rent debts.[6]

Other landlord characteristics, such as the amount they invested in the business or their motivation to enter it, factored into their disadvantageous business practices—but only to an extent. The structural and social factors discussed here—including the macro and micro processes that undermined both landlords' and tenants' financial security, as well as their trust in government—had already set many landlords on a downward trajectory in regard to their treatment of their tenants and properties. Certainly, the pace of this trajectory toward adopting unethical or illegal business practices was faster among landlords who invested few resources in the business and who came to expect little financial return from it in the long term.

That immoral or harmful business practices could be stoked among people who showed remarkable diversity across a range of factors—age, gender, educational training, racial background, motivation to enter the business, period when they purchased properties, amount of resources invested in the business, and the neighborhoods where they operated—indicates that there is a systemic problem and that it needs to be changed.

Numerous changes, both small and large, need to be made to ensure that renters have access to decent, affordable housing and to preserve the affordable housing stock. The following recommendations promise to protect all renters across the nation who collectively experience housing insecurity as a result of the macro-level shifts and local policies discussed throughout this book. The processes fueling the housing crises in Cleveland are found in other cities nationwide. A mounting housing cost burden renders tenants in New York, Chicago, Philadelphia, and other cities vulnerable to eviction. In Baltimore, Seattle, Washington, D.C., and elsewhere, rising water bills undermine renters' access to stable housing and also threaten homeowners, who risk losing their home as a result of a delinquent municipal water bill. The spread of criminal activity nuisance ordinances in Chicago, Milwaukee, St. Louis, and other municipalities throughout the nation poses obstacles to renters' access to stable, affordable housing, particularly in White and middle-income communities. Declining markets in Baltimore, Detroit, Cincinnati, and other cities undermine landlords' profit and willingness to invest in their properties so as to ensure tenants' safety. Lower-income and Black communities face the greatest fallout from the state and local laws that produce these outcomes, in line with an ongoing legacy of policymaking that perpetuates the struggles of marginalized spaces.

The recommendations presented here will require tremendous financial investment, particularly on the part of the federal government. It will require unprecedented political and social will to invest adequately in measures to support two populations that have been historically stigmatized or maligned—marginalized renters and their landlords. Yet investing to ensure decent, stable, affordable housing for the most vulnerable households is not only a moral imperative but a practical one.

Unstable, unsafe, and unaffordable housing can take a steep toll on individuals, as well as on society. Housing insecurity raises problems for individuals and families by blocking their access to employment and educational opportunities, by fostering poor physical and mental health, and by creating family instability. Furthermore, the societal costs of addressing the ills associated with widespread housing insecurity may exceed the cost of facilitating all Americans' access to decent, stable, affordable housing.[7]

Legal and Justice System Solutions

Despite landlords' pursuit of financial rewards in the business, factors beyond economic interests can motivate them to make decisions that benefit their tenants, as seen in mediation sessions. "People need the catharsis of a trial" observed a longtime Housing Court mediator in explaining that landlords' decisions were driven not only by principles of economic rationality but also by a desire to have their voice heard and to be treated with respect. The Housing Court's mediation cases were conducted on the basis of pursuing procedural justice—the belief that authorities are neutral and unbiased in their decision-making and that they include constituents' voices in the process. That orientation could help explain why the vast majority of the Housing Court's mediation cases were settled, with some benefit for the tenant, including an extended move-out date or the dropping of a claim for owed money. Accordingly, tenants could benefit from measures that incorporate principles of procedural justice, including investing in the expansion of mediation programs to adjudicate landlord-tenant disputes.

Mediation is not altogether rosy, however, and particularly not for the tenant. Power differentials between the landlord and tenant can undermine the extent to which mediation maximizes benefits for tenants. Without sufficient access to legal counsel, tenants may underestimate the likelihood of receiving a verdict in the courtroom that will provide them with benefits beyond those accrued through a mediation settlement. The permanent and stigmatizing mark of eviction that comes about through a court hearing can further incentivize tenants to settle in mediation rather than in a court hearing, where a magistrate could ask questions and solicit outside testimony that might lead to an even more advantageous outcome for the tenant.[8]

An even more proactive approach is to empower tenants to take advantage of the protections that are afforded to them by, for instance, reducing the administrative burden of navigating the system of laws. In over a decade of experience overseeing landlord-tenant disputes, a Housing Court staff member observed that tenants were often unaware of their full range of protections under the law—including the "rent escrow" process to compel a landlord to make necessary repairs and the financial resources that agencies, including the Cleveland Department of Aging, may provide to prevent an eviction or to secure housing after an eviction. Expanding tenants' access to information about their rights and protections could ensure that they benefit from them. Proactively distributing information about tenants' rights and the agencies that would assist them—whether through mailings from the court or a notice that landlords would be required to provide tenants along with an eviction notice—could enable more renters to stay stably housed.

In New York City, the Mayor's Office to Protect Tenants designed ads to inform tenants of their protections under the law and posted them in train stations and bus terminals, at small businesses, and in local newspapers. The ads present scenarios of landlords' illegitimate practices and inform tenants of their legal protections. "If your landlord says: I'm evicting you, get out by the end of the week," one ad instructs tenants, "Tell them the law says: Only a judge can evict me and I may have the right to a lawyer."[9]

Cleveland Municipal Housing Court's referral program took proactive steps to inform tenants of the resources available to them in order to deter an eviction. Caseworkers would sit in on eviction hearings to inform tenants who had just received an order to vacate their home about the financial resources available through local agencies. The program has since evolved and now informs tenants proactively about opportunities for financial assistance prior to the eviction hearing, in a note that accompanies the court summons that tenants receive several weeks before the eviction hearing. Court staff indicated that landlords occasionally decided to drop the eviction case upon learning that the tenant had taken steps to secure financial assistance through the program so they could pay rent. Clearly the landlord, in being able to collect rent and avoid the losses that accompany the eviction process, benefits from this process.

Ensuring lower-income tenants' right to free legal advice and legal representation in eviction hearings is an essential step to helping them benefit from the laws meant to protect them. Providing tenants with the right to counsel could reduce the number of eviction filings by landlords who routinely win cases because tenants are unaware of their rights—which include protection from retaliatory eviction as a result of filing a complaint about the property. In 2019, the city of Cleveland passed an ordinance that ensures a right to counsel for tenants who have one or more children, live at or below the federal poverty level, and face an eviction. Eligible tenants receive no-cost legal counsel through Right to Counsel-Cleveland (RTC-C), a partnership between the Legal Aid Society of Cleveland and United Way of Greater Cleveland.[10]

The financial and social benefits of free legal counsel can outweigh the costs to municipal budgets of providing it. Reducing the number of evictions can prevent tenants' job loss after an eviction, which undermines local tax revenue. Emergency services that municipalities provide for tenants after evictions, such as homeless shelters, further drain local budgets. After Philadelphia passed legislation to provide legal counsel for tenants who could not afford representation, the results demonstrated these cost savings. At a cost of approximately $3.5 million per year, the program reduced municipal costs by an estimated $45.2 million, demonstrating that providing access to legal counsel can pay for itself.[11]

Landlord-Focused Resources and Training

It is worthwhile for communities to invest in programs that mentor landlords on how to manage their businesses effectively. Such programs enable landlords to earn more consistent and predictable profit, tamping down the sense of financial precarity that can fuel business practices that place tenants' housing at risk. Mentoring would also provide landlords with the skills to perform adequate and timely property maintenance. The small-time landlords in particular were determined to handle repairs themselves, so as to avoid losing money through hiring costly contractors. Clearly the work performed by these landlords often fell short. Not only did handling their own maintenance create inadequate housing conditions for tenants and delays in turning properties over to new tenants, but it often created unnecessary losses.

The Rental Housing Association of Washington (RHAWA), for instance, runs the Rental Housing Academy (RHA), an education program to instruct landlords on their legal responsibilities and "best practices" to operate a successful rental business. It connects landlords to helpful information and resources through a blog that contains business-related advice; in-person and online courses on topics such as property maintenance, fair housing, and profit assessment; and a directory of contractors rated by the association as skilled and reliable.[12]

The Humboldt Tenant Landlord Collaboration (HTLC) is an educational program designed to promote positive relations between local landlords and tenants and to inform both parties about "best practices" to ensure their satisfaction in the relationship. As part of its certification program, landlords are trained in financing, mediation, equity and inclusion, and landlords' and tenants' perspectives. Upon completing the program's ten-module training, participants earn an HTLC "Good Neighbor" certificate, which landlords can present to prospective tenants in order to bolster their market competitiveness.[13]

Many large-scale steps need to be taken to protect low-income renters' access to decent, affordable rental housing and to protect the quality and availability of the affordable housing stock.

A dwindling tax base undermines a city's resources and its ability to fund a building department and other vital departments, including police and sanitation. Cleveland city officials remarked that stricter housing code enforcement could lead to unintended negative consequences, including a shrinking supply of affordable rental housing and the spread of abandoned properties. Yet, as shown here, a failure to enforce codes can be disastrous in its own right. Landlords who perceived the enforcement of housing and safety codes as capricious were less inclined to adhere to those codes; as a result, they were more likely to disinvest in their properties or even abandon them. Rigorous, proactive code enforcement, as enabled by more federal funds, is a necessary tool to ensure that investors maintain their properties in safe and habitable condition.

Community-based models of code enforcement hold promise. Authorities in Atlanta recruit and train residents to perform inspections of exterior property conditions through its Neighborhood Deputies Program. City authorities only become involved after a resident discovers, upon a follow-up inspection, that an investor has not remediated the initial violations.[14] Importantly, providing landlords with access to low-interest loans, or even grants, could prevent large-scale divestment by enabling landlords to perform extensive repair work to bring their properties up to more rigorously enforced housing codes. The city of Toledo, Ohio, provides grants of up to $14,000 to landlords so that they can remediate identifiable lead paint hazards in the property, if it was built prior to 1978, is in adequate structural condition, and is current on property tax payments.[15]

Federal funds are needed to restore aging water infrastructure. Like other infrastructure, including roads and bridges, most water systems were built over a century ago and need upgrades or replacement. Delaying the investment can lead to more costs through catastrophes that interrupt everyday activities, such as water main breaks. Importantly, investment in restoring the nation's water infrastructure would take the burden off private residents to pay rising water costs. It would also reduce landlords' incentive to engage in harmful practices like discriminatory screening and harassment out of their concerns about their tenants' water usage, over which they feel they have little control. In the short term, water assistance programs will be necessary to enable families to afford water bills and to tamp down landlords' practices meant to reduce tenants' water usage. The Low Income Household Water Assistance Program (LIHWAP) was passed in 2021, and provides funds to assist low-income households to afford water bills and avoid shutoffs.[16]

Next, there should be careful consideration of the utility and consequences of criminal activity nuisance ordinances. Despite the stated goals of deterring undesirable or illegal activity and preserving dwindling municipal budgets, CANOs may be self-defeating by deepening these problems rather than alleviating them. For instance, tenants' and residents' reluctance to call for police assistance to protect their safety can enable criminal activity to go on unchecked. The struggles faced by tenants who were evicted because of a landlord's worry about a CANO violation—including job loss, anxiety and depression, and future housing insecurity—may also tax the other municipal resources earmarked to address these problems.

Declassifying calls for police assistance with domestic violence as a "nuisance activity" is essential to ensure physical safety, as well as access to stable, affordable housing, among survivors of domestic violence. Several municipalities in Cuyahoga County have repealed or adjusted their CANOs in response to allegations of discriminatory outcomes. For instance, suburban Lakewood—where the White landlord Katie followed city orders to evict tenants who requested police assistance with a dispute— no longer considers it a "nuisance" to request or receive police assistance for domestic disputes. Suburban Bedford—where the Asian Indian landlord Gabriel turned away tenants who, he believed, experienced domestic violence—repealed its CANO altogether.

A number of legislative and administrative changes will be necessary to support voucher holders. A national source of income (SOI) protection law, which exists in a handful of jurisdictions around the country, including in Cuyahoga County, could increase voucher holders' access to affordable rental housing by banning discrimination on the basis of holding a housing voucher. SOI laws have indeed increased the effectiveness of the Housing Choice Voucher Program in some of the municipalities where they have been enacted.[17] SOI laws are not foolproof, however; there is widespread evidence that renters and home-buyers experience discrimination on the basis of race, ethnicity, and other classes currently protected under the Fair Housing Act.[18]

One of the municipalities in Cuyahoga County that have passed SOI laws is South Euclid, where the White landlord Shia rented properties and confessed, "If I have two people in front of me, and one's a Section 8, one's not a Section 8, I would probably say, 'Hey, let me go with the person who is not a Section 8.'" Yet local reporters showed that, several years after the law's passage, in 2015, the community still had not seen an uptick in the number of local voucher households.[19] Going forward, measures to remove landlords' disincentives to participate in the voucher program will be crucial to ensure its effectiveness.

An important next step toward that end is the implementation of a small area fair market rent (SAFMR) to guide the voucher program's rent determinations. Currently, the fair market rent calculation is a disincentivize to participate in the voucher program for landlords who rent properties in middle-income communities, where they can command rents that are higher than the FMR. An SAFMR would address this by allowing public housing authorities to pay higher rents in certain high-rent and high-opportunity neighborhoods. Doing so would remove the "perverse" incentive for landlords who own properties in distressed communities, and who typically have limited incentive to invest in their properties, to seek out voucher tenants. Increased rent payments through SAFMR have helped voucher holders gain access to higher-opportunity neighborhoods in some areas, such as Dallas, Texas, and Long Beach, California, though not in others, such as Cook County, Illinois. As such, it is essential to further explore what drives the varying effectiveness of these policies across markets.[20]

Measures to ensure that the HCVP meets its goals should also include reducing the administrative burden on landlords. The inspection process in particular frustrated the landlords in this study, increased their uncertainty, and compelled them to expend time and money to respond to citations for violating inspection standards they believed were enforced capriciously. Landlords also reported that communication with the PHA, primarily through its virtual portal, was typically lengthy, frustrating, and ineffective in addressing their concerns.

Increased consistency and efficiency in the inspection process is needed for subsidized units.[21] Toward that end, Dallas and other cities have adopted InspectionMate, a virtual customer service assistant, to shorten the inspection process and improve communication between landlords and PHA staff. By enabling landlords to interact with PHA inspectors and staff in "real time," InspectionMate eliminates some of the frustrations of the inspection process, including uncertain inspector arrival times and delayed or uncertain results of an inspection.[22]

In another approach to reducing landlords' problems with the inspection process, the Oakland Housing Authority conducts prequalifying unit inspections. In most cities, landlords must wait to arrange a PHA inspection until they have identified a subsidized tenant to fill the unit, a requirement that can delay the tenant's move-in by several months. Prequalifying inspections enable landlords to receive PHA approval to house a subsidized tenant prior to selecting a tenant. Through pre-qualifying inspections, landlords can look forward to a shorter window of time during which their unit sits vacant, not generating rent, after they have selected a tenant. Preapproved inspection results expire after a designated period of time (ninety days in Oakland), after which the unit must pass a new inspection to qualify to house a subsidized tenant. According to staff at the Oakland PHA, the streamlined inspection process increased voucher usage markedly.[23] Notably, streamlining the inspection process should not require significant financial invest-ment beyond what is already spent on scheduling and performing inspections.

The HCVP goal of providing quality, affordable housing to low-income tenants could also be furthered through deeper investment in housing code enforcement and water infrastructure, through the mea-sures recommended here. Rigorous housing code enforcement on the part of city inspectors would make landlords more accountable for main-taining their properties proactively, not simply in response to a PHA inspector's citation. Systemic housing code enforcement would lead landlords to consider all inspections, whether for the city or the PHA, just another "cost of doing business"; this would be an important step toward stemming landlords' disincentives to house a subsidized tenant.

Stemming rising water costs would also give landlords less cause to turn away voucher tenants, based on their unfounded belief that higher water usage and bills result from housing tenants who lack employ-ment or a sense of personal responsibility. The voucher program does not typically cover water bills apart from the rent, so until the cost of water stabilizes—ideally through federal investment—water subsidies for low-income households could facilitate voucher holders' access to affordable rental housing.

Solving the housing crises in the nation's cities also requires thinking beyond housing policy altogether. Many cities' affordable housing crises are driven by falling renter wages and precarious work, not by rising rents. The hourglass economy that emerged in the 1980s has been exac-erbated in recent years by falling wages for the non-college-educated, growing uncertainty in work hours, and a rise in involuntary part-time employment.[24] One result of tenants' mounting struggles to pay rent consistently has been landlords' increasing difficulty in generating suf-ficient revenue to incentivize their adherence to housing laws pertain-ing to screening, property maintenance, and eviction. The nation needs bold federal and state policies to ensure a financial safety net for all Americans, working or not, in order to solve its housing crises.

A renter's tax credit would signal what is long overdue: an affirmation that dignity and access to opportunities conducive to well-being should not be contingent on housing tenure. Homeowners, who are predominantly White, have disproportionately benefited from government assistance through tax credits and the home mortgage interest tax deduction. The renter population, which has fewer financial resources, receives no direct benefits from the government as a result of their tenure status.[25] A renter's tax credit would help to provide the renter population with housing security in the midst of an economy that lacks enough jobs that provide livable wages.[26]

As with the Earned Income Tax Credit (EITC), a means-tested government assistance program for lower- and moderate-income families, a renter's tax credit would put essential dollars in eligible families' pockets.[27] The value of cash assistance to lower-income renters, especially in enabling them to maintain their housing amid sudden economic shocks, was seen with the federal government's stimulus checks provided in 2020 during the Covid-19 pandemic. As several landlords, including Isaac, Herman, and Quinn, relayed to me in the summer and fall of 2020, tenants who lost their jobs and would have otherwise faced an eviction as a result of nonpayment were able to stay in place upon receiving additional money from the government.

A renter's tax credit would take the form of an income tax credit, which covers the gap between the rent amount and a certain percentage (for example, 40 percent) of a renter's household income. Delivering assistance through a tax credit would shield renters from social stigma and prevent the demoralizing interactions with caseworkers that can sow mistrust toward government institutions. A renter's tax credit would also spare voucher holders the administrative burden of navigating the bureaucracy of the voucher program and locating a landlord who will accept the subsidy. What's more, the infrastructure to support the implementation of a renter's tax credit is largely in place. Eligibility and receipt of a renter's tax credit could be based on information that renters already report to the IRS alongside several additional pieces of information, including nontaxable cash income and rent paid.[28]

Ensuring renters' access to decent, stable, affordable housing will require the reversal of those aspects of neoliberal housing policy that have had harmful consequences for some tenants.

Making more public housing units available would decrease the pressure on the private market to house poor families. Skepticism about a return to public housing is not without basis. It is essential to remember, however, that the numerous social ills associated with public housing arose because of public policy, not because of flaws inherent to the model itself. Public housing was indeed "built to fail," as was evident in the low-quality materials used to construct the developments and the subsequent subpar maintenance of them.[29] Because of the nation's dilapidated public housing, President Nixon himself declared to Congress in 1973 that the federal government was the "biggest slumlord in history."[30]

With careful consideration, public housing could be built without re-creating the missteps of the past. Several cities have adopted innovative models to construct good-quality, low-density public housing units in high-opportunity, inclusive communities. In Columbia, Maryland, the housing authority purchases and manages individual apartments scattered throughout the city and in middle-income suburbs. The housing authority in Mount Laurel, New Jersey, has chosen to construct and site low-density public housing so as to minimize stigma and undergird a sense of social inclusion.

Boston's Commonwealth Development, which is owned by the Boston Housing Authority, provides a collaborative framework to redevelop existing public housing units. The once-distressed housing project, which houses 392 very low-income residents, was redeveloped at a cost of $32 million in 1985 through the teamwork of the Boston Housing Authority, the Commonwealth Tenants Association, a private developer, and a private management company.[31] The collaborative approach produced a community of high-quality, well-maintained townhomes with yards, where crime rates are low and residents report high levels of residential satisfaction.[32]

The expansion of affordable homeownership opportunities is another strategy to reduce reliance on the private market for affordable housing. The nonprofit organization Cleveland Housing Network (CHN) Housing Partners provides affordable homeownership options for lower-income households through its lease-to-purchase plan, as financed by the federal Low-Income Housing Tax Credit (LIHTC) program. Tenants who consistently pay rent during the fifteen-year compliance period then become eligible to purchase their home. The organization commands $550 per month on average—an approximation of the monthly costs to own a home, including around $275 in monthly mortgage payments, utility bills, insurance, and tax bills. The program further prepares residents for sustainable homeownership by providing financial counseling during the five years prior to their home purchase. The program's success is clear: five years after their home purchase, 98 percent of these homeowners remain stably housed in their homes.[33]

It is essential that any analysis of the unintended or unanticipated consequences of well-intentioned policies, such as the present study, consider whether any of its own policy recommendations could inadvertently create harmful outcomes. Measures that put more money in tenants' pockets and relatedly, in landlords' pockets, such as water bill vouchers, pose less risk to tenants than policies that increase landlords' cost of doing business—for instance, stricter housing code enforcement.

As part of a strategy to prevent any unanticipated, negative consequences of enforcing laws meant to protect renters and communities, it is imperative that policymakers become more informed about landlords' business practices and the structural forces driving them. To deter unintended consequences, it is essential to create opportunities for authorities to interact with landlords and learn about their perspectives firsthand.

Today landlords' interactions with authorities are often brief and centered on a specific issue—most commonly an eviction, a code violation, or an inspection performed by a city or PHA inspector. These interactions typically involve "street-level bureaucrats" who enforce the laws, not the authorities who devise them. Accordingly, there is a need to create new opportunities to bridge the communication gap between landlords and policymakers.

The city of Ionia, Michigan, conducts a "Landlords' Lunch and Learn" event that brings landlords and local authorities together to engage in constructive dialogue. The multi-part event begins with presentations from panelists who represent city agencies and ends with small group sessions in which panelists and attendees discuss specific issues. Panelists solicit meaningful information from landlords, for instance, by inquiring about the most significant changes they experienced in the rental business in recent years. Drawing on their discussions with landlords, panelists generate several recommendations for policy "next steps" that they believe authorities should consider.[34] Notably, more than a handful of landlords in this study volunteered a keen interest in attending events in the spirit of this one—a forum in which they would be treated as constituents and have their voices heard by authorities.

The primary goal of this book has been to show how a system of laws meant to protect marginalized renters and residents falls short and even deepens their disadvantage. Notably, this analysis is not meant as an attack on the landlords who provide affordable rental housing. Nor is it an attack on the government authorities who implement and enforce laws and programs that are meant to protect vulnerable members of society. Rather, it acknowledges that the form of governance that best serves constituents is the one that accounts for their social and economic realities.

═ Study Methodology ═

AMAJORITY OF the sixty landlords interviewed (thirty-four) were found through a stratified random sample of rental property listings. In constructing the sampling frame, we relied on reports from a parallel study of a random sample of Cleveland households with young children (ages three to ten) that oversampled low- and moderate-income residents and was being conducted in the city at the same time. That study indicated that most renters searched for housing online rather than through newspapers. The most common online rental listing websites that households used, or had used in the recent past, were gosection8.com, craigslist.com, and housingcleveland.org.

All addresses from these listings over a three-month period were geocoded. Stratification was based on tract-level poverty (above or below 20 percent poor) as well as on the racial composition of the tract (Black/White).[1] This sampling approach was used to increase heterogeneity.[2] We used the phone number associated with the listing to contact potential participants. Anyone indicating that they were a landlord or property manager was invited to participate in the study. At that time (and again subsequently, just prior to the start of the interview), individuals were informed that the information they shared would be confidential (not connected to any information that could identify them), and they were promised compensation ($50). The interviews were conducted at a time and location convenient to the landlord. Interview sites included landlords' offices and properties, personal homes, restaurants, and coffee shops.

The random sample was supplemented by a field sample (twenty-six landlords) in order to include landlords who may not have been identified by the random sampling approach, whether owing to lack of a current or public listing or hesitation about participating in research. This sample was collected through contact information provided by participants in the study.

Interviews were recorded and then transcribed verbatim, and field notes captured our ethnographic observations. All respondents were assigned pseudonyms, and other identifying information has been changed.

Through an open-ended approach, we allowed landlords to direct the conversation toward topics that were salient to them. Landlords were asked to share "the whole story" of how and why they entered the business, acquired properties, set business goals, and made decisions in regard to screening, rent collection and evictions, unit inspections, maintenance, and participation in housing subsidy programs. Doing so prompted respondents to provide detailed stories, rich with information that otherwise might not have been covered solely through a more direct line of questioning. From there, the goal was to guide the conversation in order to cover all of the topics and to use direct questions or prompts in order to gather specific information that landlords had not brought up in the course of conversation.

These in-depth interviews provide a valuable window into respondents' subjective experiences, beliefs, and worldviews.[3] Though the information gleaned through interviews does not always align precisely with what respondents did, it nonetheless provides an opportunity to understand the process by which they form beliefs and make decisions.[4] This data collection approach also built trust and rapport with respondents, enabling open discussion that often led to landlords' interest in having a team member join them in the field—for example, to attend a housing inspection or to meet with prospective tenants.

To supplement our understanding of these landlords, the members of the team and I engaged in ethnographic observations of daily routines among a subset of landlords. We joined them at Housing Court hearings, where they pursued eviction or money owed from tenants for property damages. Landlords invited us to attend inspections for their subsidized units. Indeed, we watched as inspectors who worked for the Cleveland Housing Authority toured their properties, clipboard in hand, and cited them for blatant code violations. We observed landlords speaking with current tenants as well as with prospective tenants who were interested in their vacant unit. Landlords also permitted us to witness their interactions with their staff, including property managers, contractors, and groundskeepers.

= Notes =

Chapter 1: Introduction

1. Ellen, Been, and Hayashi 2013; Garboden and Newman 2012; Mallach 2007; Newman 2005; Sternlieb 1966.

2. Ellen, Been, and Hayashi 2013; Mallach 2007; Newman 2005.

3. Brooks-Gunn et al. 1993; Goering, Kamely, and Richardson 1997; Schwartz 2015.

4. Schwartz 2015.

5. Desmond 2016.

6. Desmond 2016; Garboden and Newman 2012; Garboden et al. 2018; Greenlee 2014; Mallach 2007, 2014; Rosen 2014; Stegman 1972; Sternlieb 1966.

7. Garboden et al. 2018; Greenlee 2014; Rosen 2020.

8. Kingsley 2017.

9. For an exception, see Desmond and Valdez 2012.

10. Kneebone and Holmes 2016; Logan and Stults 2011.

11. Erickson et al. 2008; Ford 2018; Spader, Schuetz, and Cortes 2015.

12. Shiffer-Sebba 2020.

13. Massey and Denton 1993; Sharkey 2013.

14. Ahern 2020; Cuyahoga County Planning Commission 2016.

15. Cuyahoga County Planning Commission 2016.

16. Cuyahoga County Planning Commission 2016; Hexter 2016.

17. Ford 2018; Western Reserve Land Conservancy 2015.

18. Ford 2018; Hexter 2016.

19. Hexter 2016.

20. Merton 1968.

21. Edin and Shaefer 2015; Kalleberg 2011.

22. Desmond and Bell 2015.

23. Joint Center for Housing Studies of Harvard University 2019.

24. Walker 2019.

25. Edin and Schaefer 2015; Tach and Edin 2017.

26. Alexander 2010; Pager 2007; Pettit and Western 2004; Western 2006.

27. Public Justice Center 2015.

28. Cleveland Municipal Court Housing Division, https://clevelandmunicipal court.org/docs/default-source/cleveland-housing-court/faq-evictions —2020.pdf?sfvrsn=6e54413d_2.

29. DeLuca, Wood, and Rosenblatt 2019.

30. Desmond and Valdez 2012; Swan 2015.

31. Hughes 2020.

32. Sampson and Bartusch 1998; Tyler 1990.

33. Turner et al. 2013; Yinger 1995.

34. Pager 2007; Pager and Shepherd 2008; Pettit and Western 2004; Western 2006.

35. Gilens 1999; Piven and Cloward 1971; Schram 1995, 2006; Soss, Fording, and Schram 2011.

36. Bandura 1978.

37. Soss, Fording, and Schram 2011; Watkins-Hayes 2009.

38. Schram 2006; Soss, Fording, and Schram 2011.

39. Soss, Fording, and Schram 2011.

40. Lerman and Weaver 2014.

41. Bell 2017; Mettler and Stonecash 2008; Soss 1999; Soss, Fording, and Schram 2011; Watkins-Hayes 2009.

42. Brayne 2014.

43. Massey and Denton 1993; Sharkey 2013; Rothstein 2017.

44. Ramsey 2018.

45. Rosen 2020.

46. Edin and Shaefer 2015; Wilson 1997.

Chapter 2: The Uneven Fortunes of Cleveland's Neighborhoods

1. Walker 2019.

2. Hexter 2016.

3. Erickson et al. 2008; Kalleberg 2011.

4. Erickson et al. 2008; Hexter 2016.

5. Data retrieved from Eviction Lab (evictionlab.org), July 1, 2021.

6.   Hatch 2017; Rabin 1984.

7.   Campion 1975.

8.   Bell 2017; Lerman and Weaver 2014.

9.   House 2021; Way and Fraser 2018; Way, Trinh, and Wyatt 2013.

10. See the Cleveland Memory Project website at http://www.clevelandmemory.org.

11. Rothstein 2017; Sharkey 2013.

12. Donnelly 2013.

13. Cleveland Memory Project (http://www.clevelandmemory.org).

14. Kirwan Institute for the Study of Race and Ethnicity 2015; Sharkey 2013.

15. Cleveland Memory Project (http://www.clevelandmemory.org).

16. Lapeyrolerie 2015.

17. Ibid.

18. Hexter 2016; Lepley and Mangiarelli 2017.

19. Jacquay 2005.

20. Desmond 2016.

21. Desmond and Kimbro 2015.

22. Desmond et al. 2013; Pribesh and Downey 1999.

23. Urban et al. 2019.

24. Ibid.

25. Ibid.

26. According to Housing Court officials, more often than not landlords also lack legal counsel. The exceptions are large corporations and businesses registered as a limited liability company (LLC), which has become increasingly common among investors as a way to limit liability for losses. LLCs are required to hire counsel.

27. Urban et al. 2019.

28. Massey 2015.

29. Dissell and Zeitner 2015.

30. DeLuca, Wood, and Rosenblatt 2019; Desmond and Kimbro 2015.

31. Coulton et al. 2010; Ford 2018; Keating and Lind 2012.

32. Western Reserve Land Conservancy 2015.

33. Ford 2018.

34. Frater, Gilson, and O'Leary 2009.

35. An important exception in the city of Cleveland is property rented by a landlord through government housing subsidy programs (such as the Section 8 program). The public housing authority that administers the

housing subsidy uses its own team of inspectors to perform annual inspections of subsidized housing units. Further, the city of Cleveland has identified "concentrated inspection areas" that inspectors surveil routinely.

36. Sampson 2012.
37. Schwartz 2015.
38. Herd and Moynihan 2018, 22.
39. Bell 2017; Brayne 2014; Lerman and Weaver 2014.
40. Brayne 2014.
41. U.S. Department of Justice and U.S. Attorney's Office, Northern District of Ohio 2014.
42. Paternoster et al. 1997.
43. Gallek 2015.
44. Legal Aid Society of Cleveland 2018.
45. Legal Aid Society of Cleveland 2020.
46. Witt 2019.

Chapter 3: "I May Just Have to Walk Away"

1. Mallach 2007.
2. Ibid.
3. Tyler 1990.
4. Bartram 2019.
5. Shiffer-Sebba 2020.
6. Merton 1968.
7. Sternlieb and Burchell 1973.
8. Sampson and Bartusch 1998; Tyler 1990.
9. Gillispie 2019.
10. Bell 2017.
11. Bandura 1990; Sykes and Matza 1957.
12. Desmond 2016.
13. Edin and Shaefer 2015.
14. Bartram 2019.

Chapter 4: "If I Got Him Paranoid Enough, I Knew He Would Go"

1. Desmond and Valdez 2012; Ramsey 2018.
2. Garland 1996; Swan 2015.

3. Ramsey 2018.

4. Coulton et al. 2010; Ford 2018; Keating and Lind 2012.

5. Hexter 2016; Mead et al. 2017.

6. Ramsey 2018.

7. Mead et al. 2017.

8. Hexter 2016.

9. Sampson and Raudenbush 2004.

10. Fais 2008; Ramsey 2018; Swan 2015.

11. Mead et al. 2017.

12. Koehle 2013; Mazzerole and Ransley 2005. For an exception, see Desmond and Valdez 2012.

13. Desmond and Valdez 2012; Fais 2008; Ramsey 2018; Swan 2015.

14. Mead et al. 2017.

15. Desmond and Shollenberger 2015; Desmond, Gershenson, and Kiviat 2015.

16. DeLuca, Wood, and Rosenblatt 2019; Desmond and Shollenberger 2015.

17. Burt 2001.

18. Desmond and Kimbro 2015.

19. Bell 2017; Kirk and Papachristos 2011; Lerman and Weaver 2014.

20. Desmond 2016.

21. Miller 2019.

22. Scott 2019.

23. Desmond and Valdez 2012.

24. Catalano 2015.

25. Hexter 2016.

26. Arnold 2019.

27. A notable exception is the property owner who accrues sufficient debt to warrant property foreclosure by the city.

28. Mead et al. 2017.

29. Schwartz 2015.

30. Alexander 2010; Pager 2007; Western 2006.

31. Fais 2008.

32. American Civil Liberties Union 2020.

33. Fais 2008.

34. Desmond and Gershenson 2016.

35. Merton 1968.

36. Arnold 2019; Fais 2008.

37. Wright and Rubin 2010.

Chapter 5: "What Kills Me Now Is the Water"

1. Water Infrastructure Task Force 2017.

2. Walton 2015.

3. Montag 2019.

4. Lepley and Mangiarelli 2017; Pager 2007; Pager and Shepherd 2008; Pettit and Western 2004; Western 2006.

5. One exception was Sid, who reported having personal experience with a tenant running the water excessively in response to an eviction. After filing to evict the tenants at one of his single-family houses, he noticed that the water meter began to spike. Local laws prohibited the landlord from entering the property when eviction proceedings were underway, so Sid asked the water department to terminate the tenants' water service. The request was denied; the Ohio Tenant-Landlord Law holds that tenants' water service may not be terminated by the landlord at any time. Later, at a second-cause court hearing, Sid received a judgment in his favor that permitted him to collect on the tenants' unpaid rent and water bills. Yet, he noted with disappointment, "I have no way to collect it. I don't know where these people went."

6. Desmond 2016.

7. Newman 2012.

8. Nickerson 1998.

9. Gilderbloom and Applebaum 1988; Gomory 2021.

10. Ford 2018.

11. Vacant and Abandoned Property Action Council 2015.

12. Ibid.

13. Ibid.

14. Ibid.

15. Montag 2019.

16. Massey and Denton 1993; Rothstein 2017; Sharkey 2013.

17. Vacant and Abandoned Property Action Council 2015.

18. Regan 2020.

Chapter 6: "You Said You're Section 8 . . . That's *Why* I Don't Want to Get in Touch with You"

1. Schwartz 2015.

2. DeLuca, Garboden, and Rosenblatt 2013; DeLuca and Rosenblatt 2017; Garboden et al. 2018; Kleit, Garshick, and Galvez 2011; Lepley and Mangiarelli 2017; McClure 2008; Rosen 2020; Schwartz 2015.

3. Hexter 2016; Lepley and Mangiarelli 2017.

4. Hexter 2016.

5. Rosen 2020.

6. Rosen 2020; Rothstein 2017.

7. DeLuca, Garboden, and Rosenblatt 2013.

8. Lepley and Mangiarelli 2017.

9. DeLuca, Garboden, and Rosenblatt 2013.

10. Tighe and Ganning 2016.

11. U.S. Department of Housing and Urban Development, Office of Policy Development and Research, "Assisted Housing: National and Local," huduser.gov/portal/datasets/assthsg.html.

12. Gilens 1999; Schram 2006.

13. Garboden et al. 2018.

14. Ibid.

15. Rosen 2020.

16. Herd and Moynihan 2018.

17. Rosen 2020.

18. Garboden et al. 2018; Greenlee 2014; Rosen 2020.

19. DeLuca, Garboden, and Rosenblatt 2013.

20. Piven and Cloward 1971; Soss, Fording, and Schram 2011.

21. Hughes 2020.

22. Garboden et al. 2018; Rosen 2020.

23. Ross, Parsons, and Vallas 2016.

24. Aron et al. 2016; Desmond 2016.

25. Massey 2015.

26. Wood 2014.

27. Rosen 2020.

28. Reina, Acolin, and Bostic 2019.

Chapter 7: Conclusion

1. Mallach 2007.

2. Bandura 2002, 1019.

3. Merton 1968; Sampson and Bartusch 1998; Tyler 1990.

4. Soss, Fording, and Schram 2011; Watkins-Hayes 2009.

5. Bell 2017.

6. Gomory 2021.

7. Hartman 1998.

8. Fiss 1984.

9. Mayor's Office to Protect Tenants, "NYC Rent Regulation Outreach Campaign," nyc.gov/assets/home/downloads/pdf/press-releases/2019 /NYC-Rent-Regulation-Outreach-Campaign.pdf.

10. Legal Aid Society of Cleveland 2020.

11. Stout Risius Ross, Inc. 2016.

12. Rental Housing Association of Washington, "Rental Housing Academy," hawa.org/academy.

13. Humboldt State University, "Humboldt Tenant Landlord Collaboration," housing.humboldt.edu/htlc.

14. Treuhaft, Rose, and Black 2010.

15. City of Toledo, "Lead Paint Remediation," toledo.oh.gov/residents/ homeowners/lead-paint-remediation.

16. U.S. Department of Health and Human Services, Office of Community Services, "Low Income Household Water Assistance Program (LIHWAP)," acf.hhs.gov/ocs/programs/lihwap.

17. Freeman 2011; Freeman and Yi 2014.

18. Aron et al. 2016; Turner et al. 2013; Yinger 1995.

19. Atassi 2019.

20. Reina, Acolin, and Bostic 2019.

21. Garboden et al. 2018; Greenlee 2014.

22. National Apartment Association 2019.

23. Nisar et al. 2018.

24. Edin and Shaefer 2015; Kalleberg 2011.

25. Schwartz 2015.

26. Kalleberg 2011.

27. Kimberlin, Tach, and Wimer 2018.

28. Ibid.

29. Schwartz 2015.

30. Bloom, Umbach, and Vale 2015.

31. Tise Design Associates, "Commonwealth Development," tisedesign.com /commonwealth-development.

32. Vale 2015.

33. Tise Design Associates, "Commonwealth Development," tisedesign.com /commonwealth-development.

34. Michigan's Campaign to End Homelessness, materials for Landlord Forum, November 12, 2008, Holland, Michigan, michigan.gov/documents /mcteh/Landlord_tool_kit_549020_7.pdf.

Study Methodology

1. Neighborhoods where more than 40 percent of residents were African American were coded "Black"; communities where more than 40 percent of residents were White were coded "White."

2. We recognize that this sampling strategy may omit certain landlord populations, including those who do not currently have a property for rent and those who secure tenants primarily through word-of-mouth recommendations. One such example is the largest nonprofit provider of rental housing, CHN Housing Partners (formerly Cleveland Housing Network). Our interview with a representative from that organization indicated that they mostly advertise through word of mouth.

3. Lamont and Small 2008.

4. Becker 1998.

References

Ahern, Joe. 2020. "Demographic Profile of Cuyahoga County from the 2018 American Community Survey." Cleveland, Ohio: Center for Community Solutions (March 9). https://www.communitysolutions.com/wp-content /uploads/2020/03/Issue-Brief_ACS-Demographic-Profiles_03092020.pdf.

Alexander, Michelle. 2010. *The New Jim Crow: Mass Incarceration in the Age of Colorblindness*. New York: New Press.

American Civil Liberties Union. 2020. "ACLU, Civil Rights Groups, and City of Bedford, Ohio Reach Settlement Repealing the City's Nuisance Ordinance." ACLU, September 22. aclu.org/press-releases/aclu-civil-rights-groups-and -city-bedford-ohio-reach-settlement-repealing-citys.

American Community Survey (ACS). 2016–2020a. "Map of Cleveland Metro- politan Region, Percent Asian." Social Explorer. Accessed March 30, 2022. https://www.socialexplorer.com/.

———. 2016–2020b. "Map of Cleveland Metropolitan Region, Percent Black." Social Explorer. Accessed March 30, 2022. https://www.socialexplorer.com/.

———. 2016–2020c. "Map of Cleveland Metropolitan Region, Percent Hispanic." Social Explorer. Accessed March 30, 2022. https://www.socialexplorer.com/.

———. 2016–2020d. "Map of Cleveland Metropolitan Region, Percent White." Social Explorer. Accessed March 30, 2022. https://www.socialexplorer.com/.

Arnold, Gretchen W. 2019. "From Victim to Offender: How Nuisance Property Laws Affect Battered Women." *Journal of Interpersonal Violence* 34(6): 1103–26.

Aron, Laudan, Claudia Aranda, Douglas Wissoker, Brent Howell, and Robert Santos, with Molly Scott and Margery Austin Turner. 2016. "Discrimination against Families with Children in Rental Housing Markets: Findings of the Pilot Study." Washington: U.S. Department of Housing and Urban Development (December).

Atassi, Leila. 2019. "South Euclid's Anti-Discrimination Ordinance Is Violated by Landlords with Impunity," *Cleveland Plain Dealer*, August 28. cleveland. com/news/2019/08/south-euclids-anti-discrimination-ordinance-is-violated -by-landlords-with-impunity.html.

Bandura, Albert. 1978. "Social Learning Theory of Aggression." *Journal of Communication* 28(3): 12–29.

———. 1990. "Selective Activation and Disengagement of Moral Control." *Journal of Social Issues* 46(1): 27–46.

————. 2002. "Selective Moral Disengagement in the Exercise of Moral Agency." *Journal of Moral Education* 31(2): 101–19.

Bartram, Robin. 2019. "Going Easy and Going After: Building Inspections and the Selective Allocation of Code Violations." *City and Community* (18)2: 594–617.

Becker, Howard. 1998. *Tricks of the Trade: How to Think about Your Research While You're Doing It.* Chicago: University of Chicago Press.

Bell, Monica C. 2017. "Police Reform and the Dismantling of Legal Estrangement." *Yale Law Journal* 126(7): 2054–2150.

Bloom, Nicholas Dagen, Fritz Umbach, and Lawrence J. Vale. 2015. *Public Housing Myths: Perception, Reality, and Social Policy.* Ithaca, N.Y.: Cornell University Press.

Brayne, Sarah. 2014. "Surveillance and System Avoidance: Criminal Justice Contact and Institutional Attachment." *American Sociological Review* 79(3): 367–91.

Brooks-Gunn, Jeanne, Greg J. Duncan, Pamela Kato Klebanov, and Naomi Sealand. 1993. "Do Neighborhoods Influence Child and Adolescent Development?" *American Journal of Sociology* 99(2): 353–95.

Burt, Martha R. 2001. "Homeless Families, Singles, and Others: Findings from the 1996 National Survey of Homeless Assistance Providers and Clients." *Housing Policy Debate* 12(4): 737–80.

Campion, John E. 1975. "The Ohio Landlord and Tenant Reform Act of 1974." *Case Western Reserve Law Review* 25(4): 876–971.

Catalano, Shannan. 2015. "Intimate Partner Violence, 1993–2010." *Special Report* NCJ 239203 (November 2012; revised September 29, 2015). Washington: U.S. Department of Justice, Bureau of Justice Statistics.

Coulton, Claudia, Kathryn W. Hexter, April Hirsh, Anne O'Shaughnessy, and Francisca G. C. Richter. 2010. "Facing the Foreclosure Crisis in Greater Cleveland: What Happened and How Communities Are Responding." *Urban Publications.* Cleveland: Cleveland State University, Maxine Goodman Levin College of Urban Affairs (January 1). https://engagedscholarship.csuohio.edu/urban_facpub/374.

Cuyahoga County Planning Commission. 2016. "HUD Consolidated Plan and Strategies: Five Year Plan FY 2016–FY 2020." https://www.clevelandohio.gov/sites/default/files/forms_publications/ConsolidatePlan2016-2020.pdf.

DeLuca, Stefanie, Phillip M. E. Garboden, and Peter Rosenblatt. 2013. "Segregating Shelter: How Housing Policies Shape the Residential Locations of Low-Income Minority Families." *Annals of the American Academy of Political and Social Science* 647(1): 268–99.

DeLuca, Stefanie, and Peter Rosenblatt. 2017. "Walking Away from The Wire: Housing Mobility and Neighborhood Opportunity in Baltimore." *Housing Policy Debate* 27(4): 519–46.

DeLuca, Stefanie, Holly Wood, and Peter Rosenblatt. 2019. "Why Poor People Move (and Where They Go): Reactive Mobility and Residential Decisions." *City and Community* 18(2): 556–93.

Desmond, Matthew. 2016. *Evicted: Poverty and Profit in the American City.* New York: Crown.

Desmond, Matthew, and Monica Bell. 2015. "Housing, Poverty, and the Law." *Annual Review of Law and Social Science* 11: 15–35.

Desmond, Matthew, and Carl Gershenson. 2016. "Housing and Unemployment Security among the Working Poor." *Social Problems* 63(1): 46–67.

Desmond, Matthew, Carl Gershenson, and Barbara Kiviat. 2015. "Forced Relocation and Residential Instability among Urban Renters." *Social Service Review* 89(2): 227–62.

Desmond, Matthew, and Rachel Tolbert Kimbro. 2015. "Eviction's Fallout: Housing, Hardship, and Health." *Social Forces* 94(1): 295–324.

Desmond, Matthew, and Tracey Shollenberger. 2015. "Forced Displacement from Rental Housing: Prevalence and Neighborhood Consequences." *Demography* 52(5): 1751–72.

Desmond, Matthew, and Nicol Valdez. 2012. "Unpolicing the Urban Poor: Consequences of Third-Party Policing for Inner-City Women." *American Sociological Review* 78(1): 117–41.

Desmond, Matthew, Weihua An, Richelle Winkler, and Thomas Ferriss. 2013. "Evicting Children." *Social Forces* 92(1): 303–27.

Dissell, Rachel, and Brie Zeitner. 2015. "Toxic Neglect: Curing Cleveland's Legacy of Lead Poisoning." *Cleveland Plain Dealer*, October 20.

Donnelly, Jennifer. 2013. "Myth, Modernity, and Mass Housing: The Development of Public Housing in Depression-Era Cleveland." *Traditional Dwellings and Settlements Review* 25(1): 55–68.

Edin, Kathryn J., and H. Luke Shaefer. 2015. *$2.00 a Day: Living on Almost Nothing in America*. Boston: Houghton Mifflin Harcourt.

Ellen, Ingrid Gould, Vicki Been, and Andrew Hayashi. 2013. "Maintenance and Investment in Small Rental Properties: Findings from New York City and Baltimore." New York and Baltimore: Furman Center for Real Estate and Urban Policy and Johns Hopkins Institute for Policy Studies (November).

Erickson, David, Carolina Reid, Lisa Nelson, Anne O'Shaughnessy, and Alan Berube. 2008. "The Enduring Challenge of Concentrated Poverty in America: Case Studies from Communities across the U.S." Washington, D.C.: Federal Reserve System and Brookings Institution.

Fais, Cari. 2008. "Denying Access to Justice: The Location of Applying Chronic Nuisance Laws to Domestic Violence." *Columbia Law Review* 108(5): 1181–1225.

Fiss, Owen. 1984. "Against Settlement." *Yale Law Journal* 93: 1073–90.

Ford, Frank. 2018. "Housing Market Recovery in Cuyahoga County: Race and Geography Still Matter: Housing Trends in Cuyahoga County 1995–2017." Moreland Hills, Ohio: Western Reserve Land Conservancy (July 30).

Frater, Mark, Colleen Gilson, and Ronald O'Leary. 2009. "The City of Cleveland Code Enforcement Partnership." http://www.communityprogress.net/the -city-of-cleveland-code-enforcement-partnership-resources-7.php.

Freeman, Lance. 2011. "The Impact of Source of Income Laws on Voucher Utilization and Locational Outcomes." Washington: U.S. Department of Housing and Urban Development, Office of Policy Development and Research (February).

Freeman, Lance, and Yunjing Li. 2014. "Do Source of Income Anti-Discrimination Laws Facilitate Access to Less Disadvantaged Neighborhoods?" *Housing Studies* 29(1): 88–107.

Gallek, Peggy. 2015. "Exclusive I-Team: Video Shows Cleveland Bailiffs in Shootout with Tenant." Fox 8, February 18. fox8.com/news/exclusive-i-team -video-shows-cleveland-bailiffs-in-shootout-with-tenant.

Garboden, Phillip M. E., and Sandra Newman. 2012. "Is Preserving Small, Low-End Rental Housing Feasible?" *Housing Policy Debate* 22(4): 507–26.

Garboden, Phillip, Eva Rosen, Meredith Greif, Stefanie DeLuca, and Kathryn Edin. 2018. "Urban Landlords and the Housing Choice Voucher Program: A Research Report." Prepared for U.S. Department of Housing and Urban Development, Office of Policy Development and Research. Baltimore: Johns Hopkins University, Poverty and Inequality Research Lab (May).

Garland, David. 1996. "The Limits of the Sovereign State: Strategies of Crime Control in Contemporary Society." *British Journal of Criminology* 36(4): 445–52.

Gilderbloom, John I., and Richard P. Appelbaum. 1988. *Rethinking Rental Housing.* Philadelphia: Temple University Press.

Gilens, Martin. 1999. *Why Americans Hate Welfare: Race, Media, and the Politics of Antipoverty Policy.* Chicago: University of Chicago Press.

Gillispie, Mark. 2019. "Cleveland Steps Up Enforcement of Trash-Can Law." Cleveland.com (January 22, 2010; updated January 12, 2019), https://www .cleveland.com/cityhall/2010/01/cleveland_steps_up_enforcement.html#: ~:text=Cleveland's%20law%20is%20straightforward%3A%20You,more %20than%2012%20hours%20afterward.

Goering, John, Ali Kamely, and Todd Richardson 1997. "Recent Research on Racial Segregation and Poverty Concentration in Public Housing in the United States." *Urban Affairs Review* 32(5): 723–45.

Gomory, Henry. 2021. "The Social and Institutional Contexts Underlying Landlords' Eviction Practices." *Social Forces.* https://doi.org/10.1093/sf/soab063.

Greenlee, Andrew J. 2014. "More than Meets the Market? Landlord Agency in the Illinois Housing Choice Voucher Program." *Housing Policy Debate* 24(3): 500–524.

Hartman, Chester. 1998. "The Case for a Right to Housing." *Housing Policy Debate* 9(2): 223–46.

Hatch, Megan E. 2017. "Statutory Protection for Renters: Classification of State Landlord-Tenant Policy Approaches." *Housing Policy Debate* 27(1): 98–119.

Herd, Pamela, and Donald P. Moynihan. 2018. *Administrative Burden: Policy-making by Other Means.* New York: Russell Sage Foundation.

Hexter, Kathryn W. 2016. "Cuyahoga Countywide Housing Study: County Planning." *Urban Publications.* Cleveland: Cleveland State University, Maxine Goodman Levin College of Urban Affairs (August 10). https://engaged scholarship.csuohio.edu/urban_facpub/1371.

House, Sophie. 2021. "Cracking Code Enforcement: How Cities Approach Housing Standards." New York: NYU Furman Center (August). https:// furmancenter.org/research/publication/cracking-code-enforcement.

Hughes, Cayce C. 2020. "A House but Not a Home: How Surveillance in Subsidized Housing Exacerbates Poverty and Reinforces Marginalization." *Social Forces* 100(1): 293–315.

Jacquay, Robert. 2005. "Cleveland's Housing Court: A Grassroots Victory 25 Years Ago Paved the Way for a Reliable, Much Needed Institution." *Shelterforce* (May/June).

Joint Center for Housing Studies of Harvard University. 2019. "The State of the Nation's Housing 2019." Cambridge, Mass.: Joint Center for Housing Studies of Harvard University.

Kalleberg, Arne L. 2011. *Good Jobs, Bad Jobs: The Rise of Polarized and Precarious Employment Systems in the United States, 1970s to 2000s.* New York: Russell Sage Foundation.

Keating, W. Dennis, and Kermit J. Lind. 2012. "Responding to the Mortgage Crisis: Three Cleveland Examples." *Urban Lawyer* 44: 1–35.

Kimberlin, Sara, Laura Tach, and Christopher Wimer. 2018. "A Renter's Tax Credit to Curtail the Affordable Housing Crisis." *RSF: The Russell Sage Foundation Journal of the Social Sciences* 4(2): 131–60.

Kingsley, G. Thomas. 2017. "Trends in Housing Problems and Federal Assistance Programs." Washington, D.C.: Urban Institute (October).

Kirk, David S., and Andrew V. Papachristos. 2011. "Cultural Mechanisms and the Persistence of Neighborhood Violence." *American Journal of Sociology* 116(4): 1190–1233.

Kirwan Institute for the Study of Race and Ethnicity. 2015. "History Matters: Understanding the Role of Policy, Race, and Real Estate in Today's Geography of Health Equity and Opportunity in Cuyahoga County." Cleveland: Kirwan Institute for the Study of Race and Ethnicity.

Kleit, Rachel Garshick, and Martha Galvez. 2011. "The Location Choices of Public Housing Residents Displaced by Redevelopment: Market Constraints, Personal Preferences, or Social Information?" *Journal of Urban Affairs* 33(4): 375–407.

Kneebone, Elizabeth, and Natalie Holmes. 2016. "U.S. Concentrated Poverty in the Wake of the Great Recession." Washington, D.C.: Brookings Institution. https://www.brookings.edu/research/u-s-concentrated-poverty-in-the-wake -of-the-great-recession/.

Koehle, Greg. 2013. "Controlling Crime and Disorder in Rental Properties: The Perspective of the Rental Property Manager." *Western Criminology Review* 14(3): 53–60.

Lamont, Michele, and Mario Small. 2008. "How Culture Matters: Enriching Our Understanding of Poverty." In *The Colors of Poverty: Why Racial and Ethnic Disparities Persist*, edited by Ann C. Lin and David R. Harris. New York: Russell Sage Foundation.

Lapeyrolerie, Olivia. 2015. "'No Water for Niggers': The Hough Riots and the Historiography of the Civil Rights Movement." *Cleveland Memory* 28. https:// engagedscholarship.csuohio.edu/clevmembks/28.

Legal Aid Society of Cleveland. 2018. "Tenant Information Line Continues Legacy of Cleveland Tenants Organization." Cleveland: Legal Aid Society of Cleveland (February 5). lasclev.org/02052018.

———. 2020. "Right to Counsel–Cleveland Launches, Providing Free Legal Help to Low-Income Tenants Facing Eviction." Cleveland: Legal Aid Society of Cleveland (July 1). lasclev.org/07012020-2.

Lepley, Michael, and Lenore Mangiarelli. 2017. "Housing Voucher Discrimination and Race Discrimination in Cuyahoga County." Cleveland: Housing Research and Advocacy Center (December).

Lerman, Amy E., and Vesla M. Weaver. 2014. *Arresting Citizenship: The Democratic Consequences of American Crime Control*. Chicago: University of Chicago Press.

Logan, John R., and Brian J. Stults. 2011. "The Persistence of Segregation in the Metropolis: New Findings from the 2010 Census." Census brief prepared for Project US2010. https://s4.ad.brown.edu/Projects/Diversity/Data/Report/report2.pdf.

Mallach, Alan. 2007. "Landlords at the Margins: Exploring the Dynamics of the One to Four Unit Rental Housing Industry." Cambridge, Mass.: Joint Center for Housing Studies of Harvard University (March).

———. 2014. "Lessons from Las Vegas: Housing Markets, Neighborhoods, and Distressed Single-Family Property Investors." *Housing Policy Debate* 24(4): 769–801.

Massey, Douglas S. 2015. "The Legacy of the 1968 Fair Housing Act." *Sociological Forum* 30(S1): 571–88.

Massey, Douglas S., and Nancy A. Denton. 1993. *American Apartheid: Segregation and the Making of the Underclass*. Cambridge, Mass.: Harvard University Press.

Mazzerole, Lorraine, and Janet Ransley. 2005. *Third Party Policing*. Cambridge: Cambridge University Press.

McClure, Kirk. 2008. "Deconcentrating Poverty with Housing Programs." *Journal of the American Planning Association* 74(1): 90–99.

Mead, Joseph, Megan Hatch, J. Rosie Tighe, Marissa Pappas, Kristi Andrasik, and Elizabeth Bonham. 2017. *Who Is a Nuisance? Criminal Activity Nuisance Ordinances in Ohio*. Urban Publications 1509. https://engagedscholarship.csuohio.edu/urban_facpub/1509/?utm_source=engagedscholarship.csuohio.edu%2Furban_facpub%2F1509&utm_medium=PDF&utm_campaign=PDFCoverPages.

Merton, Robert K. 1968. *Social Theory and Social Structure*. New York: Free Press.

Mettler, Suzanne, and Jeffrey M. Stonecash. 2008. "Government Program Usage and Political Voice." *Social Science Quarterly* 89(2): 273–93.

Miller, Donna J. 2019. "Federal Agents Search Cleveland and East Cleveland for Drug Suspects." *Cleveland Plain Dealer*, January 12. https://www.cleveland.com/metro/2012/06/warrant_sweep_this_morning_in.html.

Montag, Coty. 2019. *Water/Color: A Study of Race and the Water Affordability Crisis in America's Cities*. New York: Thurgood Marshall Institute at the NAACP Legal Defense and Educational Fund. https://www.naacpldf.org/wp-content/uploads/Water_Report_FULL_5_31_19_FINAL_OPT.pdf.

National Apartment Association (NAA). 2019. "Apartment Association of Greater Dallas Leads the Way in HCV Reform." Arlington, Va.: NAA (July 18). naahq.org/news-publications/apartment-association-greater-dallas-leads-way-hcv-reform.

Newman, Katherine. 2012. *The Accordion Family: Boomerang Kids, Anxious Parents, and the Private Toll of Global Competition*. Boston: Beacon Press.

Newman, Sandra J. 2005. *Low-End Rental Housing: The Forgotten Story in Baltimore's Housing Boom*. Washington, D.C.: Urban Institute (August).

Nickerson, Raymond S. 1998. "Confirmation Bias: A Ubiquitous Phenomenon in Many Guises." *Review of General Psychology* 2(2): 175–220.

Nisar, Hiren, Jim Murdoch, Dallas Elgin, Mallory Vachon, and Charles Horseman. 2018. "Landlord Participation Study: Multidisciplinary Research Team."

Washington: U.S. Department of Housing and Urban Development, Office of Policy Development and Research (October 17).

Pager, Devah. 2007. *Marked: Race, Crime, and Finding Work in an Era of Mass Incarceration*. Chicago: University of Chicago Press.

Pager, Devah, and Hana Shepherd. 2008. "The Sociology of Discrimination: Racial Discrimination in Employment, Housing, Credit, and Consumer Markets." *Annual Review of Sociology* 34(1): 181–209.

Paternoster, Raymond, Ronet Bachman, Robert Brame, and Lawrence W. Sherman. 1997. "Do Fair Procedures Matter? The Effect of Procedural Justice on Spouse Assault." *Law and Society Review* 31(1): 163–204.

Pettit, Becky, and Bruce Western. 2004. "Mass Imprisonment and the Life Course: Race and Class Inequality in U.S. Incarceration." *American Sociological Review* 69(2): 151–69.

Piven, Frances Fox, and Richard A. Cloward. 1971. *Regulating the Poor: The Functions of Public Welfare*. New York: Pantheon Books.

Pribesh, Shana, and Douglas B. Downey. 1999. "Why Are Residential and School Moves Associated with Poor School Performance?" *Demography* 36(4): 521–34.

Public Justice Center. 2015. "Justice Diverted: How Renters Are Processed in the Baltimore City Rent Court." Baltimore: Public Justice Center (December).

Rabin, Edward H. 1984. "Revolution in Residential Landlord-Tenant Law: Causes and Consequences." *Cornell Law Review* 69(3): 517–84.

Ramsey, Kathryn. 2018. "One-Strike 2.0: How Local Governments Are Distorting Flawed Federal Eviction Law." *UCLA Law Review* 65(1146): 1147–99.

Regan, Ron. 2020. "Federal Judge Rules CLE Water Lawsuit Alleging Discrimination Can Go Forward." News5 Cleveland, September 30. news5cleveland .com/news/local-news/investigations/federal-judge-rules-cle-water-lawsuit-alleging-discrimination-can-go-forward.

Reina, Vincent, Arthur Acolin, and Raphael W. Bostic. 2019. "Section 8 Vouchers and Rent Limits: Do Small Area Fair Market Rent Limits Increase Access to Opportunity Neighborhoods? An Early Evaluation." *Housing Policy Debate* 29(1): 44–61.

Rosen, Eva. 2014. "Rigging the Rules of the Game: How Landlords Geographically Sort Low-Income Renters." *City and Community* 13(4): 310–40.

———. 2020. *The Voucher Promise: "Section 8" and the Fate of an American Neighborhood*. Princeton, N.J.: Princeton University Press.

Ross, Tracey, Chelsea Parsons, and Rebecca Vallas. 2016. "Creating Safe and Health Living Environments for Low-Income Families." Washington, D.C.: Center for American Progress (July). https://cdn.americanprogress.org/wp -content/uploads/2016/07/14065816/SafeAndHealthyHomes-report.pdf.

Rothstein, Richard. 2017. *The Color of Law: A Forgotten History of How Our Government Segregated America*. New York: W. W. Norton & Co.

Sampson, Robert J. 2012. *Great American City: Chicago and the Enduring Neighborhood Effect*. Chicago: University of Chicago Press.

Sampson, Robert J., and Dawn Jeglum Bartusch. 1998. "Legal Cynicism and (Subcultural?) Tolerance of Deviance: The Neighbourhood Context of Racial Differences." *Law and Society Review* 32(4): 777–804.

Sampson, Robert J., and Stephen W. Raudenbush. 2004. "Neighborhood Stigma and the Social Construction of 'Broken Windows.'" *Social Psychology Quarterly* 67(4): 319–42.

Schram, Sanford S. 1995. *Words of Welfare: The Poverty of Social Science and the Social Science of Poverty*. Minneapolis: University of Minnesota Press.

——. 2006. *Welfare Discipline: Discourse, Governance, and Globalization*. Philadelphia: Temple University Press.

Schwartz, Alex F. 2015. *Housing Policy in the United States*. New York: Routledge.

Scott, Michael. 2019. "Councilman Mike Polensek Unrestrained, Unapologetic, and Unabashedly Passionate as Senior Councilman." *Cleveland Plain Dealer*, January 12. https://www.cleveland.com/metro/2010/12/councilman_mike_polensek_unres.html.

Sharkey, Patrick. 2013. *Stuck in Place: Urban Neighborhoods and the End of Progress toward Racial Equality*. Chicago: University of Chicago Press.

Shiffer-Sebba, Doron. 2020. "Understanding the Divergent Logics of Landlords: Circumstantial versus Deliberate Pathways." *City and Community* 19(4): 4–23.

Soss, Joe. 1999. "Welfare Application Encounters: Subordination, Satisfaction, and the Puzzle of Client Evaluations." *Administration and Society* 31(1): 50–94.

Soss, Joe, Richard C. Fording, and Sanford F. Schram. 2011. *Disciplining the Poor: Neoliberal Paternalism and the Persistent Power of Race*. Chicago: University of Chicago Press.

Spader, Jonathan, Jenny Schuetz, and Alvaro Cortes. 2015. "Fewer Vacants, Fewer Crimes? Impacts of Neighborhood Revitalization Policies on Crime." Finance and Economics Discussion Series 2015-088. Washington, D.C.: Board of Governors of the Federal Reserve System. http://dx.doi.org/10.17016/FEDS.2015.088.

Stegman, Michael A. 1972. *Housing Investment in the Inner City: The Dynamics of Decline: A Study of Baltimore, Maryland, 1968–1970*. Cambridge, Mass.: MIT Press.

Sternlieb, George. 1966. *The Tenement Landlord*. New Brunswick, N.J.: Rutgers University Press.

Sternlieb, George, and Robert W. Burchell. 1973. *Residential Abandonment: The Tenement Landlord Revisited*. New Brunswick, N.J.: Rutgers University Press.

Stout Risius Ross, Inc. 2016. "The Financial Cost and Benefits of Establishing a Right to Counsel in Eviction Proceedings under Intro 214-A." New York: Pro Bono and Legal Services Committee of the New York City Bar Association (March 16).

Swan, Sarah. 2015. "Home Rules." *Duke Law Journal* 64(5): 823–900.

Sykes, Gresham M., and David Matza. 1957. "Techniques of Neutralization: A Theory of Delinquency." *American Sociological Review* 22(6): 664–70.

Tach, Laura, and Kathryn Edin. 2017. "The Social Safety Net after Welfare Reform: Recent Developments and Consequences for Household Dynamics." *Annual Review of Sociology* 43: 541–61.

Tighe, J. Rosie, and Joanna P. Ganning. 2016. "Do Shrinking Cities Allow Redevelopment without Displacement? An Analysis of Affordability Based on Housing and Transportation Costs for Redeveloping, Declining, and Stable Neighborhoods." *Housing Policy Debate* 26(4/5): 785–800.

Treuhaft, Sarah, Kalima Rose, and Karen Black. 2010. "When Investors Buy Up the Neighborhood: Preventing Investor Ownership from Causing Neighborhood Decline." St. Paul, Minn.: Northwest Area Foundation (April).

Turner, Margery, Rob Santos, Diane Levy, Doug Wissoker, Claudia Aranda, Rob Pitingolo, and the Urban Institute. 2013. "Housing Discrimination against Racial and Ethnic Minorities, 2012." Washington, D.C.: U.S. Department of Housing and Urban Development (June).

Tyler, Tom R. 1990. *Why People Obey the Law: Procedural Justice, Legitimacy, and Compliance.* New Haven, Conn.: Yale University Press.

Urban, April Hirsh, Aleksandra Tyler, Francisca García-Cobián Richter, Claudia Coulton, and Tsui Chan. 2019. "The Cleveland Eviction Study: Observations in Eviction Court and the Stories of People Facing Eviction." Cleveland: Case Western Reserve University, Center on Urban Poverty and Community Development (October).

U.S. Department of Justice and U.S. Attorney's Office, Northern District of Ohio. 2014. "Investigation of the Cleveland Division of Police." Washington, D.C., and Cleveland: U.S. Department of Justice and U.S. Attorney's Office (December 4).

Vacant and Abandoned Property Action Council. 2015. "Property Delinquency and Tax Lien Sales in Cuyahoga County, Ohio." Cleveland: Thriving Communities Institute.

Vale, Lawrence. 2015. "Myth #6: Mixed-Income Redevelopment Is the Only Way to Fix Failed Public Housing." In *Public Housing Myths: Perception, Reality, and Social Policy,* edited by Nicholas Bloom, Fritz Umbach, and Lawrence Vale. Ithaca, N.Y.: Cornell University Press.

Walker, Fay. 2019. "Eviction in Cleveland." Rpubs, February 26. https://www .rpubs.com/faycwalker/Cleveland-Eviction.

Walton, Brett. 2015. "Price of Water 2015: Up 6 Percent in 30 Major U.S. Cities; 41 Percent Rise Since 2010." Circle of Blue (April 22). https://www.circleofblue .org/2015/world/price-of-water-2015-up-6-percent-in-30-major-u-s-cities-41 -percent-rise-since-2010/.

Water Infrastructure Task Force. 2017. "Understanding America's Water and Wastewater Challenges." Washington, D.C.: Bipartisan Policy Center (May).

Watkins-Hayes, Celeste. 2009. *The New Welfare Bureaucrats: Entanglements of Race, Class, and Policy Reform.* Chicago: University of Chicago Press.

Way, Heather, and Carol Fraser. 2018. "Out of Order: Houston's Dangerous Apartment Epidemic." Austin, Tex.: Entrepreneurship and Community Development Clinic of Texas School of Law (January). https://law.utexas.edu /clinics/2018/01/26/out-of-order-houstons-apt-epidemic/.

Way, Heather K., Stephanie Trinh, and Melissa Wyatt. 2013. "Addressing Problem Properties: Legal and Policy Tools for a Safer Rundberg and Safer Austin." Austin: Entrepreneurship and Community Development Clinic University of Texas School of Law (August).

Western, Bruce. 2006. *Punishment and Inequality in America.* New York: Russell Sage Foundation.

Western Reserve Land Conservancy. 2015. Cleveland Neighborhoods by the Numbers: 2015 Cleveland Property Inventory. Cleveland: Western Reserve Land Conservancy.

Wilson, William Julius. 1997. *When Work Disappears: The World of the New Urban Poor.* New York: Alfred A. Knopf.

Witt, C. David. 2019. "How a Court Can Enhance Dispute Resolutions." Cleveland: Cleveland Metropolitan Bar Association (August 1). clemetrobar .org/?pg=CMBABlog&blAction=showEntry&blogEntry=59371.

Wood, Holly. 2014. "When Only a House Makes a Home: How Home Selection Matters in the Residential Mobility Decisions of Low-Income, Inner-City, African American Families." *Social Service Review* 88(2): 264–94.

Wright, James D., and Beth A. Rubin. 2010. "Is Homelessness a Housing Problem?" *Housing Policy Debate* 2(3): 937–56.

Yinger, John. 1995. *Closed Doors, Opportunities Lost: The Continuing Costs of Housing Discrimination.* New York: Russell Sage Foundation.

= Index =

Boldface numbers refer to figures and tables.

ACS, *see also* American Community Survey

administrative burden: as obstacle to tenants' access to protection from laws, 33; as disincentive to landlords' participation in the HCVP, 110, 112; measures to reduce landlords' administrative burden, 130, 142; measures to reduce tenants' administrative burden, 138, 144

Aid to Families with Dependent Children (AFDC), 11

American Civil Liberties Union, 78

Anti-Drug Abuse Act of 1968, 63

Baltimore, 110–11

Bandura, Albert, 132–33

Bedford, CANO implemented in, 64–65

Bell, Monica, 53

blacklist of tenants, 132

Boston Housing Authority, Commonwealth Development, 145

Burchell, Robert, 42

carceral state, 11, 16

Cleveland Building and Housing Department, 21, 30–32

Cleveland Housing Network (CHN) Housing Partners, 145, 157n2

Cleveland metropolitan area: characteristics of as a post-industrial city, 4; economic rise and decay of, 22–23; eviction rate in, 21; median gross rent in, 21; racial and class segregation in, geography of, 6–9; racial segregation in, evolution of, 23–24; renters that are housing-cost-burdened, percentage of, 11; Slavic Village, 29–31; study of small- and mid-sized landlords in, description of, 4–10 (*see also* methodology). *See also* Cuyahoga County

Cleveland Municipal Housing Court: alternative dispute resolution (ADR) services, 34–37; bailiffs' work in the field, 37–39; creation of, 24; first-cause eviction hearings, 25–27; housing conditions, cases pertaining to, 28–29; important work of staff at, 21; landlords, perspective of court staff on, 51; legal counsel of landlords appearing before, 151n26; mediation option, 34–37, 137–38; as a "problem-solving" institution, 39–40; recommendations for, 137–39; second-cause eviction hearings, 27–28; two branches of, 24

Cleveland Police Department, 34

169

Cleveland Tenants Organization (CTO): establishment of, 24; on fear of low-income tenants to complain about housing conditions, 42, 54; housing complaints received by, 33; important work of staff at, 21; interviews conducted with, 15; shut down of, 39

Clinton, Bill, 63

Commission on Civil Rights, U.S., 23

confirmation bias, 99

crime control, responsibilization of, 63

criminal activity nuisance ordinances (CANOs): common elements of, 64; counterproductive effect of, 79–80; domestic violence and, 75–76; landlord concerns about/ experiences with, 66–67, 72–77; race-and class-based biases motivating, 64–65; reform of, 141; spread and impact of, 12–13, 63–64; tenants disproportionately disadvantaged by, 77–80

Cuyahoga County: emergence of CANOs in affluent suburbs, 64; median wait-list time for Section 8 voucher holders in, 106; public housing authority in, 104; racial composition of, 7–8; Section 8 vouchers used in suburban communities, percentage of, 105. See also Cleveland metropolitan area

Cuyahoga County Land Reutilization Corporation ("Cuyahoga Land Bank"), 15

Cuyahoga County Metropolitan Housing Authority (CMHA), 104–6

Cuyahoga County Water Department, 100

Denton, Nancy, 16

Desmond, Matthew, 57

Detroit Shoreway Development Corporation, 29

domestic violence, 73–79

evictions: cost of for landlords, 53; court process for, 12; emotional impact of, 24; first-cause eviction hearings, 25–27; informal, 12–13, 22, 53–54, 56, 67–71, 114; landlords' anxiety about tenant's water use in retribution for, 89–91; landlords' decisions about, CANOs and, 65–67; move-outs/set-outs, 37–39; rates of, 21; second-cause eviction hearings, 27–28; of Section 8 tenants, 110; "voluntary vacate," 35

Fair Housing Act of 1968, 28, 45, 78, 83, 103, 116, 122, 131

Federal Housing Authority (FHA), 23

financial precarity of landlords: definition of, 11, 42; housing laws and, 4, 10, 12–14, 41–42, 51; sources of, 51, 133–34; water bills and, 81–83, 87–88, 93–96 (see also water bills); as widespread in the sample of landlords, 42

financial precarity of tenants: factors fueling, 10–11; with low-wage jobs, 45

foreclosures, 100–103, 124–25

Garland, David, 63

"Glenville Shootout," 24

government: contracting with private corporations for essential services and commodities, 83; mistrust of authorities by landlords, 13–14, 50–51, 133–34; mistrust of authorities by tenants, 15, 42, 70–71. See also Cleveland Municipal Housing Court

Holder, Eric, 34

Home Owners Loan Corporation (HOLC), 23

HOPE VI Act of 1996, 3, 63

Housing and Community Development Act of 1974, 3

Housing Choice Voucher Program (HCVP): landlord characteristics and, 104–6; purpose of, 3; reform of, 141–43; rent payment under, FMR calculation of, 110–12, 142; varying success of, landlords' goals/business practices and, 128–30. *See also* Section 8 tenants

housing codes/laws: disadvantage of tenants amplified by, 4, 10; disincentives for renters to report violations of, 31, 33–34, 42, 54, 98–99; federal, 3; landlord evasion of, 4, 74; landlord frustration regarding, 133–34; landlords' financial disincentive to adhere to, 41–42, 50–51; landlord-tenant legislation, 22, 33, 36–37; local, impact of, 12–14; redlining, 23; reform of, recommendations for (*see* recommendations for improving low-income housing)

housing codes/laws, enforcement of: lenient, 42, 61–62; reactive, 29–31; reform of, 140, 143; uneven, 22, 28–29, 46. *See also* inspections

housing conditions, impacts of poor, 28

Housing Opportunity Program Extension Act of 1996, 63

Humboldt Tenant Landlord Collaboration (HTLC), 140

incarceration, rise of mass, 11

informal evictions, 12–13, 22, 53–54, 56, 67–71, 114

inspections: attendance at by small-time landlords, 96; inconsistent/capricious/burdensome, 112–13, 126, 128–30; landlord manipulation of, 114; lead paint safety standards, 122; lenient, 2, 42, 61–62; mediation accepted by landlords to avoid, 35; PHA for Section 8 rentals, 1–2, 4, 19, 104, 106–9, 112–14, 121–23, 125–30; point-of-sale, 107, 118; reactive, 16, 22, 29–31; reform of, 142–43;

residents trained to perform, 140; systematic in suburban communities, 69; threatening tenants with, 70. *See also* housing codes/laws, enforcement of

Jackson, Frank, 61

Justice Department, U.S., 34

Lakewood: CANO in, 66–67; renters in, 107–8

landlord(s): business practices of small and midsize, need to understand, 3–4, 135–36; callous measures used by, 56 (*see also* informal evictions); diversity of motivations for becoming a, 41; divesting from the rental business, examples of, 43–51; divesting from the rental business, process of, 42–43; domestic violence, attitudes towards, 74–77; evictions by (*see* evictions); financial precarity of (*see* financial precarity of landlords); harmful behaviors of, 131–33; housing policy/laws and, 4, 41–42, 50–51 (*see also* housing codes /laws; inspections); improving conditions for and behaviors of (*see* recommendations for improving low-income housing); income of, 1, 46, 52–53, 55–57, 61, 72, 74, 85, 108, 116, 118–19, 125; mediation as an option for, 35–37; mistrust of authorities by, 13–14, 50–51; motivations for becoming/continuing as a, 5–6, 41, 66–69, 83–84, 86, 93, 98, 101, 107–8, 115–16, 118, 124, 127; race- and class-based biases of, 14–15; sample of, characteristics of the, 5–6, 9–10; Section 8 program, concerns about, 108, 110–14, 122; Section 8 program and goals of, 128–30; Section 8 tenants and, 104–7, 111, 127 (*see also* Section 8 tenants); struggles with tenants, examples of, 53–56, 68–77, 89 (*see also* informal evictions); successful, business practices of, 56–61, 84, 98, 111, 127–28, 135–36; suitability for being a, 99; tax lien sale/loss of property, experience of, 101–3; tenants, dissatisfactions about/opinions of, 49, 54–56, 71, 82, 92–93, 134–35; tenant turnover as the biggest problem for, 119; vandalism, using alarms to deter, 128; water bills, responsibility for paying, 81–82, 84 (*see also* water bills)

landlords burdened by: CANOs, 12–13, 63, 65, 72–77 (*see also* criminal activity nuisance ordinances (CANOs)); collecting on debt from tenants, 27–28; water bills (*see* water bills)

Legal Aid Society of Cleveland, 15, 39, 78, 139

legal cynicism: of landlords, 41, 46, 73; of tenants, 34

Low Income Household Water Assistance Program (LIHWAP), 141

Low-Income Housing Tax Credit (LIHTC) program, 145

Mallach, Alan, 41

Massey, Douglas, 16

Mead, Joseph, 78

mediation, 34–37, 137–38

Merton, Robert, 79

methodology: ethnographic observations of landlords, 148; interviews of governmental authorities and officials at nonprofit housing agencies, 15–16; interviews of landlords, 4–5, 147–48; landlord sample, 5–6, 9–10, 147

Milwaukee Area Rental Study (MARS), 70

NAACP Legal Defense Fund, 103

New York City, Mayor's Office to Protect Tenants, 138

Nixon, Richard, 145

Oakland Housing Authority, 142–43

Ohio Tenant-Landlord Law, 154*n*5

Personal Responsibility and Work Opportunity Reconciliation Act of 1996 (PRWORA), 11

Pianka, Raymond, 29–30, 39–40, 125

Polensek, Mike, 73

procedural justice, definition of, 34, 137; benefits for tenants, 34, 137

public housing, 144–45

public housing authorities (PHAs): actions under CANOs, 63; inspections by, 1–2

race: CANOs and, 64–65, 78; discrimination in the housing market and, 14–15; disproportionate incarceration of Black men, 11; evolution of segregation in Cleveland, 23–24; geography of in Cleveland, 6–9; racial composition of Cuyahoga County, 7–8; Section 8 vouchers and, 105; stereotyped perceptions based on, 134–35; tax lien sales and, 102–3; uneven enforcement of housing codes and, 29; water bills and, 82–83

recommendations for improving low-income housing, 136–37; affordable homeownership, expansion of opportunities for, 145; financial safety net: renter's tax credit, 143–44; landlord-focused resources and training, 139–40; legal and justice system solutions, 137–39; low-income renters' access to housing, steps to protect, 140–43; public housing, 144–45; unanticipated consequences, need to avoid, 146

Rental Housing Association of Washington (RHAWA), Rental Housing Academy, 139

renters. *See* tenants

renter's tax credit, 144

rent escrow process, 33–34, 138

"responsibilization" of crime control, 63
Right to Counsel—Cleveland (RTC-C), 39, 139
Rockefeller, John D., 22
Rosen, Eva, 105
Rothstein, Richard, 16

Section 8 tenants: additional rent on the side collected from, 114–15; biases/ stigma associated with, 108–10, 113, 116; eviction of, 110; federal policy establishing, 3; financial incentives or disincentives to house, 4, 111, 116, 121–23, 126, 128–30; high standards for, 119–20; low expectations of, 123–24; minimal maintenance of housing for, 125–26; obstacles to securing housing by, 104–5; process of securing rental housing, 106–7; renting to, 1; surveillance of, 115–17, 120–21
Sharkey, Patrick, 16
Somai, Beverly, 78
source of income (SOI) protection laws, 141–42
Sternlieb, George, 42
Stokes, Carl, 23–24
strain theory, 79
Supplemental Security Income (SSI), 94

tax lien sales, 100–103
Tenant-Landlord Law of 1974 (Ohio), 22, 33, 36–37
tenants: background checks on prospective, 72–73, 75; blacklists of, 132; complaints filed by, 2; employment status, water usage and, 91–93; evictions of (see evictions); financial precarity of (see financial precarity of tenants); government assistance for, landlord perspective on, 94; housing-cost-burdened, 11, 21; ideal, landlords' vision of, 109;

improving conditions for (see recommendations for improving low-income housing); landlords' dissatisfactions about/opinions of, 49, 54–56, 71, 82, 92–93, 134–35; legal protections for in landlord-tenant legislation, 22, 33; mediation as an option for, 35–37; subsidized through Section 8 vouchers (see Section 8 tenants)
tenants disadvantaged by: CANOs, 65, 72–73, 75, 77–80; disincentives to report housing problems, 31, 33–34, 42, 54, 98–99; informal eviction/involuntary mobility, 70, 114 (see also informal evictions); landlord surveillance, 117, 132; large families, 94–95; mistrust of authorities, 33–34, 42, 70–71; race, 14–15; reactive housing and health code enforcement, 29–31; screening process for criminal records, 71; social and financial marginalization, 54–55; water bills, 82–83, 91–96; young children, families with, 122

unemployment, "double penalty" from, 91–93
United Way of Greater Cleveland, 39, 139

Vacant and Abandoned Property Action Council (VAPAC), 15
Violence Against Women Act (VAWA) of 2005, 79

War on Drugs, 63
water bills: collection of delinquent, 100–103; financial pressure on landlords and relations with tenants from, 13, 81–89, 93–96; landlord efforts to curtail water usage, 96–99; landlord responsibility for paying, 81–82, 84; metering of water usage, 87, 120; potential tenant retribution

for conviction through excessive, 89–91, 154n5; rising cost of, 81; size of families and, 94–95; small- vs. mid-sized landlords and concerns about, 95–96; tenants disadvantaged by, 82–83, 91–96; tenants' employment status and, 91–93; water infrastructure, need to restore aging, 140–41, 143

Western Reserve Land Conservancy, 28

White flight, 23